Signed Copy

GILBERT WHITE
AND HIS SELBORNE

Gilbert White & his Selborne

ANTHONY RYE

Anthony Rye.

June 21st 1971

WILLIAM KIMBER · LONDON

Published by
WILLIAM KIMBER & CO. LTD.
6 Queen Anne's Gate, London S.W.1.

Standard Book No: 7183 0431 4

For my brother Ralph

Printed in Great Britain
By Fletcher & Son Ltd, Norwich

Contents

Maps

List of Illustrations

Acknowledgements

I have to thank the Trustees of the Gilbert White museum for virtually putting the Wakes at my disposal, and especially its Curator, Mr. Cyril Northcliffe, for allowing me to consult his article in *The Hampshire Magazine* on the portraiture of White and for other patient help given over the years; the Rev. George Knapp for permission to quote from the published proceedings of *The Selborne Priory Excavations Committee*; the Rev. John Darlington, Vicar of Selborne, for allowing me to consult the Tithe Roll map of 1842 at the Vicarage, and the Charge Roll with it.

Thanks are due also to Mr Kenneth Hopkins and Mr. Alvar Lidell for their help at various stages in the preparation of my manuscript for the Press.

A little, thin, prim upright man

CHAPTER I

Gilbert White of Selborne

He was a little, thin, prim, upright man, and used to go poking about in the lanes and hedges with his stick, and then rather nattily stop to flick the dust off his shoes with his handkerchief. He was not over particular as to what things he handled – some of them were pretty strange; and he liked strange beasts, even snakes! But 'a still, quiet body, there wasn't a bit of harm in him, I'll assure you, sir, there wasn't indeed'.

'A look of complacency and an expressive eye.' He was very learned, and believed to be writing a book himself. But for all that he was a good clergyman, getting out and about in all weathers. No, he didn't neglect his duty, not Gilbert White, for all his hobby. Somebody said he was a good deal more thought of when he was dead, which perhaps was true, but then he'd never been one to push himself. Kind and courteous to all, and a good neighbour. Besides, who could have imagined he'd become so famous.

Someone could, apparently; for long before the *Natural History & Antiquities of Selborne* was published in 1789 – right at the end of his life – one who knew him well prophesied that the time would come when Selborne would be famous as the birthplace of such a genius. And now they come from all over the world to see White's birthplace, the vicarage, and his home, the Wakes. And the book – that 'little cockle-shell of a book' – that first was perused by the learned in grave, bust-haunted studies, came to be read in rough cabins by colonists, and in small rooms by those other exiles, who had left the country for industrial slums; clerks and factory workers, pining for the green fields they had lost. There was, in fact, something for everybody in the book, but it was not obvious at first. It had to be read slowly, with attention, again and again. It had to be browsed over. Then, despite its somewhat dry form of letters, its abundance of classical terms, stiff (but never arid) disquisitions and theories, some of them outdated, it was seen to

Good neighbours (from Grimm)

be a unique book, by a unique and wonderful writer. It stood as an imperative on rough shelves, with the Bible, Shakespeare, *The Pilgrim's Progress*.

To quote would be virtually to provide another of the endless editions of that book. For where White writes (with perhaps unconscious felicity) of some bird or other creature near his heart and clear to his understanding, then succeeding nature writers may despair. For then he approaches perfection in passages where the style is effortlessly sustained, the description terse, the epithets apt unfailingly, and always happy; where there is never any sense of strain, and where the author, however passionately involved, never obtrudes himself, is never dogmatic. And on all is the stamp of the mastery and discipline of his science – of a great naturalist in control.

Was White a great naturalist? He certainly inspired greatness, and is not to be thought of as minor because greater naturalists followed him. He did all that he could do in his day, and did it better than others of his day. He used universal Latin, and scientific methods of classification, and proceeded by experiment always, and observation and deduction. And nothing could be less provincial than his approach, continually seeking the maximum field to sow his ideas and reap those of others. His correspondents could be sure that if White announced a thing a fact, that thing was true as far as wonderful powers of observation and acute, reasoning intelligence could make it so.

But the key to his success is not here. White was happy and able to suffuse that happiness throughout his book. It was a happiness peculiar to the eighteenth-century rural England with which he balanced so perfectly – unvexed, earth-rooted, content. We might say he was a lucky man too, if his life seemed less evidently planned by providence. Selborne bore him, drew him, held him. Everything shaped and turned to the end that he should settle there and ripen and perfect work which could not be done elsewhere.

Grandmother White was a local farmer's daughter. The grandfather, Gilbert White the elder, was Vicar of Selborne, and in his vicarage in 1720 White was born. Much of his boyhood he passed there, and at nine he came to live permanently at Wakes, the far humbler Wakes which later he owned and added to, which has become *the* Wakes. Dedicated to Selborne, he resisted academic allurements, though Oxford certainly offered success, of a kind. Selborne's vicar he could never be, since he went to Oriel not Magdalen, in whose gift the living was; and even this perhaps is fortunate, for as vicar he would no doubt have married and reared a family. The conscientious priest and parent would have swallowed the naturalist and inspired dilettante. Curacy was another matter, and he was Faringdon's curate for many years, and for long terms curate-in-charge at Selborne. Faringdon is only a mile or two away – practically, in summer, it was a single Cure. But in winter it could seem more like twelve miles and sometimes a passage had to be dug before him, through the snow; sometimes riding the hollow way was like breasting a small swift river, with the mud and stones and slime up to the horse's belly.

The Old Vicarage (after Grimm)

Wakes from the rear, 1776 (after Grimm)

White reflected almost all the moods of his century; he responded with enthusiasm to its taste, had the improving eye for garden *chinoiserie*, for rural classical and rustic gothic. He was always building little summer-houses, arbours, alcoves, in his grounds and about on the Hanger; and a hermitage – his 'pensile bower'. Is there a happier illustration of the eighteenth century at play than this hermitage of White's with its hermit-on-demand, brother Henry, stealing off and dressing-up, to emerge suddenly, with youthful beaming face over long false beard, when visitors – especially young ladies – were slyly led that way by Gilbert? He was a dipping antiquary, with a proper sense of ruins; a lover of twilight and eglantine and country cottage sentiment. His summer evening was Collins's and Gray's. With tempered romanticism he sought out 'horrid' prospects, dashing torrents, sounding floods, all

Harry alert

of which, tempered, Selborne has. He was Echo's patron always, and a gentle, genteel Pan.

All these pursuits and pleasures Selborne and destiny afforded, and in return he gave us his book, that is to say, himself. There was little of him evident besides. Few are the things of his possessing in the Wakes today, but his home remains there, buried in extensions. And Selborne remains: 'White's Selborne'. Except for a part here and there and near the church, the village, like the book, may not at first seem so remarkable. At least it may not appear to justify White's claims for it. You know, he called it wildly majestic:

> 'See Selborne spreads her boldest beauties round,
> 'The vary'd valley, and the mountain ground,
> '*Wildly majestic!*'

(White called the South Downs mountains, and majestic ones too.)

Could such terms be justified? White could justify them perfectly. He knew that, properly regarding nature, man is miniscule. Scale becomes unimportant, ceases to affect. The Hanger has grandeur, properly surveyed – and White was a prime surveyor – and so have the lesser heights at Temple and Wick Hill, and the views from them towards the South Downs, or over black Wolmer Forest, are magnificent and unrivalled in kind. The valley is indeed varied; criss-crossed at intervals with other, smaller valleys, their steep sidelands bearing beech and ash, field maples, hazels, oaks, in vast masses of shifting light and shadow, in autumn kindling to flames. The noble, dominant hill sends, as he tells us, a stream from either side to meet in greenest Dorton and flow as one, with all the variety of interest of a pastoral stream's progression, between the Short Lyth and the Long Lyth and Dorton Wood, down to the ruined Priory. But you must be steeped in this too, to realise its beauty. No use keeping to the street. You must climb the Zigzag and the Bostal and descend to thread the valley of the lyths, cross or circumvent the upland fields, penetrate to each shadowed angle of the bourne. As you go you may feel you have, for company, the little, thin, prim, upright man with not a bit of harm about him. Some have been conscious of that presence, but it would be a subjective ghost merely. Such perfectable, perfecting spirits will not much linger in fields of their growing, and happy White, doubtless, has gone elsewhere. He had no ties to hold him, his work done. He left no wife, no children. Like Jane Austen he solaced himself with an abundance of

Shooting

nephews and nieces, so that with these and visiting and corresponding friends the seclusion of his choice was never solitary – and it was Selborne's. Perhaps he was not quite harmless, to our view. Some of the birds he so loved were not felt as so much a part of himself as to prohibit his shooting them in defence of fruits and vegetables. For Science also he shot and stuffed them. There was no other way. But between 1720 and 1793 a man could correct sensibility with sense and not do violence to his nature. He lived at an equipoise, conscience untormenting, with all the honesty and absence of cant of the best spirits of his age, free to ripen in a freedom we can hardly conceive of. And of all mortal lives that ever were lived, I feel, none was more innocently and fruitfully spent than his; no place more propitious than Selborne.

* * *

So much for the general view. No one, I suspect, will quarrel with it who cares for White and natural history and the countryside. But granting that no man's life is uneventful to himself, was White's as quiet and agreeable as all that? Did he go smoothly from that very admirable family I shall be describing, through college, into the Church, discreetly avoiding matrimony, retire, and then, comfortably off, fulfil himself with bouts of hospitality, and solace himself with decorously amusing little festivities, all the time pursuing his hobby at ease, collecting material for his one short book?

Under the surface, inevitably, things are not quite the same. Though he was on the whole a sane serene person, his life a full and happy one – which no doubt accounts for that 'look of complacency' which sounds so horridly to our ears – White did not have it nearly so much his own way. He had his struggles and perplexities, his perils and avoidances.

He did not by any means get off uncriticised, even in his own day, when he was attacked for pluralism and selfishness; our own has provided strictures less plausible. Some people say White was lazy. This is so very odd and contrary to fact that at one time I really thought the idea originated with D. B. Wyndham-Lewis ('Timothy Shy') who wrote an amusing piece of light verse about twenty years ago which, after castigating some imaginary clergymen of the Church of England for imaginary Shy-like deficiencies, ended:

> Rev. G. White, this goes for you:
> Aint you got no work to do?

But the superstition that White was lazy seems to have been started much earlier by James Russell Lowell of Boston, Mass. He was very severe on White in his book of essays, *My Study Windows*. (Not the best place, perhaps, from which to look at White.) Lowell is well known

Courteous to all

as a good and loyal friend to the young Henry James, who had a great regard and affection for him, but said of him: 'His weak point will always be his opinions.'

There will be no difficulty in showing that White was busy enough, but the question of how quiet and peaceful a life he led does require looking into. Also, national figures should be above suspicion, and a hero had better be anything else but lazy and self-indulgent, or smug. While it might be unwise to risk any disturbance of that pleasing image of playful yet innocently industrious country ease – and a pity to do so anyway – there is something about that 'not a bit of harm, I do assure you' that is mildly offensive; and the picture so far drawn, with its opinions and fancies assembled from old quotes of those who knew him actually or by repute, from what 'the old men say their fathers told them', from the gleanings of family piety, seems not quite adequate.

CHAPTER II

The Importance of being White

SELBORNE and Gilbert White are complementary. Selborne would not be famous without White; White could not have written his famous and fame-making book without Selborne.

White stands, indeed a man so famous (but often only as a name) as to be beyond the need of further attempt to illustrate: we are shortly to celebrate the 250th anniversary of his birth who wrote the fourth most published book in the language. But Selborne stands, like too many other villages, at a point where its existence is continually threatened under pressure of modern needs and changes – genuine needs, fashionable expediencies, sudden, arbitrary decrees, and all the immense development and departure in agriculture.

Apart from its geography, which is peculiar, what has so far miraculously preserved Selborne as White knew it is White's fame. It is the Mecca of naturalists and nature-lovers the world over, who come to benefit from its beauties and inspect his green living outdoor laboratory and carry on his work. Therefore the completer the understanding of White and estimate of his stature the better for this cause.

Selborne itself, I feel, needs further justice done to it. It is my hope, knowing it intimately as I have done all my life, to give something more of its also unique quality. But a man's first debt, I suppose, must be paid to a man, and I therefore go on with a further probe on White and an enquiry into the value of what he made his life-long study. For it is vital to recognise at the outset the supreme importance of natural history, which is the study to comprehend exactly all things alive; ourselves with all the rest and in relationship with all. While we are pressing to this end with every God-given faculty at stretch, like White, we cannot remain materialistic and self-centred to the point of destruction: and this is the easiest and most delightful way by which we can achieve the sense of identity with all creatures, and the comfort, the assurance that we belong to a scheme of creation, no longer wandering foot-loose in misery and anger. It is the one thing by which we can remain kindly and sane.

* * *

'Not a bit of harm in him, I do assure you!' It would almost seem that within fifty years of his death, the period when most of the descriptions I assembled were gathered, White had come to typify just those peaceful devoted old naturalist-parsons and back-row savants poring about in the hedgerows which, in fact, his book and his method had called practically into being, or, since something like them had existed before, had at least caused to multiply a hundredfold. Calm and peace and innocent observation, and a little, less innocent, collecting of birds and butterflies – one remembers how revolted W. H. Hudson was by the parson who suddenly shot out his hand to secure a passing moth; the type had indeed developed, had become fixed in the public mind, and this important interim phase, when the *Natural History of Selborne* was rapidly gathering way, when the new editions and reprints were already many, every bright young improving naturalist using the book to give himself a leg up, with sometimes needed notes and introduction added, aided by retired country gentlemen anxious to improve their local image, had certainly much modified the public idea of a naturalist.

The field naturalist had become respectable. He was still sometimes a figure of fun. Witness in the *Ingoldsby Legends* the unhappy Sir Thomas, who was drowned in a pond while fishing for tadpoles, and, involuntarily, captured eels. (It is a miraculous example of the sick joke, by the way, for those who think we invented that.) That is to say, the early Victorians might still look on him as an eccentric being, but he was no longer a Dr. Smellfungus, something to disgust.

And then, suddenly, under the impact of Darwinism, he became a thing to fear and mistrust, and in those very circles where White's influence had been most felt. Darwin's evolutionary theory, his *Origin of Species*, naturally affected the clergy first, for whom hitherto natural history had been a blessedly cheap, innocent occupation, through which they might easily reach to the hearts of naturally pious but not sufficiently orthodox strayed sheep. Now all was changed, and the clergyman, if a gifted naturalist, as was Kingsley, reacted often violently. Kingsley was tough and agile and angry. He attacked the 'modern' naturalist. His *Water Babies*, ostensibly for children, is one of the most tendentious books ever written. Questions which White and his contemporary naturalists had never had to entertain, and which Darwin himself must only have glanced at nervously and suppressed, were now brought into the open and furiously debated. Hopeless controversies were engaged in by learned folk at cross-purposes. It was Bishop *v.* Biologist, and the new natural science invariably won.

Or for a long time it was to seem so. Darwin and T. H. Huxley, his mighty advocate, died with the great hopeless argument still raging. Valiantly they had followed and fought for truth, but they had been decently sad about their victory. They had not wanted to murder spiritual life, which was virtually what they were accused of. Very touching is Huxley's attitude towards the religious faith of his wife, which he wished he could share. And he said:

> I have never had the least sympathy with *a priori* reasons against orthodoxy, and I have by nature and disposition the greatest possible antipathy to all the atheistic and infidel school.

Darwin had lived to deplore the attrition of his more spiritual faculties. He could not read poetry, he could not listen to music as he had before scientific study so intensely possessed his mind. And Darwin's great peer, Alfred Russell Wallace, who had come to Evolution by his own quite different road, arriving simultaneously as it were, overcame the difficulties the Theory raised against orthodox religious beliefs with a single sweeping gesture of what might seem – what must then have seemed gigantic simplicity: he became a spiritualist.

Not one of these very great men, of course, thought it necessary to deny the importance of what to their antagonists was so desperately at stake. It was a struggle of Titans, grand and rugged in their enormous simplicity, against the young splendour and irresistible strength of the up-and-coming Jove. And so simple, then, was that side also. The Theory that was Jove's thunderbolt was aimed and struck only at fundamentals: it was not possible to square new-found facts with Eden, a seven-day creation, the bodily survival of death. But the scientist, then, could not have thought it irrational to wish for survival into heaven, for to have done so would have been to deny the value of life itself – the life whose marvellous and intricate beauties and sufficiency it has always been the aim of naturalists to throw new light on.

CHAPTER III

Mulso: The Faithful Friend

THE man who so boldly prophesied that Selborne would be remembered as the birthplace of Gilbert White was John Mulso, his almost life-long friend. Probably no one knew White as a human being better than he did. They had been young men, they had been gay together, sharing freedoms it would have been impossible for White to share with his much younger brothers. Out of such mundane beginnings had grown settled in Mulso the conviction of his friend's extraordinary powers, a something which set Gilbert apart from himself and others. The only thing Mulso seems to have been in doubt about – and this was because White was so quiet, cool and reticent – was whether his friend had sufficient faith in himself; whether what he had could sustain him to the end so clearly foreseen by Mulso, who was always, always egging him on to complete the book whose parts in manuscript he had been allowed to read. White's own admission of procrastination and occasional confession of diffidence regarding his book must have increased this doubt, but White did not really much procrastinate; he simply insisted on leaving himself maximum space for the execution of what he probably knew would be a unique work; and it will be seen that in the cause of science he was clearly not diffident at all.

What is so very remarkable about this understanding of John Mulso's, of the importance and intrinsic delightfulness of what Gilbert was doing and to do, was that he himself was of the most worldly kind of eighteenth-century clergyman, genial, witty, self-indulgent, flippant, for ever hunting successfully after what was then called 'fat goose living'. His uncle was to become Bishop of Winchester and the nephew made the most of it. For a long time he was urging White to cash in on it too, and to take every chance of advancing himself at Oriel College, Oxford, urging him in these directions with just as much jolly vitality, vivid brilliant phrase, as to the completion of the book.

Urging White too to take a wife, but with discreet merriment here, sound worldly wisdom but never to impertinence; until he had at last to resign himself ruefully to the probability of White's remaining single, never to taste of the Mulso happiness (itself long waited for) with a very stout, very lazy, lovely valetudinarian wife reluctant to exchange arm-chair for carriage. The truth is that Mulso as clearly perceived White's potentialities in these mundane fields. He wanted to do everything for the friend he loved as well as admired, and there seems little doubt that White could have succeeded in the realms of Church and College had he wished. It is that he did not so wish, though so well-equipped, but stood so level and composed between the two worlds that, I imagine most fascinated Mulso. And it is because White was like that – because he was a sensualist-materialist with a difference – that he is so useful and so important to ordinary men and women. John Mulso was delightfully, triumphantly ordinary in this sense. His friendship was important for White, I suspect, as a congenial and never failing corrective always at hand.

We owe very much to John Mulso. He was irrepressible and he never failed and his letters are a continual source of information about White. White's letters to him we most strangely have not got, but as Mulso always concentrated on answering to their content, their loss is not so serious perhaps as his would have been. White's affairs were always in apple-pie order, Mulso's haphazard without a doubt, and thus his letters were secure and White's simply lost, I suppose. White seems to have taken this golden friend very much for granted. He did not, in the phrase of their once mutual friend Collins, 'meet his friendship with an equal flame' and Mulso several times complained at the extreme coolness and formality he unaccountably displayed. Mulso always began his letters 'Dear Gil:' and ended with something like 'believe me to be very heartily, Dear Gil, your ever affte friend, J. Mulso'. His style is usually so playful that one does not know quite how seriously to take his objections, but the fact is that White sometimes addresses him as Dear Sir, or My dear Sir, – but hear Mulso: 'Dear Gil – (for I cannot bring Myself to write Dear *Sr* as you do to me, at least 'till you are a Dean, Arch Deacon or Bishop,)'. 'I am, Dear Gil, Ever affetely Your's, J. Mulso. (PS) I observe that you have changed *Dear Mulso into* Dear *Sir*. Do you chuse that word in ye place of *Gil*?' And finally, 'I thank you for your family Anecdotes; it is in ye Style of Friendship, & gives me much pleasure; it is indeed a little check'd by ye wonderful

TO WHITE DENIED

'*The Curate of the parish returned from duty*' (after H. Singleton)

Formality of your Conclusion of your Letter "*Your most humble servant G.W.*" which would have sent me, with my poor Billy, on a freezing Voyage to Arch-Angell round the *North Cape* of Indifference, if ye Body of your Epistle had not been like your former Self, domestic, obliging, friendly and ingenious.' And he signs off: 'Your old and hearty Friend'.

How mortified he would be to know these letters lost – he of all men – to the interested posterity he foresaw.

TO MULSO REFERRED ·
'*The Vicar of the parish receiving his tithes*' (after H. Singleton)

What could it have been in particular about White as a naturalist which inspired John Mulso – who was no naturalist at all – with such a prodigious faith in his destiny? For an answer to that we must go to the Letters to Pennant and to Barrington, of which the Natural History is composed, remembering that Mulso had had the opportunity from the beginning of following the progress of that book.

Mulso was a clever man; he had no small powers of mind himself and with a generous temperament admired the powers of others. However his worldlier self would have liked Gilbert to become a bishop or, next best, Provost of Oriel, and however worldly a parson he was himself, he evidently admired his friend's integrity, the something wholly religious about him, his concentration, the feeling he gave out of complete dedication, even more than he must have appreciated the supernormal gifts he had of the senses. And above all he would have appreciated the originality of Gilbert's grand but simple scheme. For although it may not be obvious to us now, it was highly original, the idea of a natural history as complete as could be, of one small place; the idea that each man's concentrating on just this, without wasting precious energies on vast generalisations and trying to compass the whole world, which no man however gifted could do, would be to the utmost benefit in the long run to natural science; that only in this way, in fact, could the best results be obtained.

CHAPTER IV

The One-Book Man

It seems possible that White really was diffident, as well as modest, but more likely that he was merely rightly hesitant before embarking on what he felt was a supremely important and difficult task. Diffident, that is to say, about writing the kind of book *he* wanted, which it is clear nobody concerned with him had any idea of. Who could have realised what a perfectionist he was? Not even hero-worshipping, prophesying Mulso. But when one studies the genesis of his book, his seemingly gradual emergence as an author, what becomes absolutely clear is White's determination that such nature books as he envisaged should be written. By himself or another did not signify. At the same time, of course, he had been fitting himself to perfection for the take-over, whenever that might be. The time did come, and it came remarkably late, yet one must feel that it came exactly right, as if at the dictates of providence.

Agitated Mulso, not knowing the interior method of White, was often puzzled and exasperated by what his friend himself called procrastination. Mulso had been very patient; White was being so much more so. As the years went by agitation grew to frenzy. For White to set everything aside to help his brother John over John's own natural history book might be understandable; and you might have to excuse White for knocking off to extend the Wakes so as to entertain large and increasing numbers of brothers and their wives, of nephews and nieces, and friends and their families, including Mulso's own. Interest in brother Thomas's proposed *Natural History of Hampshire* was alarming for a while, but excusable, like the interest in John's book, and anyway it soon came to nothing. But he had been encouraging Gilbert since they were both youngsters, first in his verses, then in a travel book he himself proposed, finally in natural history. He knew the man had all the knowledge and all the notes, but what was he doing with them? Brother Benjamin was to blame for not insisting on publishing his brothers' books (for the sooner John's *Fauna Calpensis* was off the stocks, the sooner Gilbert could start concentrating on his own again). Brother Ben had had 'fine pickings out of you naturalists of late years', Mulso says, and adds that John (who was not flourishing) 'ought to be under Ben's pay'. It may be mentioned here that John, inspired to natural history by Gilbert and by him encouraged to write a nature book about Gibraltar, the *Fauna Calpensis*, had turned out a brilliant naturalist. But he could not write a book.

Volatile, impulsive Mulso had no conception of the caution of the brothers White, nor perhaps of their intense *esprit de corps;* or if he guessed at these things it was all the same hidden; and here they were, almost in their fifties (Mulso was a year the younger) and no solid progress made. He could not know in 1769 that the serious intention towards the *Natural History of Selborne* had crystalised, the form of the book been chosen, the Letters selectly embodying the notes begun, and that all was as much due, possibly, to the cunning and acumen of brothers Tom and Ben as to Gilbert White himself.

* * *

And then of course he did know, and all began to fall into place, and as the manuscript Letters to Pennant and Barrington grew he was given the chance to read and to marvel afresh, and to comfort himself with the thought that in a few years he might have before him completed this work which he had had such faith in, even in its full extent and scope of matured comprehension, as White was now making clear to him.

And then, just as he was getting comfortable, in 1775, with the corpus of the book complete, a new hold-up occurred: White insisted on its being illustrated. Mulso did not at first see the necessity, and when he did, did not approve the choice of artist. He was quite wrong; Gilbert as usual knew exactly what he was at in hiring Hieronymous Grimm – an artist who, like himself, could adequately blend the ideal with the factual. True, Grimm is not very exciting, but those who know Selborne well find and instantly recognise, in the topographical details, touched lightly, gracefully yet *honestly*, of these twelve pen-and-wash drawings, very few of which were finally engraved for the book, that certainty as to the reality of the scenes depicted: the veritable perdurable Selborne now as then.

Grimm came, in 1776. The July seems to have been rather wet, but he performed expertly for a fortnight and was gone. It was in the next year that the Great Parlour was building; and then, in 1777 the most awful blow fell. It was proposed to add the *Antiquities* to the *Natural History* and this meant incalculable delay.

Poor Mulso! He 'would not go 2 miles out of his way to see the finest ruins in England' – and here, by God, there were no actual ruins to be seen! He had no use for what he called 'the rusts and crusts and frusts of time'.

'For heaven's sake don't waste time on the Size, Markets, the Tolls, the Souls, the Priories & Religious houses of Selborne . . . let it be short if it must be.'

He cajoles sweetly, fears that the 'sweet and elegant simplicity' of White's observations will be overwhelmed by the 'Rubbishy Antiquities'. Yet – and here it comes: 'Yet it may save some future biographers trouble when they celebrate the place where such a genius was born.'

September 1780: 'Pray does your book come out this winter? I really cannot hold out any longer. If you spoil the genuine elegances and neat simplicity of the original design by a farrago of Antiquities routed out of the Rusts & Frusts of Time, I shall not esteem it so well as once I did, & so I tell you.' All, threat or flattery, was in vain. The long cool look which White seems always to have directed on life passed cursorily over Mulso and, with perhaps a faint indulgent smile, he went steadily on to make, by the courtesy of Magdalen College, the necessary researches. More years passed. Mulso became almost tearfully reproachful.

June 1781: 'The good old Bishop has died', robbed of pleasure by the publication's withholding or deferring: 'Are you cowardly or are you over-nice and curious? Make haste my dear old friend, or you may rob the nephew too. Do you save it up for my chair-days?' Those 'chair-days' were not so far off, as perhaps poor Mulso divined. In 1781 White visited him and no doubt temporarily allayed his fears that he would not survive till publication, but in June the next year comes something like genuinely irritated explosions: 'Another winter is passed without your *essays*. You are a timorous & provoking man. You defraud yourself. . . .' And in August: 'Am I to dye before your little favourite work comes out? *Des aliquid famae*; and don't be so tedius and phlegmatic.'

But at last, in September 1787, Mulso is able to say: 'You delight me with the account of your being in the press.' Delays are really over, apart from such as normally attend publication, and on 15 December of the following year, in bed with influenza, he holds the handsome volume in his trembling hands and owns, gallant man, that the Antiquities have 'such a grace in your manner of treating the subject, as would give a pleasure and a hunger to a man not an antiquarian'. But I imagine that he still thought of them as like a Gothic porch clapped on to a Palladian mansion.

One final note of genuine pathos. 'I a little repine that my name did not stand in a book of so much credit and respectability; and I am ready to say with Tully, *Orna me.*' But such precious help as Mulso had given for so long is not of the kind that is professionally acknowledgeable.

CHAPTER V

The Modesty of a Falcon

'TIMOROUS and provoking' – 'tedius and phlegmatic'.

Certainly these quotations from Mulso Agonistes tend to give the impression of a vacillating White, continually postponing and not particularly caring; the very opposite, if I am right, of the truth. He does seem indeed to have been modest and reticent and unpushful to a fault, but perhaps only if he were opposed by someone singularly importunate (if good-naturedly so) who was trying for no really good reason to hustle him. There is the Letter too, to Pennant, accusing himself of diffidence, which is similarly open to misunderstanding or exaggeration. This letter was written in July 1771 and in it he discusses with Pennant, with whom he had been in correspondence for the past four years, the possibility of his publishing a book of his own. By this time it had presumably ceased to be a mere possibility, but relations with Pennant had become rather strained. To say that the latter had been picking White's brains long enough might be being too harsh, but I will suppose White now to be feeling a trifle cagey with him.

White wrote in July 1771: 'As to any publication in this way of my own, I look upon it with great diffidence, finding that I ought to have begun it twenty years ago.' And then he goes on to delineate his plan – his own idea of his book. 'But if I was to attempt anything it should be somewhat of a Nat. History of my native parish, an *annus historico-naturalis* comprising a journal for one whole year, and illustrated with large notes and observations. Such a beginning might induce more able naturalists to write – of various districts – so in time that much to be wished for full and complete nat. history of these kingdoms.' Pennant did not take the hint.

Or did White wish to give Pennant a kind of rebuke? Their correspondence was just closing, whereas that with Barrington, begun two years after the start with Pennant, was now in full swing. To Barrington a year before, he had *first* announced his own intentions, without any 'if', but about that time to Pennant he appears very critical, at least by implication. Referring to the latter's fourth edition of the *British Zoology* about to appear, and which for years he had been supplying valuable notes intended to correct faults in previous editions, White hopes that Pennant 'will continue to *revise at leisure* & to *retouch it over* 'til you have *rendered it as perfect* as the nature of the work will admit of'. (These italics are rare with White.) And what had been the result? Pennant had done nothing, simply sent White the manuscript as before, for White to make the corrections for him! 'I must correct over again what I have corrected', wrote Gilbert, to his brother John, ' 'til I am quite sick. The printing also is very incorrect.' To add insult to injury there was the bare mention of his name in a list of others, in acknowledgement of his immense services. White also would have said, '*Orna me*'.

In short I claim that White's 'diffidence' was, here at least, deliberately and defensively assumed towards one who had caused him a certain amount of pains and disappointment and irritation, but who was not only a popular author, to be wary with, noted for his readable, gossipy travel books full of agreeable animal anecdote, but also one of Benjamin's best-sellers.

Since we have now got into the world of booksellers we will take a closer look at Gilbert's book.

CHAPTER VI

The One-Man Book

WHEN a man has spent his whole life writing a book, it is best to look at it with attention if you want to find his character. In this case it is not a big book, and the character, I think, shines out very distinguishable.

The first thing that meets you is that utter absence of false-modesty I have earlier mentioned. In the cause of natural science White speaks out fearlessly; quiet impersonally, because there is here no need anyway to intrude the personality. There is no dogma, no controversial pugnacity, just an entire firmness of conviction that where he does inform he does so because he teaches from absolutely proven experience.

There were many eminent naturalists before White and alive with him, and one of them, Linnaeus, was very great. White does not scruple to point him out in a fault. How could he? The names of many, temporary pundits, occur in the *Natural History* and it is evident that they all had been studied with the closest attention. How fortunate, we see, in this respect, that naturalists had the benefit of Latin, the universal tongue, which ourselves seem about to chuck out of the window. At the same time how very glad we must be that he didn't write in Latin himself. (But glad still that he was a good Latin scholar.)

Scopoli's new work is awaited eagerly. Scopoli's new work arrives; there is good in it, but he is criticised for false facts. Brisson is named. He has compared from memory 'whereas I have compared the birds themselves'. Brisson perhaps was French, and White is severe on them: 'The French are prolix in their natural-history generally'. Was this aimed at Buffon? There is a Kramer, and he fell short in style it seems. Names of many naturalists forgotten or shadowily remembered occur – Derham, 'old Moufet', Geoffrey.

Actually Derham – William Derham (1657–1735), though fusty enough to us, would have been a different proposition for White. For he was a child, in a sense, of the great Ray, sometimes called the father of British biologists, who, with Willughby, meant so much to White. And Derham had had something of his own method (but nothing of his imaginative, magical writing touch) and, like Ray, strove to show nature as of God, and that divine harmony was discernible in everything. A clergyman, like White, Derham, Vicar of Wargrave, had gone outdoors too, but without such senses as White could employ. He had been Boyle lecturer for a year. He was not just a naturalist to be read in passing. Derham had written books: *Physico-Theology* and *Astro-Theology*, whose titles show what kind of mind was his. He and Ray may be taken as the spiritual parents of Paley, of the *Evidences*. White did not differ from these men in his basic aim. What would render him effective in the future, where Paley was no use, was the feeling and understanding of the living reality he was able to bring home in pointing out the creatures they all sought.

As I have said, it was not by accident that White was a clergyman; but then you would never detect anything of deep religion in his book; only an occasional thing like a reference to Ray's *Wisdom Of God In The Creation*, or calling (P. Letter XX) a deer's newly-discovered scent glands 'a new instance of the wisdom of God'. His religion was so still within him, his reticence, his discretion so entire, his sense of proportion so perfect.

* * *

As for Pennant himself, of course, he crossed swords with him in the matter of the migration or not of ring-ouzels; Pennant had thought them exclusive to the North. And when White says (Letter XXI) with regard to Scopoli's work mentioned: 'Monographers, come from whence they may, have, I think, fair pretence to challenge some regard and approbation from the lovers of natural history; for as no man can alone investigate all the works of nature, these partial writers may, each in their department, be more accurate in their discoveries, and freer from errors, than more general writers; and so by degrees may pave the way to a universal correct history', it is pretty clearly aimed at Pennant's weaknesses. 'Not', he adds, 'that Scopoli is so circumstantial and attentive to the life and conversation of his birds as I could wish: he advances some false facts; as when he says of the *hirundo urbica* that "*pullos extra nidum non nutrit*". This assertion I know to be wrong from observation this summer; for house-martins do feed their young flying——'.

No one ever *was* as attentive as he wished. No one would get out of doors and study the creatures in their habitat accurately, with detachment, not allowing themselves to be led away by preconceived theories. No one really cared, except for his own reputation . . . so vain. One senses that Pennant, for instance, really exasperated him with this stubbornness about the ring-ouzel, not accepting his proofs, in a running fight lasting to the end of their correspondence. No matter, he would get those facts into his own book at last.

However, Pennant had succeeded in identifying the *falco* White sent him – after a considerable time of silence. It turned out to be a peregrine falcon. This occurred early in their correspondence, and more usually people sent things to White for identification. One of his greatest feats in this direction was the identifying of a wall-creeper, a rare bird from the Continent scarcely ever seen here. White sleuths it down meticulously and inevitably. He had never seen it before, of course, and only saw a drawing of wing feathers now, but it just had to be the wall-creeper. He was shown a large and curious horn:

> There can be no doubt that the horn shown to me at Mr. Lever's Museum, vast as it was, belonged to the Genus Bos: for it was Concavum, antrosum, versum lunatum laeve: whereas had it been related to the Genus of Capra, it would have been concavum, sursum versum erectum, scabrum. Neither can it by any means belong to the Genus of Cervus, for then it would have been solidum, corio hirto tactum, apice cresens: nor for as strong reasons to the Genus of Cuis; for then it would have been concavum retrosum versum, intortum rugosum.
>
> It must therefore of course have belonged to the Genus of Bos.

This kind of thing may have been routine stuff to the classically trained naturalist of White's day, and I do not know that I am right in regarding it as a fair example of his method, scholarship and *humour*. It was recorded in his Journal, and I fancy I detect in it the equivalent of a twinkle, as though he had sat down to amuse himself. Certainly he had plenty of humour, playfulness, fun; but of that later.

Local sportsmen when they (inevitably) shot some bird they had never seen before – the fascinating Stilt, for instance, on Frensham great pond, and the mysterious hybrid pheasant, so hard to place, and which was painted by a Farnham artist, and included in the book, the painting itself hanging long at the Wakes afterwards, and many another odd creature – when these were shot they were generally brought straight to White. He had, so to speak, his spies everywhere. He lost no chance of advancing science, he delighted in oddities, rarities, anecdotes. And in that little chosen field, his native parish, he made discoveries of his own. They are not many, and not sensational: the harvest mouse, almost the smallest mammal in the world; the great bat, which he called *vespertilio altivolans*; the 'grasshopper lark' (which we call the grasshopper warbler) and perhaps greatest, the three warblers he distinguished by their songs: chiff-chaff, willow warbler and wood warbler. These had been classified by Linnaeus as one species, *Motacilla trochilus*. Everyone had been hearing these three birds, but they saw only one (they are very hard to distinguish), and it remained for White to think it so odd that one bird should have three songs and to get up and investigate it thoroughly.

This novel outdoor enterprise and expertise made White famous long before his book was published, but as nobody likes being told better unless he is as dedicated as White, it was necessary to use the greatest tact with his main correspondents. Barrington was evidently more amenable than Pennant – he was less professional, had less to lose. Daines Barrington, who was one of the 'Old Benchers of the Inner Temple' later immortalised by Lamb – I hope it is not unkind to mention that he was the one who had the sparrows poisoned – had the pet theory that swallows hibernated in mud. Thus many have interpreted it, and fixed Gilbert White with it too. An absurd theory, but not much more ridiculous than the belief that White could entertain it. The point was that White was not going to say it was impossible that some swallows stayed behind until he *knew*. (And let me say that there is still some doubt about this question.) He thought they might lodge in barns or deep in the crevices of cliffs, or in thick undergrowth such as the sheep-bitten beech growth on the Hanger in Selborne, among the roots and tangle. And it was this last which led him sometimes to an appearance of subscribing to Barrington's idea of their hibernating like some fishes in the mud. For as was very well known, swallows congregating on the eve of migration did go down at nightfall into the reeds. But I am not going to defend White from an absurdity – it is true he did say 'if they do' (migrate) in the Letter XVI to Barrington: I am afraid it was a sop. But he perfectly knew the movements of migrating swallows generally, who told his brother John to date their passage for him to and from Africa over Gibraltar. The swallows generally were his speciality; papers on them by him were read before the Royal Society and printed for its use; the letters about them in the *Natural History* form examples of his most exquisite writing. Of course the question ought not to be laboured; but you would be surprised how many people have approached me with this objection: that White was a poor naturalist because he believed swallows hibernated in mud! And having gone so far, let me add that it is plain – and an endearing thing about White – that he would have loved to be sure that some swallows did 'remain loyal' to our country, to stay and share its long cold winter with him – the birds beyond all he loved. But he did not go in for wishful thinking, and died with the problem unresolved. It is a little example of that life-long discipline White imposed on himself in the cause of science, which, I maintain, the study of his book bears plainly out, which is a most admirable part of his steady, well-based character.

Again you will easily see how careful White had to be with Barrington, who was also one of his brother's most influential customers, which brings me back to the provenance of this correspondence, that is to say, of the book. To what extent was it all arranged by Benjamin and fostered by Thomas? This we may discover better when we come to consider White in relation to his family – that wonderful eighteenth-century family of partizan pride. It is obvious that he was helped very much.

CHAPTER VII

The Book

BUT these drier facts about White and this number of mostly long-forgotten and mostly undistinguished naturalists of the past, his relations with them and with their fusty books, can have little to do with the charm of his personality and the success of the *Natural History of Selborne* – though they probably helped the latter a great deal in the beginning. The facts and discoveries need not excite us now, for as Hudson said a century after they had been made, they 'have been tested and sifted and all that were worth keeping are to be found incorporated in scores of standard works on natural history.' It remains to emphasise again that his greatness lay in taking the study out of doors, making ordinary men and women as well as savants familiar by close direct confrontation with the live fellow creature in its lovely and sufficient forms.

Many another person of course had been poking and peering in hedges and ditches before White, but mostly, except to some degree botanists, unavailingly, because they were cut off from the Buffons and Scopolis in their libraries. Now the position was rectified: a real scientist had joined them and gone at once to the front, one who demanded that knowledge should be come by their way, insisted that it was the best way, if not the only way. It should not be derived from dead, pressed, deformed specimens transported to the dimness of indoors, subjected to the speculations of indoor minds, illustrated often in the most shockingly inadequate manner, and finally buried in expensive inaccessible libraries.

For White seems to have paid almost as much attention to the layout of his book as to the matter it contained. He was dissatisfied with the illustrations of his period – and no wonder. To put it simply if crudely, the living works of God, stricken from their habitats, their 'conversation' for ever interrupted, if they had once been observed in all their quick joyous, shining exercise of God-given life – these living works of

God arrived all squashed, and were handed over to a lot of poor hack artists, drudges. These did their best perhaps, but no best was possible. The interested who turn to such eighteenth-century nature books as *Bingley's British Quadrupeds* or *Goldsmith's Animated Nature* will be impressed by the large quantity of animals shaped like stoats or dachshunds. Even the Ringtailed Lemur, most graceful of animals, with its upright poises of more than human dignity, its restrained perfection of gesture, comes out with a great long body, shortish legs, nose like a greyhound and a long *straight* tail. Only by the rings round eyes and tail can it be identified, which in fact was about all these poor fellows in their dark caverns of Fleet Street basements had to go on. All this became unfashionable after White. And to him we owe, I think it fair to claim – though at long remove – the changed feeling which is substituting photographs for the illustrations depicting mostly stuffed specimens in our bird books, and the growing custom of replacing with painted clay models our decaying bird specimens in museums, so much more life-like, so that perhaps models of insects, too, will come to fill the cases; for certainly it is not beyond our technique to reproduce the carven carapaces of beetles, and even the wings of the Lepidoptera. And we may owe to him and to the most enlightened of his followers – though he did shoot specimens and cause them to be shot for him, for then there was no other way – that nowadays the bird-watcher with binoculars has almost replaced the sportsman with the gun, at least for natural-history purposes. Nature study, while more scientific, is more alive. There has come a new climate of understanding. We have above all the nature film.

* * *

The second most important thing as to the character of White from his book is his style. Nothing is more revealing of its author's nature. It is something absolutely of himself, unique, and I should say it is one of the chief reasons of his abiding popularity, the secret of his power to entertain.

As to that, even to this day, there is no doubt. Would you like to know of the curious Reaumur, who hatched the large eggs of the forest-fly in his bosom? Of hail-stones – pieces of ice three inches in girth – in the great thunderstorm of 5 June 1784? and of the summer preceding that year, with its horrible phenomena, when from 23 June to 20 July the sun at noon looked as blank as a clouded moon, shedding a rust-coloured ferruginous light on ground and flooring, and why this was? Of how really enjoyable, how fat, good, juicy, tender, thin of rind or sward, bacon can be if obtained from a very old sow, notably prolific, as thick as she was long, and whose belly swept the ground, and who, when she would converse with a boar, would quietly undo the gates between and march up hill to one, returning calmed, and closing them after her? Of what it means to sit in the Hermitage and hear three swivel-guns discharged out of the Hanger Alcove; and how a gentleman of means and leisure may build his own echo, so as to sit with friends of an evening, when the air is most elastic, exercising his skill in classical verse, answered to a last syllable? How swifts copulate on the wing? How goldfish die, and why; and why it is we like them so in a bowl; and how to add to the pleasure of that with a new dimension, but to know just how far to go with that kind of thing.

Of course you would: and like to hear of the village boy who lived only on honey, catching the bees alive, careless of stings. And of the poor leper disgustingly encrusted with brown scurf. Or the extraordinary forbearance, in the eighteenth century, of the keeper at Frensham pond, with regard to a flock of black-winged stilts – rarest of visitants. And what happened on the night of the furious storm and the Hawkley land slip, which tore a cottage in half almost, and a barn quite, and deposited everything some forty feet below, but level, and not much disturbed, except that the pond had deep and shallow ends reversed. Of mother-love and its fury and courage, and what truth there is in a viper's young all trooping into her mouth as into an air raid shelter; and whether a woodcock really does carry her chicks in her bill.

These are for a sample – a tithe of the anecdotes which cram the marvellous book. Or you may prefer something which shows the clear clean reason at work not always perhaps to quite the right or modern conclusion, maybe, but that is all long done with and irrelevant now; and the exquisite passages on the *hirundines*, perfect despite their slight bias now and again towards Barrington's pet foible (and perhaps we must say White's too): essays on bird language of song and alarm-note; on the flight of birds; the reasons for their flocking; their feeding habits. About pulveratrices, and how, though these never wash, some that do wash dust as well, such as the sparrow. And a side glance made at Arabs as pulveratrices, with allusion to Mahomet.

The variation seems enormous, the sense of space infinite; he is

View of the Lyth and Dorton from Huckers Mead

interested in everything that lives and the atmosphere surrounding, the air it breathes, the water it drinks, what it eats. And he makes all come alive. And through everything, as one reads on, one is aware of the harmonising spirit, the humanising touch; the voice quietly not insisting, but insinuating always that we are one.

The humanising touch. As when he tells of stone curlews crying in the night, coming from the high lands of the hill and fore-down on spring and summer nights, 'down towards Dorton; where, among its streams and meadows they find great plenty of food', which fills you with the sense of lying still, listening in the darkness, under a cottage gable in Selborne's hollow vale. And with something else, when he has earlier told you that they cannot help but be loud-crying in the night, for companionship, and for fear they lose each other: when he has told of the wonderful spirit of sociality in the brute creation.

For men themselves are never divorced from his study. Much that fascinates was merely meant for use. For humble cottage uses, which so much appealed to Cobbett: how to make cheap light by peeling rushes and dipping them in mutton or bacon fat; and beautiful neat little soft brushes of chestnut-coloured 'hair' shredded from the stalks of the great golden maidenhair, *polytyicum commune*, or silkwood – which gives its name presumably to the field where it was grown behind the old mill, so that White calls that little river valley with its waterfall 'Silkwood Vale', though really its name was Mill Bottom.

Yes, Cobbett must surely have been led by these trifles, with his desire, so strong under pressure of future industrialism, to revive cottage economy. He approved of White and visited Selborne many years later. He came via Hawkley Hurst and the Empshott way, and was enormously impressed by the violence of the country lying convulsed below him. He reined back his horse on its haunches and looked sideways at his groom – a man who came from almost equally imposing and even higher country at Inkpen Beacon – to see how he reacted. (And he suitably did.) And George Borrow, too, I feel certain, was electrified by the strangely-named Curleoples, of the brave wild half-animal gipsy race, and took the hint White gave regarding this name. To the lonely youth Hudson, in far-away time and country, we know what an instant link was the Selborne Cobweb Shower. To Hudson such things, though very well known and on very much larger scale in the pampas, were also a wonder and a mystery for ever.

Though I said I would not quote in the beginning, since to do so would be, in effect, merely to add to the already enormous number of editions and reprints, and because I want you to obtain a copy and read for yourself, so cheaply and abundantly printed is it, I must, of course, quote some part at least of some things. Letter XXXIV to Pennant for instance contains something which that reference to gipsies brought instantly to mind – though it may not be at once obvious why – about peacocks and their nuptial behaviour.

> By a strong muscular vibration these birds can make the shafts of their long feathers clatter like the swords of a sword-dancer; they then trample very quick with their feet, and run backwards towards the females.

This which powerfully and instantly begets a vivid image, is the fruit of intense observation and innate fellow-feeling, and cosmic understanding as well. Thus do nature's high-bred wooers teach us how to woo. In these few vivid lines I get the sense and image of Spanish gipsy dancers who have interpreted, probably through these and other birds, nature's own way of approaching love – love vibrant at its highest on the physical plane, with a shimmer and a shudder and stamp of heels, a click of castenets. Clumsy indeed, crude, lustful, is the pelvic roll and thrust of negroid dancing, though equally expository, equally true. I do not know anything which reveals White's art so well as this marvellous little passage, where he betrays nothing either of his powers of intellect or of the senses. It is obvious that he was acutely possessed of both. Now Flaubert, too, did a wonderful job with peacocks at what might still be well termed 'amorous converse'. It comes, if I remember, in *L'Éducation Sentimentale*, but Flaubert remains always the cold, brilliant, self-conscious observer, and the spectacle, the eroticism is not moving, but rather somehow sad. Though we are sure that Flaubert was a good man and loved life, it seems he could not get that loving through his art and into his novel as White into a natural history book.

* * *

What a natural history book! It seems his sensibility was as acute as his senses; that he was a romantic, quick of heart, full of concealed nervous excitements and enthusiasms. He possessed great tenderness. He concealed this: remember that he was a very small man, only a little over five feet in height, which I think is of significance here, for though small men are notoriously aggressive, and even at times fierce – the grandest fighters have always been small men – it was obviously, for Gilbert White, imperative to keep calm and cool. For that aggressive spirit which leads to self-assertion he could have, as we have seen, no use. No need for him to be competitive. That he was so cool and balanced in his activities as normally observed, will be shown in his ordinary, his man's, existence; and quietly, only in certain phrases, is this tenderness revealed.

Flycatchers: they hover before the nest in the vine, in the fierce sun, fanning and shielding their naked nestling. And it is known that the spotted flycatcher is very unusual among birds in having no song. But it does make a sound – 'A little inward wailing note', says White – and I find in this choice of words an example of innate inner tenderness. The sounds are distress notes, expressive of deep anxiety.

The naturalist has, of necessity, almost professionally to maintain a spirit of detachment towards the sudden deaths of creatures, engaged as we all are in a system of mutual destruction from birth. It is a godlike aloofness but never estrangement, very hard for some of us to comprehend; but those who cannot or will not accept this tragedy are those, often, who cause more misery and confusion, even if it is only that people of sensibility are condemned with sentimentalists by the strictly scientific of mind. White of course had this habit of detachment professionally, but I see in his descriptions of the missel-thrushes who fought so bravely in vain for their young,* and the raven whom parental solicitude also destroyed, in the wood called Losels,† something beyond the drama and excitement which, together with the facts, exercised his pen so well; something of human sympathy, of appreciation, human to human, when it was unthinkable to point animal to animal. There are cases where he seems to step aside deliberately to draw our attention to the 'humanness' of animals. The most famous perhaps is the friendship between the hen and the horse – the kind of thing we find as children in fairy tales; but this is in a natural history book. And in the melancholy account of the Duke of Richmond and Gordon's moose‡ I find something of the same kind but more subtle – I hope not too fancifully. On Michaelmas Day of 1768 he had a chance to go to Goodwood to see this animal, but it had died. White was baulked of the living thing he had hoped to study, but he determined at least to study the corpse. . . . 'I found it in an old greenhouse, slüng under the belly and chin by ropes, and in a standing posture; but, though it had been dead for so short a time, it was in so putrid a state that the stench was hardly supportable.' If some of those who accuse White of laziness were to go into greenhouses and investigate putrid mooses it would be a good thing. White, the hero, like the painter, Stubbs, with his horse, gives a wonderful factual detailed account of this fearful cadaver, and was only just defeated in the end when ' – in my haste to get out of the stench, I forgot to measure that joint (the tibia) exactly'. Yet after this nauseating experience bringing him nose to nose with corruption – with Nature decidedly at her worst – White has the spirit to say: 'This poor creature had at first a female companion of the same species, which died the spring before. In the same garden was a young stag, or red deer, between whom (mark that 'whom') and this moose it was hoped that there might have been a breed; but their inequality of height must have always been a bar to any commerce of the amorous kind.' Is this compassion, are these musings, wholly of a natural-historical kind?

A journalist friend of mine remarked the other day, rather in the way of admiring White for it, that he had gone in for sensational gossip. Startled, I asked for an instance and it appeared that the Bee Boy had struck him like this. The immortal Bee Boy (Letter XXVIII to Barring-

* Letter II to Pennant. † Letter XXII to Barrington.

‡ Letter XXV to Pennant.

ton), a creature miserably deprived of most normal faculties to the extension and modification of one. It was White's description of this unfortunate, undoubtedly, which gave de la Mare the idea for his poem beginning 'There were two fairies, Gimmel and Mell/Loved earthmens' honey passing well'. They would come with cunning and slit the skeps, you may remember. And White: 'He was a very *Merops apiaster*, or bee-bird, and very injurious to men who kept bees; for he would slide into their bee-gardens, and, sitting down before the stools, would rap with his finger on the hives, and so take the bees as they came out.' Intoxicating words and image, for any poet.

So many things we start when we write a natural history book – if we are White. And had this, this additional, this bonus-quality, after all much to do with natural history? It is natural history, all the same; for White, an enthusiast for Pope, would have known all about 'The proper study of mankind——'. 'Man' comes under his lens in many instances and poor creatures alienated in far-away countries found themselves here again in home surroundings, even if the instance given was only about Warreners on a heath, fearfully bitten by harvest bugs.

White the scientist never loses touch with humanity, and in this, too, he is unique in his time.

* * *

Yes, indeed, the whole of White's book is quotable; and it is easy to come on copies in second-hand bookshops all over the country, and you may buy it new, and cheap. You must do so and read for yourself.

You will find how in many a light delicious phrase White inspires us as usually only poets can. 'This wonderful procreant cradle' is how he describes the harvest mouse's nest – a phrase which competes with the 'pensile nest-like bower' (in a poem indeed this time) with which he describes the Hermitage he and his brother had built on the Hanger. The sedge warbler is 'a delicate polyglot', which means that it did not just mimic sounds at random. (John White in Gibraltar said only 'a polyglot'.)

When Hudson says of this book, after searching for the reason for its immense success: 'I believe that there is no mystery at all about it; – the personality of its author is the principal charm of the Letters, for in spite of his modesty and extreme reticence his spirit shines in every page; that the world will not willingly let this small book die, not only because it is small, and well written, and full of interesting matter, but chiefly because it is a very delightful human document.' (*Birds & Man.*) I am sure this is right, that he has put his finger on it; and that this amounts to saying that it is White's happiness that does it. It found its way to us through the style.

White was a great and happy man. We know that because he wrote a great book. He was a great writer.

CHAPTER VIII

A Nest of Whites

THOSE twin luminaries, two flowers of Hampshire soil, Jane Austen and Gilbert White, offer certain interesting similarities. Each is an example of extreme sensitivity coupled with earth-rootedness; in each life we can if we like detect the hand of providence. One cannot well imagine either living at any other time or in another part of the world.

White's time was 1720 to 1793. As I have said, he perfectly balanced with it, and yet he just sufficiently carried forward into the succeeding age, as Jane Austen, with her serious sense of religion, also did. His birth just then, as if in preparation for the coming of Darwin, while at the same time providing those who wished among the religiously sensitive with a gentle antidote against the terrible shock of evolution, was providential. The place 'selected' for his theatre of operation was providential; his profession of clergyman was providential; above all, his family was providential.

For the Whites, like the Austens, and for that matter the Darwins themselves, and the Wedgwoods, seem to have been one of those families which the eighteenth century specialised in for the nurture of genius; families whose members were mostly all sane and cultivated; who all admired and helped each other.

It is not to be supposed that they quite realised what swans had been hatched among them; nor indeed is it obvious that either Gilbert or Jane understood that they were swans at all. Both were so modest and retiring, yet both seemed innately, perfectly to understand at the outset what work they had to do. Furnished with such clear vision as from birth, nothing that was to happen on the way forward seemed capable of preventing their fulfilment.

* * *

Again, as in Jane Austen's case, there is no adequate portrait of White, only a pair of casual sketches. No portraits of the grand-parents of White on his father's side hang among those of so many other relatives at the Wakes, but elsewhere there is a portrait of Gilbert White, senior, and a fine one. Hardy and stern to grimness he looks, Gilbert the 1st, whose engraved stone in the chancel floor is so confusing to the visitor. He may not have been so very far removed from Fielding's Parson Trulliber (chiefly remembered for his prowess in the pigsty, and for throwing stones at birds in the fruit-garden), but he was a scholar and conscientious priest before being a good husbandman and repairer of his church walls and roof. He was a Fellow of Magdalen College, Oxford. His father had been Sir Sampson White who, as plain Mr. White had helped to buttle at Charles II's coronation feast, presenting him then with a golden bowl on behalf of the citizens of Oxford, of which city he was Mayor. He had been knighted for it accordingly.

Gilbert, senior became Vicar of Selborne at thirty-five in 1681, and he died at the vicarage in February 1728. Since his grandson, born in that house in July 1720, was for these first eight years of his life only a visitor to Selborne, his parents living at Compton, near Guildford, he might not have known his grandfather very well. His grandmother Rebekah, however, who long survived her husband, dying in 1755 (at the age of ninety-one), he knew very well indeed. For after the vicar's death she removed to the cottage he had evidently provided for the purpose, called Wakes – that is, late the property of a man called Wake – on the other side of the street, and there her son John, with his wife Anne, and Gilbert and all the rest of their growing brood came to live with her. Rebekah White was a Selborne woman, born Luckin, daughter of a farmer at near-by Noar (or Nore). This was a very special gift to White; no wonder he was able to get on with his neighbours. He thoroughly understood their interests. His Selborne roots went deep, for the Luckins, whose home called Norehouse still stands by the road to Galley Hill, were people long established in the place. So you see him rooted in and fixed on Selborne, that fertile place, notable for the diversity of its flora and fauna; that village ground where a few hundred paces could as vastly change the mental atmosphere as the view; with differing soils, and extremely differing within the compass of a few miles; the perfect examplar of the average of all that fertile England could afford the curious, budding naturalist.

Gilbert's grandfather made the lawn at the Vicarage, as Gilbert himself was to make one at the Wakes. The old man was skilled in all sorts

The Vicarage terrace as it was

of husbandry, and must have given his son and grandson many tips, as Rebekah would give innumerable household hints and points of folk-lore and old remedies. It seems likely that White's chief remembrance of his grandfather was either of a tremendously imposing, robed figure at the altar, or else of somebody perpetually digging at his vegetables. But grandmother White would be remembered as one who had taken the mother's place and looked after them all when that poor soul died at a relatively early age; in fact she may have been filling that position for a long time, perhaps from the start of their all living together. It may strike some people that it was rather a queer arrangement. A large commodious house was to be exchanged for a much smaller one – admittedly under necessity – and into it, with Rebekah, were to go eleven people: John and his wife; Gilbert, Tom, Benjamin, Rebecca, John Junior, Francis, Anne and Harry. From Tom on they came at about nine-month intervals, so that indeed some were very young children. And this is leaving out of consideration what servants there might be to live at Wakes as well. One must think that the original Wakes had been enlarged provisionally by the grandfather at some time before his death; but the added wing looks to be of about 1680. Without that wing, so far as can be judged of the cottage before, it would have been impossible.

But whatever arrangement, we may be sure that it was sensibly entered into and made to work, because of the character and common sense of the grandmother and the good nature, cheerfulness and good sense also of the family generally. Grandmother White was shrewd and would have known when to give way to be comfortable; her son's nature was notoriously gentle, and so was Gilbert's. There seems to have been a particularly close and friendly relationship between grand-mother and eldest grandson, which grew stronger when this pair came to share full responsibility in the household after Anne White's death. By that time Gilbert was nineteen, just going to Oxford, but he must for long have exercised a benevolent control over his brothers and sisters. He came early to be in effect head of the family, for his father had never cared to take much responsibility.

So the legend goes. John White, senior, is reckoned to have been a man of interestingly passive or negative character. He was a barrister, but he never practised. The Bar would be a lonely place if all young barristers married heiresses, even if only modest heiresses. Anne White was a small heiress. In days when a man who had means might choose to lead a quiet country life he need not be thought peculiar because he did so.

As a *White*, in contrast with his active enterprising forebear, the cup-offering Mayor, his practical, hard flourishing parson father, and his sons, in the light of what they were to achieve, John White does seem relatively ineffectual. But he was loved and respected. Mulso remembered him kindly, and that he used to play the harpsichord, and since to make music is so unusual a thing in an Englishman, no doubt the fact impressed the minds of his contemporaries and followers; but as a counter to this he was a J.P., or had been one (though one does not know when or how frequently he sat), had a sixty-foot well dug at Wakes, had a considerable say in the laying out of the new garden there, and saw to the remetalling, with a sum his father left for the purpose, of a considerable length of road in Honey Lane – the 'road to the forest' (Wolmer Forest, where Selbornians had rights of turbary, or cutting peat). Honey Lane is called that because the clay there in places was sticky to the feet. A harmless man, John White would have shared the oblivion which the times conferred on simple happy and contented gentlemen who stayed at home, if fate had not selected him to be the father of Gilbert. But I have no doubt that the latter inherited from him his sweetness and calm, his love of poetry and music, and that more elevated gardening taste refined upon Gilbert, senior's, who had made the Vicarage garden out of a 'rude field with a stone-pit in it', as White said proudly later, and with a terrace, and a superb yew hedge. But it is perhaps of interest that when it was a question of finding a suitable job for another John White – 'Gibraltar Jack', son of Gilbert's brother the Rev. John White, Gilbert said, in turning down the idea of the lad's becoming an apprenticed attorney: 'As to law, I have nothing to say about it; lawyers get all the money. Your father, you know, did not approve of it.'

It is Gilbert's opinion here which matters. He is otherwise merely repeating his father's general one. But is there any special significance in the 'lawyers get all the money' coming from the eldest son of an heiress?

Anne Holt had certainly been a minor or 'small' heiress. Her money came to her from her mother, who had been an heiress too, of course, and not a minor one. As Miss Hyde, this lady had married the Rev. Thomas Holt, and it was to him that the bulk of her fortune came on her demise, and when *he* died it passed to his half-brother, also a Thomas. It next came to Anne's second son, Gilbert's brother Tom. Anne by this time was dead – she died of measles, fairly young, in 1739 – but why did this fortune go to Tom alone, and everyone else, so to speak, by-passed? John White inherited almost nothing from his wife, and he left almost nothing when he died. One might well ask: 'When is an heiress not an heiress?'

Of course we are here in a world of dusty parchments and owlish legal eyes; the world of marriage settlement and entail into which it is impossible at this late date to attempt to enter – at least for the 'layman'; but it is of great importance to the proper understanding of future happenings to White. Simply, Anne's fortune was what she brought under her marriage settlement, and this and only this she and her husband had to enjoy and to dispose of. They had many children (perhaps not their only extravagance in early married life) and they must have given most of this away to these as occasion arose, for education and to start them on their careers. We know this was so in one case. But the real, the parent fortune, the original Hyde money, was obviously subject to entail, but why it should have zigzagged and hopped as it did – passing latterly, it seems, only to Thomases! – is a mystery which would lead us far back in time. We only know that no one in the nest of Whites seemed to see anything odd about Tom's being preferred, and that Gilbert was regarded by his father and everyone else as the 'general heir of the family', which appears in the event to have meant very little, and here I must leave it for the present, apart from saying that it is very important to remember that 'everybody' 'knew' that Gilbert was eldest son, heir to John White, from whom he would inherit Wakes, and that his mother was an heiress.

As we know, he did inherit Wakes. It is not much good being owner of a place like the Wakes, you may think, without enough money to keep it up. Well it was not the Wakes we see now, and it was managed in the event, and we shall see how it was done. No doubt it was all for the best, but it is another thing which demonstrates that his life had its stresses, and another illustration of the workings of providence.

* * *

There has been no secret for years now about the Whites having been poor . . . well, not poor exactly, but financially always at a stretch; but we must remember that at the time it would have been imperceptible. People were very secretive then about their means and all private affairs. It is no secret now because in consequence of contemporary mistakenness on the point, leading to trouble at Oriel about White's not giving up his Fellowship, on the score of not being well-off, and the virtual repetition of charges against him many, many years later, his great-grand-nephew, Rashleigh Holt-White, produced financial details in defence of White's reputation.

But what of John White? Doesn't it in some way bear out the idea that he was odd – to stay there doing nothing, when he must have known something of what the future held in store for his eldest son? He was indeed strange in one thing: at that period it was rare to meet a man with no family ambition at all; to whom Wakes was nothing but a makeshift, not a place to hold on to, to be maintained as a seat for his heir. To him, it seems, an eldest was no more than any other child.

Yes, I think in this John White was strange; and that Gilbert perhaps took after him more than his mother – (though the intellect which all of the male Whites possessed, like a serviceable instrument, is likely to have come from the Holts). White, possibly, left to himself, would also have been untroubled by ambition: his ambition came from without – or from within. Take your choice. At any rate its force was in 'otherness'. John White's directions in his will, that he should be buried absolutely without ceremony, without memorial stone, are markedly like his son's. I wonder if some instinct told him to remain passive in face of the carefully designed legalistic system which was to help perhaps to keep Gilbert single and close to Selborne during vital preparatory years?

CHAPTER IX

The Boy on the Terrace

WHAT did White – the child White – feel about leaving the vicarage which, after all, in spite of his having been only an occasional visitor, he must have looked on as his real home? I think it was the place he held to be the best in Selborne, as Selborne was the best place on earth. I think that his grandfather's garden with its terraced view stood for him, when he was a child, as paradise.

Looking back in advanced age he spoke of that view as commanding 'so romantic and picturesque a prospect that the first master in landscape might contemplate it with pleasure; and deem it an object well worthy his pencil.' It seems that the master he had principally in mind was Rubens. The praise is perhaps a little stilted, as if he were repressing his emotion.

At the time of leaving for Wakes, of course, he was still very young, but in the life of so extraordinary a sensitive there may be said to be practically no youth. I see him on that terrace, looking at that prized view, a little lad dressed up as children were in those days, to appear a miniature adult. He would often have been running back there, for after his grandfather's death an uncle, the Rev. W. H. Cane, took on as vicar. In fact from his birthplace Gilbert would never be entirely separated, since he used to function as curate-in-charge for long periods for absentee vicars, and when he did he would lodge there, and in the one lasting instance when there was not an absentee he was in and out just the same, since that Vicar, the Rev. Andrew Etty, and his wife, became firm friends.

And the view of which this connoisseur of vistas thought so highly? A grassed terrace, the ground falling steeply before it, looked out over a small valley to slightly rising fields of corn and meadowland. The hedgerow immediately opposite, and further hedges dividing these fields beyond, were thickly grown with trees – oak, ash, field-maple, witch-elm, thorn, and a sprinkling of wild cherry. The valley was about a hundred yards across in the part opposite the centre of this terrace, which was backed all along by the tall yew hedge, well clipped. And just off to the right of you, beneath, was a division of double hedge running aslant down the sideland, not very straight, so that it met a range of fencing which slanted correspondingly up the other side, the two composing a vee. This little valley narrowed and steepened as it rose away to the left, westward. That part below the vee was one of the several small fields joined to form what was called Church Lytton Closes – today all Church Meadow, and open; the part above the vee was known as Kimbers. Right down between ran a small stream which you could only occasionally see flashing among the tall-grown sallows on its banks. If your eyes followed the valley round to your left, the part they rested on was called Webb's Mead, and a small bridge went over the stream there, just where the Alton road crosses it today.

There was no road to Alton that way then, and only this wooden cart-width bridge, not massive, but fairly high, because in winter the swollen river came roaring under. The view over that way to westward was all open countryside to the rooftops of Norton farmhouse, with Bush Down beyond it. You looked out on this view from a summer-house or small wooden gazebo let into the yew hedge, and everywhere you looked was full of contrasts: billowing rounds, shimmering, shivering falls, smooth flexuous lines of branches, or boughs sharply angled, and layering plane on plane of foliage, light on dark, all different textured. The little valley whose sides fell away so deeply was full of shadow, or striped with gold and shadow, or brimmed with light on early summer mornings; but however it was, whatever time it was, it was always sharply incised. At sunset the light fell warm upon the terrace.

And the little fields in front of you were mostly only rough pasture, ropey and chewed about by what we should call rather stunted cattle. The landscape was knobbed and blobbed over with bushes and shrubs, such as elder, and the spirit went up with a joyous sensation of lightness and freedom, soaring with the stout taller columns of some shade-tree shooting high among them; or it rested as lightly on the mass away out to the left of high Foredown – 'the' Foredown, separated from its chalk-hill parent mass, the Hanger (which you could not see, since it lay behind you) by the Northfield Lane going up between to Newton Valence.

It was not so much of a view, after all. It was small-scaled and untidy

The boy on the terrace

– rough. Great clumps of dock stood out, their dark broad glossy green leaves prodigious in the rich soil, like small palm trees buried up to the neck, and the burdock stood branching like a shrub. But on everything light shone and moved also. The flutings, pipings, moaning of many birds accentuated the silence. It was always a busy stillness, even on the peacefullest evening. Beasts lowed and whinnied and brayed, cocks crowed, hens crooned or had bouts of hysteria. Down Webb's Lane, through which you got to the bridge from the street at Gracious Street, came ducks and a few geese, trooping to the stream in Kimbers. On the higher ground beyond, in fields running back along behind the Short Lyth, there were spaces short of trees and somewhat tatty. Hieronymous Grimm, standing at the top of Huckers Lane far over to the right, on the saddle of the main valley out of which this valley groped like an arm – one of several – Hieronymous Grimm, in 1776, about to take a 'sweet view of Dorton and the Lithe', was to make it all look very bare and scanted there, and it is not likely to have looked any different in the 1720s, when we are looking with White.

But if you knew you could go down into that greenest depth, to the fresh stream, skirting or threading the hanging coppice of oak and hazel on this side, and be up to your chin almost in gold – buttercups – as you had been to your knees earlier in kingcups, and be among all the other field flowers – Meadowsweet, Herb Robert and Ragged Robin, Bistort and Scabious and such, and among rushes and reeds; knew, when you entered that rough pasture field called the Lyth, you'd be sure to hear the happy summer sound of the field-crickets who sat at the doors of their little caves; knew the mighty beeches that fledged the Short Lyth and the Long Lyth further down, and all the mossy caverns among those trees – if you had all these and a thousand things else in your heart and soul and mind, then it might well be the finest view on earth – of its kind.

So it always seemed to me in my own youth, right into the twenties and on into the thirties even: the loveliest spot in Selborne. Indeed I believe it to have been more beautiful then than in White's time. Nor is it so bad today. A single enclosure of old days adjacent to Webb's Mead, called Goslings Croft, has given its name to a council estate which has spread back from the road in the direction of the top of the

The Penstock in the vee

Lyth, over those levels that were looked across to from the vicarage terrace. Too near? Perhaps: but it is not so much man as time which has disturbed the valley and prospect. For certain huge trees, willows and poplars, which towered up and made it a cool and silver silence only to look, were thrown down in a gale in the early thirties, having grown long past their prime. They lay there for years, up and down the hillside, lost their bark, and resembled the white bones of Titans.

★ ★ ★

And then how White must have loved that old house – the Tudor Vicarage Hall so lamentably pulled down (but it must have been by then in a shocking state of disrepair) by the rich vicar of mid-Victorian times, Parsons. This indeed was the first great crisis time of change in White's Selborne, when the new pretty church school was built down Malters Lane, since called School Lane, and the new road to Alton was made, rendering obsolete that most difficult one of his time which went, hollow and serpentine and almost unusable except in summer, all round by West Worldham down to Truncheons. It was cut down right-handed from the Street, near the Plestor, obliterating the primitive bridge, and making direct for Alton, following the route of the footpath to Hartley Farm. That was about 1850.

The ancient vicarage Grimm has shown to us on three faces. It had a date 'sometime in the reign of Elizabeth' cut over a door leading to stairs out of the hall (perhaps those of old to the Solar) White tells us; and he tells us that the original Hall, which went right up to the roof, had long since been divided so as to make a floor above with partitions for the parson's and his family's bedrooms. One senses that he took great pride and delight in the old house, which was just such as children can lose themselves happily in, all up and down, with plenty of small out-of-the-way rooms, attics, cellars. On the front to the Plestor, where it had a wide court, the sun would flood in in the mornings. Grimm shows us this front of stone – 'a plain stone building' White calls it, but round on the east side it is half-timbered, with tall twisted Tudor chimneys, and the wall-backs of a hearth promising prodigious winter fires. There are many gables.

★ ★ ★

But Gilbert would not, I think, have played much. He would have been a solitary little boy, there in the old vicarage or at Wakes. For

Tom, the next eldest, was nearly five years younger.* Yet he did play, if only by himself, or fulfilled his playtime vicariously through watching others. And right at the end of his life, when the well his father had dug at Wakes was being cleaned out, we find wistful journal-entries about old favourite marbles recovered, to glint and roll in the sunlight after half a century's dark; wistful entries, too, recording the commencement of whip-top seasons on the Plestor. Perhaps the studious, gentle, musical father brought his son companionship, walked with him on that terrace, pointing out beauties, perhaps birds. For all the birds Gilbert loved and was to write about with such delicate precision and felicity haunted this purlieu. That would be a rational supposition, I think; and that John White also imparted something of the legal disciplines of mind he had been trained in. Playmates Gilbert must have had of course among the village boys, but village boys' hours of playtime are few, and the time came fairly soon when he was dispatched to school in Farnham, whose 'sweet bells' he was to hear again at the far end of his life.

'A sweet romancy place' John Aubrey had said of some favourite seat in the West Country, using the term as he alone did almost, in his time, a hundred years before, with any hope of being understood. It was beginning to be widely understood while White was growing up, and those who felt its power and charm fullest, of course, were the true natural poets, Thomson particularly, and Collins and Gray, with the immured demented Christopher Smart unheard but not quite undetected. The knoll on which Selborne church and Vicarage stands was and is a truly 'romancy' spot, and Gilbert was acutely aware of it. He was not a poet on a par with those named, being too much influenced by Dryden, Pope and the Augustan school out of which these others were groping with occasionally brilliant effect. But White was contemporary with them, and to some degree open to the zeitgeist; nature had to be present in anything he thought, though in verse his expression could rarely rise to his feeling. Perhaps 'What time the timorous hare limps forth to feed' does faintly foreshadow 'The hare limped trembling through the frozen grass'. I think so. But having heard and wishing to communicate of quails, no Regency poet could ever have talked of '. . . the *soft* quail *relating her tender pain*'. At least one hopes not.

* Three children had come between Gilbert and Thomas – John, and two girls both named Anne – but all three had died in infancy.

White, it is fair to say, was not a good poet, but he was an accomplished enough writer to pass for one among people with a taste for verse in those days. And his verse is entertaining and even delightful for many not poetical reasons. It gives engaging pictures, like little vivid vignettes, of polite eighteenth-century people enjoying themselves in various 'with it' ways, whether merely picnicking, admiring views, breathing in the fresh flower-and-leaf-scented air, or indulging the warmed fancy with a 'pleasing kind of pain', '. . . a soothing melancholy joy'. We are not to make fun of this sort of thing, for out of it grew the splendour of the 'Ode to a Nightingale' just as surely as out of White's new appreciation of nature's 'minute particulars' (to use a phrase of Blake), and power to inculcate a sense of harmony with creatures, came 'He prayeth best who loveth best', and Wordsworth's 'Ode: Intimations of Immortality', and all of his best, and, when the general sense of it all had ripened and toughened, the 'Ode to the West Wind' of Romanticism's despair and sublime courage. The heroic temper of times far more nearly our own.

* * *

There is a legend that White wrote his 'Naturalist's Summer Evening Walk' in the summer-house on the Vicarage terrace. He might well have written his poem 'The Invitation' there too, indeed all his poetry – there is not much of it, and it all seems in a way to be one poem; and he was always farming what he had of material here carefully through the years, taking bits out of one poem and putting them in another. For of course what afforded infinite variety for nature study was quite restrictive when it came to his own private feelings and predilections and reveries. But what stands out clearly from it all is the extent to which he was steeped in the atmosphere of this knoll, this circling mound with its ramparts and bastions, that looked so much like a fortress-mound and may even have been one: Adam de Gurdon's (of whom more later) of which hero of the thirteenth century he gives account in the Antiquities, and hints at in verse. And then the terrace, pendant over the valley, is the very place to see white owls skimming. Some nested, as he fascinatingly describes in Letter XV.B, in the church tower (which he gave a spire to, round which swifts screamed) – and to hear drowsy dor-beetles 'brushing' by, and see 'the feeding bat glance through the wood' – observation here as well as literature – and where at night you heard curlews calling to each other.

And in the 'Invitation', which begins so valiantly with 'See Selborne spreads her boldest beauties round,' he dilates, in a passage later removed, perhaps as being too domestic or pretentious, on what must be Vicarage garden joys:

Plan the pavilion, airy, light and true;
Thro' the high arch call in the length'ning view;
Expand the forest sloping up the hill;
Swell to a lake the scant penurious rill;
Extend the vista, raise the castle mound
In antique taste, with turrets ivy-crowned;
O'er the gay lawn the flow'ry shrub dispread
Or with the blending garden mix the mead;
Bid China's pale, fantastic fence delight . . .

The lines I have italicised might be in allusion to Wakes – 3 and 8 certainly are, but the rest is all the Vicarage. We note too that though he never mentions Wakes in his verse and gave it only a tiny far-away illustration, as intended in the *Natural History*, the Vicarage by contrast is sung of – 'Nor be the Parsonage by the Muse forgot', etc. and appears in three of Grimm's pictures.

* * *

Lawn and terrace were merely the mightiest creations of the grandfather White; he also appears to have turned part of the ancient burial ground into a flower garden and shrubbery, between the church and the south end of the terrace, (what with vegetables and fruit trees there was by no means too much space), as was discovered years later by a future incumbent having a bowling alley dug there. A great many bones were unearthed. It was on the verge of this garden and shrubbery that the lengthening view was called in, the valley vista framed, and here was a rose hedge (China's pale, fantastic fence) planted. These things can be seen in Grimm's picture from across the valley. But that castle mound in antique taste with turrets ivy-crowned brings us forward and away from the place first preferred in Selborne, away down into the vista to Priory, with which his youthful mind was ever preoccupied, and into the world of 'The Invitation'. And there we have monks (lazy ones, I am sorry to say), and, as well as white owls, 'cowl'd spectres skim the folded plains'. This last word is a little confusing, being a local term. The place White is referring to is merely the left-

'Cowl'd spectres skim the folded Plains'

hand one of the last pair of intersecting valleys between the village and Priory, where anything like a plain is as improbable as on the top of Skiddaw. This 'plain' is or was a common pasture, and you meet the sense in such a space as Cowplain near Portsmouth. It lies well past the end of the Long Lyth, and the region has been suspected of hauntings still. It is still known as 'the plains'. The plains lie above and near to the one authentic Priory fish-pond – what White called Combe, or Combe Wood pond – fed by a small rivulet coming down from Milking, or Milk Wood Hanger above. White was always watching the swifts, swallows and martins feeding there, and at 'Knight's' ponds, by the Grange, high upstream in the village. The monks, of the Order of St. Augustine, black-robed Canons, must certainly have been often about there, and there it is that a small miracle to do with the providential taking of a great fish is said to have occurred in the Priory's heyday. But we shall be returning to the Priory later.

Meanwhile, in case anyone should have jumped to the conclusion that because White in the 'Invitation' talks of 'The lazy monk within his cloister'd cell While papal darkness brooded o'er the land; 'Ere Reformation made her glorious stand;' he had necessarily been subjected to any intense propaganda by his grandfather, the old Vicar, I must explain that the monks of Selborne really were lazy, and that our monastery did in fact peter slowly out without aid of Reformation and long before it. The records of Selborne Priory are more complete than anything else of the kind, I understand, since Wayneflete, Bishop of Winchester, carried them all off to the care of his newly-founded Magdalen College after the affairs of the Priory were wound up. In these records the sad story of decline is fully enough revealed – though we should not, probably, put too much importance on the visitations which produced such severe rebukes, since these no doubt came by routine to all monasteries and were constant alike in stricture, automatically, like school reports.

How deep must have gone the attraction of the past for White to have insisted on adding his Antiquities, defying Mulso and defying Time – for time was really getting on when he came to that decision! He had, advanced, that sense of the past, of the romance of it which is like a thick odour of musk to those fortunate enough to possess it; a sense of the past – a still quite recent and then very rare acquisition indeed. For the rationalising, exquisitely civilised, materialistic eighteenth century generally regarded the Middle Ages as hideously barbaric, and even country life at any time odious, grotesquely primitive and slightly ridiculous all round, saved solely by the fact that the money mostly came from there. But White, we see plainly from his verse – that tiny closely cultivated plot – cherished what flowers of historical romanticism blew there. He told of 'Madding Croisades' setting the world aflame. Long before *Ivanhoe*, that was. Yet it is plain that all these things, though fascinating, meant little enough to White. They were a boyhood recreation (though he never forgot them), dreams of small significance to his life-work. The only real things in his poetry are the creatures he had had to watch at 'conversation' in the wild in furtherance of the great pursuit towards which the summoning horn had probably not blown, or blown very faintly to the ears of the child standing on the terrace, the scent of the hay and laughter of the haymakers, and the creak of the wagons creeping home under the Lyth coming up to him with happiness.

CHAPTER X

A White on the Wing

NOW to transfer to Wakes, and a different atmosphere and another world, though only the other side of the street; where the Hanger is king of scenes, up which to climb, with Arbour Hill to sit and dream upon – outward-going dreams – looking over to Wolmer Forest and Blackdown beyond. And there are other vantage-points possible to be used for look-outs on that 300-foot high, precipitous, shaggy eminence; eyries to be schemed about and to occupy the imagination with the nature of distance, and future, and freedom.

For the removal synchronises with Gilbert's departure for the outside world. Gilbert is going to Farnham, to school. And so he will have tucked away down inside him the moods and soft influences and dramatic suggestion of the close recessive luxurious hidden valley ground. Hanger and Highwood and Common claim him now, with a prospect of plains indeed, but not haunted ones, or if haunted, haunted by the nightjar and the raven and the great grey shrike; and where the nearest thing to poetry proper is a wonderful cobweb shower.

But all that mild moony dreaminess and suggestibility he put aside now was nevertheless real in him, though it belonged to a secondary and lesser part of himself. It was only to be rested in abeyance, waiting till he needed it, and could be called for all through life. For hear Mulso, years and years afterwards: 'I see you under the beeches of the Lyth: you are in more soft and mild attitudes; a sort of pastoral spirit possesses you. You hardly want to look over the blue forest, so contented are you in your green recess; you see even the possible lake before you, and almost hear the waterfall from the imaginary rock,' (some people I have met returned from their outing disappointed and mystified at not finding that lake and waterfall).

Those attitudes more soft and mild must have intrigued Mulso, ever admiring and observant of his friend, by their contrast with the alert and bustling White with the matchless observing eye – a man almost as

Returned from school

extrovert as himself. For Mulso, White as undergraduate was very much the outdoor man, as keen on sport as on natural history, who used to shoot any small swift bird in summer to keep his eye in for winter, who was so good a horseman that later he nicknamed him the 'huzzar parson'. The small bright cheerful man was a thorough good fellow, even something of a flirt, being known as 'busser White', when to buss a girl was to kiss her. Mulso's brilliant and witty sister Hester, called Hecky, who later became the erudite and improving blue-stocking Mrs. Chapone of the *Letters*, also used to like what she called 'careering about with Whitey-bus'. Mulso, must, of course, have been used to the fact that White was a poet – always had been since they first met at Oxford – and thus would be expected to pose a little. But now, in the 1730s, when he was still a boy at his first school, there was a set of little people left behind in Wakes to whom his dreamy side had probably never been revealed. *They* would have thought him purely practical no doubt.

When the admired eldest brother returned for the holidays, what excitement there had been: little bodies thronging the forecourt – then a good deal deeper – pressing against the white pales which kept away the cattle from polite grass-plot and gravelled approach; looking out for winter's shambling pony or summer's growling trap. Little brothers and sisters, now growing up: Tom and Ben and John avid to show what new discoveries *they* had made while Gil had been out of the running at school; but mostly eager to go again where only he could lead them, to places otherwise out-of-bounds: to the deepest holes under the bank at the turn of the stream far down, where the big fish lay; to adventure more dangerously to Wolmer Pond – or even Frensham, to try for moorhen or grebe, or a mallard, if he thought there might be a chance of getting away with it. To poach a Fallow fawn maybe in Alice Holt – a red deer calf in the forest . . . but that could hardly be breathed.

No doubt later on, when he had got to Basingstoke, Gilbert told them how a few bold spirits at the school, he with them, had sapped the old tower of the Holy Ghost Chapel so that it altogether collapsed with a roar that wakened the town, but by good luck not until they had cleared off. This seems to have been the only thing in the nature of a boyish prank which Gilbert ever indulged in, and he must have been very proud of it since he put it into one of the Letters of his Antiquities.

Though deeds of daring counted, field-sports absorbed these children more. But as they grew older, of course, and Gilbert was moved further away to Basingstoke, and as the three next eldest to him became themselves able to afford energy for the intellectual world – which it was always easy for a White to do, it seems – he had no need to hide

Fishing

his fondness for poetry; nor would he have done. Meanwhile these two great friends-to-be were a long way apart. White had first to get from Farnham to Basingstoke and from Basingstoke to Oxford.

* * *

At Basingstoke, under the Rev. Thomas Warton, the poetasting youth must very soon have felt that he was already half-way there – half-way, with Joseph and young Tom, to Oxford, and John Mulso, and Collins on Parnassus.

It is not known whether at Farnham White attended the Grammar School, but it is thought he did. At Basingstoke he was under a remarkable teacher who kept what may be called a glorified crammer's establishment rather than a school, on the outskirts of the town. It seems that the earlier belief that he went to Basingstoke Grammar School is unfounded, for the Rev. Thomas Warton never was head – or otherwise master of that school. He was Vicar of Basingstoke. You did not necessarily have to go to a school to be educated in those days – and the Grammar Schools, incidentally, were then falling rather into disrepute – and the Vicars (all scholars of course), were given to taking private pupils for entry into the universities. The Rev. George Austen, for instance, had a number of boarding pupils at Steventon, and White's youngest brother, Henry, did the same. George Austen taught his own children among his pupils, including perhaps Jane: the Rev. Thomas Warton had his brilliant sons, Joseph, and Thomas, junior.

These Wartons cut a large figure in the literary history of the eighteenth century. They were all very puissant in literature. Thomas, senior, had been Professor of Poetry at Oxford; Joseph, perhaps rather less distinguished in literature, became headmaster of Winchester, holding the position for very many years and being revered for it – you will see a fine marble bas-relief to his memory in Winchester Cathedral; Thomas, junior, relatively rather the wild one of the trio, passing as a 'modernist', a link in the transition from Augustan to Romantic, outdid his father in becoming not only Professor of Poetry at Oxford, but Poet Laureate also. He seems to have been a jolly, dissolute fellow, given to carousing with boatmen.

Into this propitious family circle White by chance or providence fell, at about the age of fifteen. Joseph was two years younger than he, and Thomas, junior, eight years younger – but so brilliant that all three would almost certainly have been classed together. After a year or two

Joseph went off to Winchester, where of course he fell in with two equally scholarly lads, John Mulso and William Collins. Collins was first on the Roll of Winchester Scholars, Warton second, Mulso third. So that when White arrived at Oxford, rather later than usual on account, it is suggested, of being held up by his mother's death, and was obviously introduced by Warton to Collins and Mulso, and when Thomas had caught up with the rest, White found himself one of a brilliant literary coterie.

William Collins was by far the most gifted of this set, as he was the most ambitious. There is that poignant story about him at Winchester being seen looking downcast and troubled. He said he had had an evil dream: that he had climbed a tall tree, and that the bough had broken and brought him to the ground. His listener tried to laugh his oppression away, but 'Ah!' said Collins, 'You do not understand: that tree was the tree of Poetry.' And he had not been able to take rightful advantage of his superior position as head scholar of the school. This should have assured him a place at New College, Oxford, 'with the advantages of a "Fellow" or Scholar', says Mr. Edmund Blunden, in his *Poems of William Collins*, but there was no vacancy. So he went instead to Queen's College, as a Commoner, but his brilliance got him to Magdalen as a Demy-scholar. What would have served White so well was thrown aside by Collins, who would not be 'Japanned', as some put it, and left Oxford at once after taking his degree. Collins published poems while at Oxford. He hungered for London and poetic fame. He became the friend of Johnson, who loved and admired him greatly but did not realise what an exquisite ear for poetry he had. In London his friends kept in touch with him as well as they could – Mulso particularly – and ominous at times was what they heard and told. Collins haunted the theatre, went behind the scenes a lot, frequenting players – actresses. He seemed flighty and erratic, dressed stylishly and wore a feather in his hat. He got into debt and came back to Oxford to collect subscriptions for a proposed *History of the Revival of Learning in Europe*. He was saved from this necessity by a legacy sufficient to keep him for life, but his beautiful *Odes*, published not long before, had failed to 'take', and he burnt remaindered copies – an extraordinary thing for a poet to do; but then, he would go further than that: Collins would put MSS. straight into the candle flame, smiling into the horrified eyes of a friend as he did it.

And so gradually he became mad, as they said, and crept back to his native Chichester, and died before he was forty. But before that last phase of misery began he somehow dragged himself to Oxford again, doubtless to visit Tom Warton. White saw him there, under Merton Wall, in circumstances it will be interesting to consider later. And so ended the life of a great English poet, illustrating better than Burns and Chatterton what Wordsworth had in his mind fifty years later, when he sang in 'The Leech Gatherer':

> I thought of Chatterton, the marvellous boy,
> The sleepless soul who perished in his pride;
> Of him who walked in glory and in joy
> Following his plough along the mountain-side;
> By our own spirits are we deified;
> We poets in our youth begin in gladness;
> But thereof comes in the end despondency and madness.

For poor Chatterton died by his own hand in a fit of childish pique fatally magnified, and Burns died of whisky. Collins, for all his pride, was not as careless of genius as that, though 'poets ever were a careless kind' as he said.

⋆ ⋆ ⋆

Gilbert White was not that sort of creature at all, and it may well be admitted must by comparison appear sober and prim and steady, and headed for a quiet life. Only for a few moments shall we find him come near to Collins. He belongs to a lower stage in the hierarchy altogether than the poet who wrote such lines as

> The oak-crowned sisters and their chaste-eyed queen

and

> In his bewitched, low, marshy willow brake

and

> The shadowy kings of Banquo's fated line

by that mysterious process which allows genius to recreate where it finds in the past – in this case the Elizabethan or Miltonic past, endowing the generation of Keats, more than three-quarters of a century distant.

But it is the privilege of rare remote, most highly gifted spirits to founder. And you see, if you have, like White, the sure knowledge within you of a shining thing accomplishable with ordinary talents (but concentrated, elevated to the highest degree), you will scarcely be tempted into courses which may lead to disaster. *He* had an aptitude for the country life; he had no hankering for London, or desire to cut a dash; and possibly no deep-rooted strong ambition more than the ambition to see a great, simple and very worthwhile thing done as he knew it could be done – by himself if necessary, by somebody, at any rate. Of Collins's ambition I think he could not have dreamed, nor would have approved of its intensity and overweeningness if he had done. And yet I think all his ambition lay that way.

I do not know to what extent White's observant eye may have been startled by the displays of Collins; how far he might have been warned from him, who was, I imagine, a poet-rival. But not for White to leave Oxford in a hurry. He dared not be so reckless. On the contrary he stayed, took Orders, became a Fellow. And when his degree was being conferred he also received, and from the hands of Pope himself, an inscribed copy of the latter's *Iliad*. How much is to be made of this? The exact circumstances are obscure. Was it a prize of sorts? Was the Rev. Thomas Warton possibly a friend of Pope's? Had he favoured his former pupil and used influence?

One circumstance which may have bearing is that old Stephen Hales was a close friend of Pope and had been also, for years, of the White family. He was the Vicar of Faringdon, near Selborne – White was later to become his curate – but was most often to be found at Teddington. Perhaps this signal honour, then, had been arranged between John White and Stephen Hales as a happy surprise and compliment for Gilbert, in recognition of his great knowledge and appreciation of the beauties and subtleties of Pope, which had certainly become well-known among his circle of friends at the university, and probably beyond; the Mulso family, for instance, held him in the highest esteem for it. We shall never know, and anyhow nothing came of it as affecting White's career as a poet. But what did come of it was the one authentic attempt at a portrait of him, sketched on the flyleaf of Volume III of the *Iliad*. This curiously effective amateurish drawing has 'Portrait of Gilbert White' under it, and is initialled T.C. almost certainly by one who was senior Proctor at the time, Thomas Chapman.

I like to think of this sketch having been attempted as the crown of some little celebration by his friends of Gilbert's poetic triumph. The face is oval, the head small and the brow narrow and not high, it is held a little back; there is a rather strained expression; the large longish eyes look brilliant, and might be dark; the long hair of indeterminate shade is swept back on to the neck and tied somehow. I think this drawing is intended to portray White reading aloud from the poem.

The portrait sketch in the Iliad

We might think that Gilbert White was absolutely immersed in poetical affairs all his time at Oxford, but of course he was not, but employed his always active breezy outdoor self vigorously as well. For this we have not only Mulso's occasional hints in his letters but White's own careful account books to testify to, which reveal his pursuits of riding, shooting and fishing equally with his purchases of books. He was then as keen and able a fisherman as shot. These accounts are in his usual beautiful clear hand, which he acquired early and kept to the end, like the clear careful habit it served. I think every educated person was trained to keep accounts in those days, so it need not be taken to indicate any particular neurotic closeness or cautiousness. We see how carefully he lived, it is true; how meagre his furniture was – almost confined to essentials, table, bed and chairs (except at the time he was Junior Proctor). He caused his parents as little expense as possible, that is evident, saved in any way he could, let off, for instance 'my little additional room' for 10/– a year. All items, his 'cloaths', books, fishing-tackle, gunpowder, shot and flints, are carefully put down. It is evident that White was training himself to live economically. One should not need the great-grand-nephew's exculpatory figures to conclude the Whites were not affluent. Would Gilbert have been sent to Winchester if they could have afforded it, one wonders – a thing which at first sight would seem so obviously desirable? Well none of the brothers went to public schools. We never hear that their father did. Perhaps he disapproved of them.

I myself am not sorry that he did not go to Winchester, but had instead, I think providentially, the benefit of Warton, senior, as it were privately first, and became friendly with the sons in a more intimate, homely setting first, and had not to be at stretch, competing with Joseph Warton and Mulso, and Collins, in the prestigious, expertise-ridden atmosphere of Winchester, perhaps the most intensive forcing-house of scholars in the country. For the same reason I am glad that his arrival at Oriel was delayed.

He was content at Oxford, as his temperament allowed him to be in most situations. As happy writing his verses and comparing them with others' as debating the merits of the classics and holding forth on the adroit felicities of Pope, arguing discreetly with young Thomas Warton, who talked a lot about nature but would not take the trouble to learn anything real about it. And I guess he was happiest of all with his fishing-rod and his gun, which connected him intimately – too intimately, many will think – with the freely shining forms. He was sharpening his senses, learning how to look, and where, but probably not, just now, noting anything. His first nature notes had been taken years before in Rutland staying with Thomas Barker, later his brother-in-law, but they are isolated. '1736 – March 31. A flock of wild Geese flew N. – G.W. 1736 – April 6. The cuckoo heard. – G.W.'

Although he had developed into a rather dapper young sportsman, typical of his country breeding, he had never lost and never was to lose the schoolboy's excitement, the village boy's expert eye – like a savage's in his jungle. It is notable how many naturalists have begun as sportsmen. White, Darwin, Hudson, Jefferies – modern natural history began in the field and has to this degree been connected always with field-sports. They all grew learned from the creatures they killed. This is how they discovered how wild life was lived. From the game-keeper and the poacher, it is notorious, the raw stuff is gained, which the scientist later transmutes and expands. For many, many years had White been perfecting himself this way, when he set himself seriously to his task.

CHAPTER XI

Planning at Wakes

WAKES was a theatre, a show always on, the scenery changing which would one day become fixed. All the White boys, with their father, discussed what was most effective to be done. Some difficulties seemed insuperable, others might prove amenable to future hoped-for change. Every point was debated keenly, and the only shadow was that so many of the actors knew they would presently not be available to help, practically or otherwise.

Wakes' back garden was much larger than most of those on the south side of the Street, but in one point it was just like them. The ground sloped down in an awkward way against the house, with only a narrow path intervening. It led to dampness and flooding. This ideally would require levelling to put right, but it was a task beyond John White, either because there was some supineness about him, some tendency to mental fatigue, or because grandmother White wanted things left as old Gilbert had left them. The soil, too, was the most horrible stiff clay; and where to put it when it was dug away?

And then, if you did have a levelled lawn, what would keep Farmer Wells' cattle out? I wonder which one first suggested a ha-ha – a ditch, that is to say, which would have exactly the preventative effect of a wall while leaving the eye free of uninterrupted spaces. This wonderfully simple idea had only recently been invented and was being much talked about.

There were many more ifs and buts. They needed something, of course, to compensate for the lost lawn and terrace and knoll-elevation at the Vicarage. Wakes could have a beautiful prospect – if only it could be opened up. The ground had a certain peculiarity, as what ground did not in Selborne? It rose away behind the house and then went into a shallow decline, a dip which looked as if it might once have held water, and then rose up smoothly again right to the verge of the Hanger. It was really just the opposite effect to the Vicarage garden.

This, between the Wakes and the Hanger, was a quite large area, but unfortunately the major part of it, not considering at the moment what lay away to either side, was the property of other people; Farmer Wells in chief. Great thick hedges striped in between, but on the other hand there were not enough shade trees. Why, it could be a park-like expanse! On the other hand, thought Gilbert, as it was it was very good for birds. He himself had been allowed to plant an oak on the confines of the garden and it was doing well, and he was proud of this.

To any other family but the Whites it would have seemed that they were not, at Wakes, going to have anything approaching the beautiful Vicarage garden, ever. Apart from the soil, with which nothing much could ever be done, this would not have been fair. It was just that the two places were so utterly different. It wanted getting used to, that was all. It took time to get used to the tremendous presence, the tremendous potentialities of the Hanger. But that was not exactly a substitute for a garden.

But as to houses there could be no two opinions. Wakes was palpably inferior. Merely as a dwelling place it had strong drawbacks. Water ran off that slope at the back, was held a while in the path, then soaked through into the ground floor and into the cellarage. The stabling was barely adequate, and there was no proper brewhouse. A brewhouse was essential in Selborne, and anywhere else in a hop-growing country, where quite small out of the way patches could be made to grow hops. Then, though the Vicarage might be very old and quaint, how large, comparatively, and imposing it was; and Wakes was pretty old, for that matter, and in fact might in part be quite as old. What old Wake had found and added to – or was that Gilbert senior? – had been nothing but a little ordinary cottage of two rooms below and two above, with a lean-to coming right down at the back almost to the ground. It had the stairway not much more than a ladder, in the usual way, going up almost straight through the ceiling, by the side of the fireplace. And the taller, added wing, that was after all pretty rustic, rugged, hardly genteel.

There was a general opinion that nothing much could be done to Wakes by way of making it genteel. Only Gilbert had not yet quite made up his mind on that matter.

CHAPTER XII

Selborne Squireless

It will have been noticed that there was only one house of size and appearance in Selborne village, and that the Vicarage.

There were roomy farm-houses, of course, and sturdy yeomens' appropriate houses, and within a mile or two an occasional Great House, such as Sir Simeon Stuart's at Hartley Mauditt. The Vicarage at Newton Valence was a good brick, sash-windowed, corniced house. But here in the village itself, just this one. It had been a Hall – a Tudor Hall, and perhaps it had replaced something which had housed Adam de Gurdon, and known greatness, as Sir John Norton's house, where Norton Farm now prosily stood, had housed a King and a Queen – quite a number of Royalties had been around here in ancient days, on account of the hunting, for one thing, and possibly the Priory. Ela Longspee, Countess of Warwick, whose grand-parents were Henry II and Fair Rosamund, had a chantry in our church, in the south aisle.

The point of interest is that in Selborne the Vicars were the nearest thing they had to a resident Squire. Naturally, since the chief landowner was Magdalen College. The President and his Bursar came down every year to hold the Manorial Court in the Great Tithe Barn down at the Grange, and there was much excitement and jollity, the children were given a holiday and danced round the maypole on the Plestor; and this went on right into our century, only being discontinued with the passing of the Birkenhead Reforms, in 1925.

One consequence of absentee landlordism – for absentee Magdalen had to be, though very good landlords in other respects – was the remarkable freedoms Whites were able to take with the Hanger. They were descended from a Vicar of Selborne, and it almost seemed as if they had acquired hereditary rights!

I have never quite understood this. The Vicars' and Magdalen's interests in the hill were, of course, one, and there was certainly not much advantage in having a Hermitage and an Alcove on it. And the White family owned no part of it; were only, as owners of Wakes, entitled to Common rights like the other copyholders, which did not include building ornamental structures and cutting paths all over and up and down it. Yet Gilbert, as curate in charge so often, an acting-vicar, seems to have concluded that a good way of looking after Magdalen's property here – as in effect a sort of steward – would be to do just this. As his grandfather, presumably, had placed an arbour in Arbour Hill, so he built a hermitage and cut a zigzag to it, and the Bostal later with its alcoves (or alcove or new hermitage). They did what they liked, and nobody stopped them, or even, it seems, protested. And when the Whites were gone the useful pathways stayed, but the structures were left to vanish quite away.

Of course, permission *must* have been granted; but it by no means obviously might. Once a year only the President came down, attended by his Bursar, and sat in the Tithe barn down at the Grange, and held court, and was regaled, and very possibly never went near the Hanger.

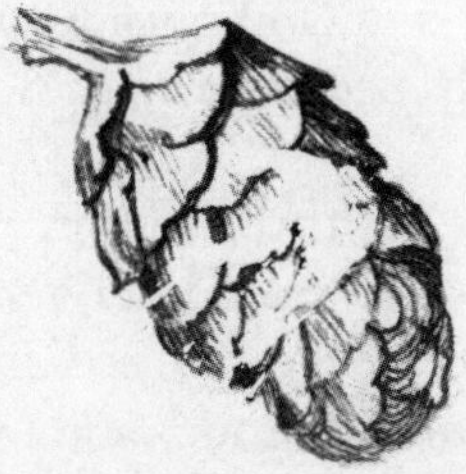

Not having a resident Squire must have affected the village in various ways, and certainly would affect the Whites. You notice an unusual number of small farmers, for an English village – almost everyone seems to have farmed, including Gilbert White. Then 'we abound with poor' he says, and this might have been largely for the lack of one central employer who would have spent money in the village. Selborne, too, seems to be remarkably independent-minded. It was so in White's time, when they pitched the stocks into the stream; it rose to a fierce height after he was gone, at the height of agricultural distress; it has been shown up to quite recent years, when a field-gun placed on the Plestor as a memorial of the great war, was pitched down the ramparts into the stream. With the rise of the Liberal Party Selborne became Liberal, and I regret to say that some large chunks of earth were liberally thrown once last century at a visiting Conservative agent, and struck the then Vicar by mistake. What its politics are just now is perhaps less certain.

There was not the least bit of a Squire about White, nor, though he was a J.P., does there seem to have been about his father, who must I think have functioned on the Bench very mildly for his son to have been so popular; able to hob and nob so freely and happily with his neighbours: Mr. Carpenter the cobbler across the way, Mr. Burbey of 'the shop', Mr. Benham and Mr. Berriman, small farmers, and Mr. Hale, and so many others. It is this free and un-self-conscious intercourse which seems most remembered of White at the time when interrogations were made in the village after his death. He would take his home-brewed ale over to the shoemaker's bench, and they would 'discuss it', and compare, and of course compare and discuss crops, vegetables, their merits and otherwise, and the floods and droughts, and whether so-and-so was likely to recover. And the same thing went on up and down the village, in and out the cottages; in parlours where he also sat to comfort the sick and dying, and outside under the thatch eaves up at which he was continually peering to see how the swifts and martins were doing.

I think he was less at ease in the pulpit. His sermons were dry and uninspired, and were repeated over and over at regular intervals, as the custom was. Probably he felt oppressed in the priest's vestments as much as in the poet's figurative robe, and tended to become as stilted. But when it came to the practical side it was another matter. A splendid rider, White got about and visited all over a parish which was then a very large one – the bounds took two days to beat – and on one occasion, at least, snowdrifts hedgehigh on the route between Selborne and Faringdon were accepted as a challenge. He got to church on time, with his faithful henchman, Thomas Hoare, and Dame Loe (who kept a little school) to dig him free in the deepest places, (theirs seems to have been the major heroism) only, I suspect, to find the church empty on such a day. Still he would go: it was his duty as curate. And for this kind of thing he was paid £20 a year! And to the poor who 'abounded' he did more than give good words. His accounts, which of course he never dreamed would be made public, tell his tale of alms donated. The best-known entry is that which records a small gift to 'Tull's

Gilbert White hobnobbing

naked wench'. He faithfully administered his grandfather's bequests, as his father had done.

Carpenter, Hoare, Loe, Stevens, Hale, Knight, Tull. The names float up and are fixed, imploring the trite image of flies in amber. These and others are still to be found, or were until recently, in and about the neighbourhood. A Tull died the other day in Alton. In White's time a Tull farmed at Wick Hill. This Tull of the naked wench was obviously one of the poor, and thus almost as certainly a poacher, and improvident, a frequenter therefore of the White Hart, the inn at the east end of the street, facetiously known even into the present century as 'The Poachers' Rest'. The brave souls were not taking their rest *after* poaching, however, but snatching an hour or two between day and night, to discuss where best to go, after which quarry.

* * *

I have given a trifling hint that White may have poached a little in boyhood. Of course I meant only to suggest that he may have dreamed as a boy of taking a fawn! But if, as it evidently was, taking game was desirable to him, then the comparative landlessness of Whites would have been irksome to him. He could not have got enough of the sport he loved – though he used occasionally later on to be asked to shoot with Lord Stawell, over at Alice Holt, and presumably by others, being so practised a shot.

Once grown up he could not possibly have approved of poaching. But he exercised his usual detachment here as elsewhere, and it is interesting to read Letters VI and VII to Pennant, where he treats of the famous 'Waltham Blacks' (who used to black their hands and faces as did Commandos, and for the same reason) and other more local instances of poaching. He does make it plain that he abhors one aspect of cruelty involved, where the hooves of fawns are pared where discovered soon after they have been dropped, so that it was because of the depredations of the Blacks that the shrunken residue of the once splendid Wolmer herd of Red deer were removed to another Royal purlieu, less accessible, and unquestionably we are meant to regret this as he did.

The Waltham Blacks caused the emptying of Wolmer Forest and of Waltham Chase, and afterwards, directly named for them, was passed the Black Act (Statute 9 Geo. 1, c.22) – that cruel Act, by which men were hanged, and transported, and brought together in conflict in deep woods at night, many being killed on either side. When a Bishop of Winchester, Dr. Hoadly, was asked to restock Waltham Chase with deer he refused, pointing to this Act, which he said had caused trouble enough already.

I believe that White, by printing thus gratuitously what Dr. Hoadly had said, makes it plain that deep, perhaps not so very deep down in him, he viewed the poacher with sympathy and compassion. He knew how strong was the hunting instinct in men; how impossible it was that they could easily believe it right they should be deprived of natural food, now arbitrarily become 'game'.

'Our old race of deer-stealers are hardly extinct yet' he tells us – and surely here is a note of secret satisfaction? – 'it was but a little while ago that, over their ale, they used to recount the exploits of their youth'. It looks as though he sometimes entered the White Hart, if so it would have been when very young. For a Graduate, or even an Undergraduate, and especially, of course, for a clergyman to have done so, would have been not at all the thing.

But to return to the consequences of a squireless Selborne, it must surely have had indirect effect upon the Whites as a family, in that century, and especially at that time in the century. A beautiful balance obtained in these narrow social village circles, however in some ways objectionable or offensive such balancing might appear to us. Educated folk – 'gentry' – depended on the local Great House and the Vicarage for social entertainment. For most of White's time the Vicars, except for Andrew Etty, were sickly and absentee. He had to go over to Newton Valence and Richard Yalden to find someone to talk to intellectually, if unvisited by college friends or members of his own family. Old Dr. Hales at one period would have suited well enough, but he was very old, and not at Faringdon frequently, nor for long. He was anyway two generations at least removed, and his mind was a natural-philosopher's rather than a naturalist's, which accounts for White telling Barrington that it had been his misfortune never to have had anyone to discuss natural history with.

This not having a Squire, then, and hardly anything of a Vicar, certainly threw the family back on its own resources. It might well have made them incult. One might expect the young men all to have developed into a series of Tony Lumpkins. On the contrary. The Whites were noted for their accomplishment, for their ease of discoursing on recondite subjects with scholars and scientists as with peers. And they had a very marked capacity for entertaining themselves and their friends and neighbours, possessing easily at hand a fund of charming gaiety.

They led, of course, the full country life; but they never went in for hunting fox or hare. At a time when leisured youth was bitten with these sports all over England these youths, not in this sense leisured, and, as we find, not over monied, were out in the world in London or at Oxford. Gilbert White, incidentally, disapproved of fox-hunting parsons, and gradually dropped all his sports. He only shot birds off the fruit trees. He always kept by him, though, a clever sporting dog, his mongrel Rover, his pretty, spot-faced, long-eared spaniel, Fyfield.

CHAPTER XIII

A Nest of Bottle-Tits: eighteenth-century Wakes

It is not possible to say how all these young Whites fitted in to Wakes together, because we do not know what the capacity of the house was at that time. The description I gave so confidently a while back is of the mere core of the ancient building only (with of course the 'new' wing). From now on I shall call this original portion the central block.

The ground floor of the 'new' wing comprised one room and passage to the stairs which may have been the father's study, as it later was Gilbert's. Above was another large single room, and on top of this attics, how many is unknown, but probably only two. The second-floor room was the principal or 'great' parlour until in 1777 White added a more commodious reception room at the other end of the house. Other bedrooms than the two attic ones seem unlikely to have been more than three – in the second storey of the central block. How were grandmother, John and Anne White accommodated? Where did eight children, two of them little girls sleep?

They must have been like Long-tailed tits in the nest. But it is possible that the girls and their attendant were housed (like some of the domestics, presumably) in cottages pertaining near by.

The quite large Georgian block which later threw the rest out of balance, which one might take for granted had been built by grandmother White, would seem in fact to have been built in 1794, immediately after White's death. A plaque with this date and initials E.W. and M.W. was discovered only recently (about 1956) in the brickwork. The initials, E.W. and M.W. are those of a nephew and niece who came to live at Wakes after White's death. Who actually built this wing I do not know. It certainly looks older, but styles of architecture often overlapped in those slow-moving days. Until this date was known there was no need to make a mystery over the accommodation at Wakes when the large family went there, as this addition is large.

Today the ground floor of this part is occupied by the dining room. It fills the angle-space between the central block and the 'new' wing of 1680 or thereabouts. By certain remarks of White in his letters it seems that in the early days, and all through his life, a kitchen occupied this space, entered probably from the common sitting-room of the central block. A late seventeenth-century kitchen to such a cottage would be probably fairly roomy, with its large oven, bread-oven, loft for smoking bacon built in above, and most probably too there would be a scullery attached and outjutting into the yard, which was to the east of the house.

It is most unfortunate that pictures of Wakes were not made (if we except the distant and part-obscured one drawn by Grimm) before White became famous. In the next century several were made, but all from the Street side show it with this tall addition of 1794. White's Great Parlour addition of course is also shown. The pair of additions prevent one understanding what was formerly the exact construction at either end. We cannot tell how high the old kitchen part went; whether it had a second floor. It is likely to have been something of a lean-to kind, and duplicated at the west end. This would make three such lean-to's, counting the one at the rear of the central block which I have mentioned. The excellent view of Wakes from the garden side, done about 1840, just excludes a lean-to which certainly did exist until fairly recently to the eastern side of the 'new' wing. It appears in a sketch of 1901, and also in an early photograph. This was pulled down later in the decade to make way for a modern kitchen wing with bedrooms over, by the Pears family, who caused so many curious modifications to the Wakes. I may add that lean-to's are a common feature about Selborne cottages, and one to exactly this effect may be seen down at the rear of Dortons. The 1840 drawing shows Wakes just as White must have left it, except that the top of the tall part of 1794 comes up well above the roof-line. Dr. Bell, the naturalist, bought Wakes when the last of the White family had gone (having occupied it for 111 years), and added just one more reception room on at the Great Parlour end, and gave it a very large modern window which White would certainly I think have approved of, for to him windows were 'enlarging', meaning to the spirit of him looking through them. It is worth noting, that in what was White's study in the 'new' wing is a blocked-up door. This would enable him to slip out into the garden without going through the house.

* * *

Before I leave this description of the possible appearance of eighteenth-century Wakes, the disposition of its rooms etc., I want to settle one thing which of late years has tended towards the belittling of Gilbert White. It is a small point, but necessary, I think, to put right.

Some fifteen years ago a radio 'feature' was made about White. It was very entertaining, but would probably have soon been forgotten if a local enthusiast had not put it on tape and had it played through at the Wakes, now a public museum, on particular occasions of visits by special parties. This recording has become quite popular, and up to a point deservedly so. It deals ably and instructively with White up to the time of his building his '*Great*' parlour. Then the script-writer, who did not really know or care what kind of a man White was, began to amuse himself in amusing us. White becomes a poor little fussy neurotic man, bustling about in distress, occupied with unworthy, slightly absurd ambitions, which go somewhat astray. The plaster won't dry, the chimney smokes, and so forth, there is anxiety – it is all perfectly true, and yet quite misleading as to the character of the victim. For what has been cleverly and amusingly done is to take his notes of the undertaking – an important enough one privately for White – as jotted into his Journal – and run them together to dramatic effect, and everywhere where White has written the words 'my great Parlour', (which actually is not very often), to act them with an awed and breathless emphasis, to ludicrous effect: 'My GREAT parlour' – so.

The fact is that for White to want this new and larger parlour was as sensible and worthy as the other wise wants and ambitions in his life. His nephews and nieces had all grown up, and were marrying and producing great-nephews and nieces, and what it amounted to was that together with their parents, and other more or less regular visitors, a large room would sometimes be necessary to entertain them all decently in. They used to have musical evenings, and charades, and dance. And to use the words 'great parlour' was in those days no more than to make such a contrast as we should between drawing-room and sitting-room. The new wing consisted of one storey. The previous great parlour upstairs in the old 'new' wing was now to become his bedroom, and the house would have exactly the same number of reception rooms as before. The original sitting- or living-room in the central block, entered direct from the front door, was doubtless draughty and otherwise inconvenient. It was unfortunate that the summer when he began this project (for which he sold some timber) was the wettest they had ever had. It made everything, of course, more difficult.

As for White's wanting to aggrandise Wakes and thus himself I am certain he had no such idea. I rather suppose, as I have indicated before, that he and all the Whites thought it rather an inferior house, which it is still – though in its weird long agglomeration it amounts to something of considerable charm somehow, in a particularly English way. It is, anyway, invaluable to lovers of White, because it does manage to incorporate almost everything architecturally which was there in his time. What Gilbert White did concentrate on and try to make more imposing and more beautiful was the garden. And what he did to that garden we shall later see.

* * *

There are these attempts to pettify White, even to denigrate, which crop up from time to time and are mostly just whimsically perverse, and the unfolding of his life and intentions does away with them automatically. That last Great Parlour business was a fairly innocent example.

But White shot at birds, and had them shot for him, and he weighed his tortoise by displacement in water, so he was cruel, and something of a hypocrite. He had a living at Moreton Pinkney, near Oxford, which he only went to to collect his money – a pluralist, then. He suffered from coach-sickness, therefore he was a weakling. And then he spent his time peering after soulless animals when he should have been attending to his human flock, and was absorbed in writing his one book, which he put off as long as he could, so he was lazy. Of course there is a little truth in some of these strictures, but one knows it has been distorted preposterously, and the victim carried clear out of the context of his times. There is something laughable, for instance, in our being solemnly assured that White fell rather short of our ideal of a Wild Bird Protectionist!

But this and other of the strictures I have listed, or things like them, were levelled or strongly implied in a document which proceeded from the British Museum, so that we must really sit up and take notice, for here White is supposedly being judged by his peers.

The museum had staged an admirable little exhibition of MSS. and books in the King's Library, to mark the occasion of the 200th anniversary of the meeting of White with Pennant, and a brochure was got out to accompany it, giving a brief account of White, Pennant and Barrington in relation to each other. Unfortunately some sort of rivalry was pretended between them in this brochure, most unprofitably, especially in comparing White with Pennant. It resulted in quaint, even grotesque effects.

It is fair to say that White was able to sharpen his faculties on his correspondents, but it cannot seriously be pretended that he owed Pennant much. Is there not something perverse in trying to make Pennant out a naturalist of equal worth with White, i.e. as an observer of natural phenomena, when what we have to judge from of White's was all done to put Pennant right, or make him wiser? And who reads Pennant now?

One would not want to be running Pennant down, a valuable man and gifted in his different way, most popular with his contemporaries, including, up to a point, White (and very popular with his publisher, Benjamin); but he was 'less of a field naturalist than a collector of specimens and a collector of information' says Mr. R. M. Lockley, naturalist and White's latest biographer. Seriously to suggest, that without Pennant's encouragement White's book might well not have been finished is astonishing, and shows a complete misunderstanding of the facts. It is true that White did write (to Barrington) 'In obedience to your repeated injunctions I have begun to throw my thoughts into a little order', but that is not the same thing. It must be realised how these letters were self-edited and rearranged. A polite formal courteous element was necessary, he thought, in this version of the letters for publication, and I am afraid he was here just being polite and indulging an inclination to flatter a trifle, for reasons before hinted at. To this extent possibly he does a little deserve what is given him in this unlucky brochure. Still one asks one's self why there should have been so marked a slant against him in it, everywhere, by implication.

Pennant was a 'great' traveller (but in the days of Mungo Park also), therefore White must be no traveller, inhibited against it by coach-sickness, a malady here enlarged so that it 'would have prevented him from undertaking a work on a national scale'. (You will remember that in a letter of 1771, and elsewhere, White had definitely stated that this was not his purpose.) As a fact White travelled widely about England on horseback, which requires a good deal of stamina.

Pennant was famous, so White must be unknown outside his family. It might have been useful to recall what sort of family that was; how it connected him with Linnaeus; with the Royal Society, before whose members some of his work was read, for whose annals some was printed; how it provided him with a first-class publishing house; an expert publicity agent to some extent in Thomas; how much his brother John had distinguished both their names by his Gibraltar study, even though he could not publish that book.

All this suggests a rapid superficial study of White's life by whoever was responsible for this British Museum brochure of 1967. One might have guessed that, from certain small pin-pricks of faults, such as that White's uncle Charles had resided at Wakes, which he never did, though he was for a brief time its owner and White inherited it after him, White having been living in it virtually as owner and master since the time his grandmother White died.

But what I find so very hard to understand is why, when a man is known for the freshness of his observations and the freedom with which he made these known to his fellow naturalists, it should have been thought necessary to go about and rake up a supposed instance of his having got something out of another author's book, as if he had pilfered it.

You would certainly have to rake about. Here the raking is very superficial. That other man was Pennant, it is suggested; and the note, presumed his and previously published in his *British Zoology* (though not actually specified here), comes in the famous Letter XXII to Pennant about nightjars, and how one of these birds fairly shook the Hermitage with the volume of its sound. That note certainly was White's, and so would appear to be all the rest in this short passage of the *Natural History*. So far as is known Pennant never came to Selborne.

Was the pre-eminence of White resented? One knows that in an age of anti-hero such feelings do operate. In ordinary walks of life I have found people who hate some tall tree and want to cut it down, because they know it will be living long after they are gone, or hate some prolific weed because it so triumphantly grows and insults their own puny vitality. Probably I am naïve to be so surprised that academic circles should seem to have felt that way too.

CHAPTER XIV

Whites on the Wing

We need not think of them all as being too uncomfortable there at Wakes, the more than dozen of them in the inadequately bedroomed house, since in general people were accustomed to crowding then – it kept the rooms warmer in winter in the entire absence of central heating, for one thing. Not so very long before, travellers had taken it for granted that they might have to share beds at inns with total strangers, and sharing beds in one's own home was a commonplace. Perhaps it was not so very different for the little boys herded together from what many of us experienced in our dormitories at school. They were rid of fear of ghosts and other night fears at least, and had always the company of each other, to exchange their whispered family jokes punctuated with explosive snorts of laughter, and discuss the day's doings and make plans for tomorrow.

And anyway the situation was fluid: White's were on the wing continually, death or vocation claiming. Gilbert's early dispatch to school or tutorage in Farnham set the style for all the boys. Tom and Ben were sent to Bishop's Waltham, not much further away, and probably the next pair down, John and Francis, went there too. Little Harry was sent for some reason a longish way off, to Kingston-upon-Thames, but his turn was not for many years to come, for he had not been born till Gilbert was in his fourteenth year. All these boys, so lively and mischievous as we may hold them to have been, grew into able scholars easily. John and Henry, like Gilbert, went to Oxford and became clergymen; Tom, though he did not go to university, is described as an elegant classic. Once educated, none of them was allowed to hang about. Off to London went Tom and Ben, and the next we hear – and it seems in no time at all – the one is a successful business man in ironmongery, the other a partner with a Mr. Whiston, publisher and bookseller, at the sign of the *Horace Head*, in Fleet Street.

What a clever lot they were. They have notably fine foreheads, Thomas and Benjamin, and so has John. If the sketch of Gilbert is at all to be relied on, his forehead was narrow and his head smaller altogether. He seems to have been of a finer and more nervous make. However, he was every bit as business-like. When he was twenty-five he went to Thorney, near Ely, to attend the death-bed of that Thomas Holt who was going to leave his entailed property to Thomas White. As one of the executors and trustees, Gilbert stayed on to wind up Mr. Holt's affairs at Gore Farm, and did the job with perfect efficiency, surveying the land, selling off the live and dead stock, discharging servants.

How did he get this expert knowledge? It is not known, but I think the father might here be given credit. It is probable that he taught his eldest son, who was going to have to look after land property; that to this extent he lived an active life vicariously through Gilbert. It was he who ordered White to the death-place at any rate.

And as both the daughters made good marriages, doubtless he supplemented all that useful education they were receiving from their grandmother White with a few graces – lessons on the harpsichord, poetry, elocution. It is true that from a hint in one of Mulso's letters we surmise that he was not a very proficient reader of music at sight.

All the Whites were exemplary, with the sad exception of poor Francis of whom so little is known. He seems to have gone to London, to some unspecified employment, to have married, produced an infant girl who died, and followed her very soon. His widow does not appear in the family story. But John White, junior, too, at one time gave trouble. He was dismissed from Corpus Christi – where he had gone with a scholarship – and left the university owing debts – this we learn from himself. Whatever it was he was sent down for, it could not have been anything very heinous, for he took Orders and turned up very soon in London as a 'very smart parson', as Mulso describes him, without much more to do than preach one sermon a week.

Disorderly conduct was what the college authorities convicted John of; he accuses himself of 'an imprudent and incautious procedure at my first stepping into the world'.

John's chief penalty, I suppose, lay in forfeiting a Fellowship. He did not throw off the misadventure lightly. I think on the whole he must have been the brightest of all the Whites – a little too bright perhaps. He had mathematical as well as classical ability, and concerned himself with electricity besides. (When you think of Shelley experimenting with his electric coils at Eton, do you ever think of the John Whites who preceded him?). John came home at once after his fall and began to put into operation his scheme for making the Zigzag – an affair of delicate scientific grading. There was not a sign yet of the natural history prowess he was going to show when he got to Gibraltar. Sadness and dissatisfaction waited on his end.

Thomas White became a member of the Royal Society. He developed a special knowledge of trees, was a good all-round botanist and horticulturalist, and something of an apothecary. It was Thomas who is said to have planted that knotty and warped old sycamore on the Plestor with a bench round its gnarled roots. The great old oak of some 500 years, which it was meant in some way to replace, and which had been in the centre, as White records, and fell in the year of the Great Storm of 1703 and which his grandfather in vain had hoisted into place again, had had a two-tiered stone seat round it, like a plinth, on which old villagers had sat to watch their children at play – reminding one of Blake's 'echoing green'. It is sad that the substitute no later than the 1830s was to be described as crooked and cankered; but the Whites had done what they could, and it remains a much-loved old relic of a tree, for all its failings.

The gorse on the common up on the Hanger was of his sowing. He reviewed Gilbert when the time came. Thomas wrote on a great variety of subjects, in the *Gentleman's Magazine*. His, in youth, is a thoughtful, sensitive, intellectual face – he looks well-bred, less beefy than Benjamin, whose own brow may have been as high but is not so discernible since it is partly concealed, in his miniature, by a low-crowned curly-brimmed hat. Whether Tom was as good a business man as Ben I don't know, but there was no difficulty in disposing of his business when he retired, which happened in 1776, when on the death of the last of several annuitants, he came into full inheritance.

As for Harry, the baby of the family, who seems to have been loved by all and the special favourite of Gilbert – and of Mulso – he wound up very soon with a living at Fyfield, not too far away, and was happily married, with many children (so that he, like Gilbert, had to extend his house to contain them all, and because he took pupils). He did well – though it needed a constant effort – till he died still comparatively young (for a White) in 1788, aged fifty-two. Gilbert often stayed at Fyfield, which is in Wiltshire, and the two exchanged nature-notes on husbandry. Harry, too, is now known to have kept a journal, which is found to be of considerable value.

How clever they all were! I suspect that even poor Francis came unstuck through attempting something too enterprising and brilliant. And they each wanted and attempted to express themselves in writing; all to some extent indeed did, with the exception of Francis, and Benjamin who went one better, some would think, in becoming a publisher. And as the years go on, it is a happy thing to see how they clung to the old home in spite of possessing flourishing establishments of their own. Wakes was theirs in effect to use for long vacations, summer or winter, they and their wives and all their multiplying children, and in consequence it was always a joyful place, echoing with childish laughter or howls of dissension. And they in turn, especially Thomas and Benjamin, the ones best able to afford it, helped to improve Wakes, to extend its grounds, until I believe they could all look over the ha-ha through the vista – 'my outlet' – and view one long park-like expanse, from the boundary of the Ewell to the extremity of the Pound Field, or Punfle, as we call it today. Bit by bit, as Farmer Wells and his sons became willing, these fields were added, and an early dream realised as on this earth it seldom is.

CHAPTER XV

The Garden Created

AND each time they returned, these exiles, they would find some improvement made which they had heard of from afar in a way which had raised delicious expectations: new shrubs planted in 'basins', which were large holes dug in that vile soil and filled with rich humus; new shade trees which most of them would never see at height; all kinds of new exotic flowers such as nasturtiums. which White once misdescribed as an Indian plant; (but perhaps the even more expert Thomas, who had a fine garden himself at Lambeth, and may have given these nasturtiums to Gilbert, had made the mistake first, for the plant was then very rare and romantic and new). And in the kitchen and fruit gardens, what wonders! Melons – cantaloupes and succades, or squashes – were gone in for intensively, and a brick wall built for them to climb up and ripen against in the full sun. New kinds of grapes were tried, with experiments such as dipping the vine roots with 'mummy', just as we would do with some new patent fertiliser.

Vines always grow well in the rich, self-fertilising, grey malm which presumably was imported here for them. Cobbett himself remarks on the vines of Selborne – out-of-door grapes, the best he had seen in England or anywhere, you would almost suppose, for, getting carried away as usual, he exclaims 'I have never seen such quantities of grapes upon any vines as I see upon the vines at Selborne'.

Now in all these improvements, which were carried out over many years and with long intervals between them in the case of the major ones, such as the building of the haha and the lengthening and widening and above all levelling of the lawn, the digging and filling of the basins, White unquestionably played a working part. He for permanent helpers only had his henchman, Thomas Hoare, so far as is known, and an old, mannish weeding women called Goody Hampton (like a man in woman's clothes, White told his niece Molly) to help in this big garden. Tough, wiry must the little man have been.

But of course there was labour to be recruited from outside in the village. There was a John Breckhurst, who was employed once to plant trees on the Plestor, so why not here; and a Lasham (there is a present cottage called 'Lassam's' in Selborne Street) was paid for cutting a vista for the Obelisk; and above all there was Larby – poor Larby, who had the toughest job of all in '81, when the Bostal was begun, at the foot, where it was all clay again. Larby began too low and did not climb steeply enough, and could make nothing of it. So what White describes as a troop of Myrmidons took over. White probably then took no very active part in the work, for he was sixty – when sixty *was* sixty.

Who were these 'Myrmidons'? The term always puts me in mind, in this context, of those muscular and beautiful young Oxford students who did a little navvying in the streets of that city (surrounded perhaps by admiring young ladies) about a century later under some scheme influenced, I believe, by Ruskin. Now about this time, 1781, when the Bostal scheme was afoot, White did have about eight or nine young relatives undergraduates of Oxford: did they all come on a visit?

The ha-ha, of course, and the melon-wall – of which only a small section remains – required some expert labour. The ha-ha was begun in 1758 or thereabout, in a month of wet weather which must have been good for the mortar, as it was later in the case of the Great Parlour's building. It was in the extended or 'new' part of the garden, between Bakers Hill to the east and the Wells's farm to the west bordering Gracious Street, the first of those fields behind Wakes which the family of Wells was to cede, that the ha-ha and other great features were effected. Admiring eyes fell on huge oil jars erected on stone plinths, turned into vases out of which creepers and climbing roses trailed. These and one or two more obelisks were set fairly far out in the newly acquired field, distant beyond the ha-ha. A series of gates too, one before the other, seems to have been placed so as to give a clear look through towards the Hanger, but this feature is not easy to grasp. Nor yet what exactly it was that Mulso saw with his inner vision when he said: '. . . place me at my proper distance, and let me see your Antonines and Trajans with their Egyptian Hieroglyphics'. Mulso had a most wonderful knack of matching his rich enthusiasm with phrases.

* * *

All this intense activity, which began about 1755, the year of Rebekah's death, may well have been to take White's mind off gathering trouble;

his father's illness, his Oriel perplexity impending – less deep but perhaps more worrying than the other natural griefs. Indeed it is notable that the death of one dear one and the illness of the other synchronise with this labour. I revert to my idea that Rebekah may have disliked changes, and I think that there may have been a pathetic hope of pleasing the failing father with a realisation of some more of their joint projects before it was too late. After all it had been he who first laid out some seven acres with walks, and planted trees. A very beautiful sundial, of unusually fine white stone and graceful shape, was erected in the centre of the ha-ha terrace, and there was a magnificent stone urn, which may be seen at the end of the path leading down the garden to the house, in one of Grimm's drawings of years later.

This ha-ha, dial, brick path and stone urn, then, were all visible in 1776; but we cannot possibly know what Wakes' garden looked like ten years previously. All I can say is, for reasons which will be revealed in place, White's new garden was probably completed by 1763.

How did it compare with the garden we see today?

We can say that we have most of the skeleton of it; but we can say more than that: we have a very definite impression of its exact identity.

The original lawn was much restricted over all, and would have ended in a hedgerow whose appearance it is difficult to envisage. It may have been only a fence, but beyond this certainly was a field, and hedgerows and more fields past that. In the place of the now broad Wakes parkland we should have seen long strips of, probably, grazing-land, and all much more shut in. And it was in this rougher piece of grass beyond the verge of the old lawn, so much higher in relation to the house, that the terrace was made from east to west along the ha-ha, and at the eastern end of the terrace walk stood something which would have brought more exclamations of surprise and pleasure even than the ha-ha – the first or Garden Alcove.

This Alcove and the Hermitage on the Zigzag are the only two of White's structures of the kind of whose appearance we can form an idea, though we can guess fairly plausibly at what the Bostal Alcove looked like. This last he most confusingly called later on the Hermitage, sometimes referring to the original as 'the old Hermitage'. One can get into a terrible tangle about these various light structures here and there about the Hanger and garden, and I don't propose to go too deeply into it but only to say that I think that when White mentions his Garden Alcove he means this at the end of the ha-ha terrace, because that

The Garden Alcove

was in the garden; and the other, which is more often heard of but is quite unpictured, often spoken of as being where White 'sat and watched the birds', though it undoubtedly stood where it is said to have stood by Rashleigh Holt-White, was not in the garden at all, but in the field in a part not acquired until after an 'alcove on the Terrass' is mentioned by Mulso.

White, of course, was always watching birds, everywhere. This summerhouse, or arbour or whatever it was, in the Great Mead, was very likely to have been what he went to when it rained. It was reached in its meadow of wet soaking grass by a narrow brick path continuing that which ran (and still does) from the garden door at the rear of Wakes direct to the Garden Alcove. There is a legend that White built this little brick path so as to keep his feet dry, which seems very reasonable – yet I have met one who even found this a point of irritation, as indicating a fussy, valetudinarian little man! Anyone who has walked even a short way through wet grass knows what it can do. I believe that White constructed this Field Alcove, as I had better call it – for a summerhouse was often called an alcove – towards the end of his life, when he might want to slip out to a convenient hide not too far off, for perhaps a short while, and not have the bother of changing into stout footwear. Besides, when White spoke of a Garden Alcove he meant an alcove in a garden; not on the Bostal, not in a field.

There has been talk this year (1969) of reconstructing the Field Alcove in its old place and repairing the old path to it which is still faintly discernible under the grass. This, in memory of Gilbert White, is obviously a good and appropriate idea, to be realised in 1970 when the two hundred and fiftieth anniversary of his birth is to be celebrated. We do not know in the least what the structure looked like, but what does that matter so long as something quiet and rustic answering to a bird-watcher's hide is built?

Not that the Field Alcove was necessarily rustic. The Garden one certainly was not, as to aim, though it is all of wood. You will see that it is classical in design, pedimented – the wood of the moulding here was to gape, and flycatchers built in it – tall and fairly commodious inside, with a bench all round against the wall. In shape of body it is a true alcove. Here people sat, sheltered from the wind, the sun welcome on spring days as it set over the foredown in front of them – the sunsets of lengthening days always recorded by White, long looked for, pined for. And they would listen while one of them recited poetry or read passages from erudite authors, and perhaps play a little music. They took tea with perhaps a little less ceremony than the Chinese and Japanese had taught them to do pictured in ceramics, but with true decorous enjoyment. Decorously too always (if there were ladies present – and there generally were) they joked, were witty, teased each other affectionately.

Was that garden so long striven for, so thoughtfully planned on the new principles of Cobham and Brown (but not yet Repton) to afford something of the naturalistic and the romantic without in the least sacrificing the civilised – was this garden of the Wakes comparable with that of the Vicarage? Well, it was so very different. But it was triumphantly a compensation. It was like the mind of the developed man, against the dream-and-beauty-drugged child and poet-youth. White was the sort of person to whom it is given to realise dreams – such dreams as are honest and modest, unpretentious and realisable at all on earth; such happy ones are few.

The happiest chances might come in Wakes garden: you might have three nightingales singing here at a time; hoopoes might build in your outlet; you might, wonder of wonders, have *forty* ravens playing at once all day over the Hanger.

* * *

As to the fruit and vegetable side, it would make one happy if one could conjure a pleasing Marvell-like picture of White stumbling among melons, with ripe fruit dropping into his mouth, but it could not have been much like that – though how they must have enjoyed their fruits in season, carefully watched for, anxiously always, with eye to the weather, and so manfully toiled for on top of all the rest.

How anyone could imagine White lazy defeats me. For just think of all this, much of it dull routine; bone-wearying, sinew-cracking work, for nearly three-quarters of the year; and add to it all his parish work – devotedly and conscientiously performed; and his perpetual going of the rounds about Selborne, up and down literally, with his eyes open, his senses at stretch, and then to come in and make his notes, and put these in shape and expand or elaborate them for others in exquisite form, in his careful beautiful clear long-hand; his correspondence, continuous, with brothers and sisters, nephews, nieces, friends: not just any expressions, however affectionate, would do for a Gilbert White.

No, there is simply no end to the possibilities of employment for him; and everything, by all evidence, was performed.

But he took all his life to write one book. Well, this book demanded a life and White had energy for more than one life, and he led them on different planes – often together.

CHAPTER XVI

Embattled White

WHEN this overcrowded Wakes began to empty, White, by so much the eldest child, was already a conspicuous absentee, and had indeed been only a part-time resident for a considerable time.

At the end of 1739 Anne White died – the first to go. Gilbert was then only a youth about to set off for the university. Fifteen years passed, during which many of the others were launched from home, and old Rebekah White died. She was ninety-one – she who had promised her husband on his grave tablet that she would soon follow him! Fifteen years, and by then what change! White was a man of thirty-four, his Oriel life entering on its last phase. He had become B.A., M.A., a Fellow, Junior Proctor, Dean; in 1746 had taken Deacon's Orders, and since held several curacies – but never very far from Selborne – and travelled about generally, with his eyes open, on his horse 'Mouse'. But he was not yet really settled to anything. Not yet, nor for some years to come, was there any sign that he was to be the 'Father of Field-Naturalists', author of the fourth most published book in the English language.

Significantly on his mother's death, ancient though she was, John White fell seriously ill. He recovered but was never really strong again. He lived on three years, a more shadowy and enigmatic figure than ever, White making chances to be near him in this decline, and died in 1758. Wakes went then to Uncle Charles at Bradley, who had to die before Gilbert could actually inherit it: but Gilbert had been virtually master of Wakes from the time his grandmother had departed. Henceforth what he had to do was to see he stayed there. It was essential, and it took some doing, and he had to do it alone.

It is a truism to say that every man's life is a battlefield, and I don't want to make out that White's was anything of a Talavera, but only to show that before he could settle to his life-work he had certain strenors and perplexities to endure, and griefs to suffer, and ambitions to forego. These years of his early manhood show vacillation, but they also show that *innately* he was all the time conscious of his destiny – of what it was intended he should do.

It was not so very obvious. White certainly played with the idea of making the most he could out of his Fellowship. He certainly tried to get himself elected Provost. He was for a long while immersed in Oriel politics, and seems even to have led a faction. The only thing is that he did all this in a remarkably half-hearted way – for a White; almost as though he knew all the time that it would be useless.

He had had to take Orders, the cynical would say. It was the one course that all who distinguished themselves at universities had open to them. It was how they were to live; almost like a business career – and indeed Mulso does once refer to 'our business' in reference to some one of the hazards which pursuit of it entailed. But there is not the slightest reason to doubt the genuineness of White's call. Mulso was always congratulating him on his selfless and conscientious life as a curate, and his own infrequent observations on the subject confirm it, as well as his acts. Mulso approved of it all, even while continuing to urge his friend on to 'fat goose' livings. No doubt he thought him enviably free of the necessity of hunting after these – White, the heir, the future inheritor of Wakes; and we know that he thought him lazy and lacking in enterprise.

But of course White's trouble, and all his hesitations – his struggle with what Mulso regarded as a hydra of Oriel opponents (with which he held him well qualified to cope) were simply due to the fact of his being unable to be Vicar of Selborne.

I suppose there is some quite simple reason for his going to Oriel and not Magdalen. It may merely have been that there was no vacancy just at the right time, as in the case of Collins. But going to Oriel and not Magdalen put White in a most difficult position, when all is considered, for what it almost amounted to was that he was not going to be able to be a resident Vicar anywhere, nor ever marry into his own class.

He could always have accepted a good Oriel living and married some nice serviceable girl and settled down in the usual sensible eighteenth-century way wherever within reason it took him, and then of course he would automatically lose his Fellowship and there would be no fuss. And I dare say he must often have wanted to do these things, just as he must sometimes have hankered after being Provost of Oriel (a thing plainly within his grasp) since he had an ordinary man's desire for security and comfort and the power and prestige which gives to some extent control over destiny. But for White it could not be; his destiny was not of that kind. He had to be at or near Selborne and he was going to inherit Wakes. So he must remain a curate, and compromise. If he could ever become Vicar of Bradley, where his uncle Charles White was, which was in the gift of his uncle's friend and patron, Sir Robert Henley. . . . But he must not think of something so far away and depending on a kinsman's death.

White was an ordinary working priest, in 'the dirty boots and dripping bob of a weather-beaten curate', as Mulso put it, from the time he first rode home in triumph, his undergraduate career finished (carrying his beloved gun in a long leather holster), to the time when he made his last entry in the Register at Selborne church in his still, as always, beautifully clear hand-writing, nearly fifty years later.

First he was curate to his uncle at Swarraton, which Charles held with Bradley. It is quite near Selborne. Then he went to Durley, again to his uncle, who held this living too. It is near Bishop's Waltham and again within easy reach. West Deane, where he next went, is in Wiltshire, and this curacy is the furthest away he took. But he did that chiefly to oblige his friend Richard Yalden, who held Deane with Newton Valence, and later when Yalden had to be absent White took over both parishes temporarily. And in intervals of course, he did terms of duty at Selborne itself, removing into the Vicarage, his old home, but only to sleep there. When the chance of being curate at Faringdon came along he must have jumped at it, for he could always manage the two, should occasion arise. It would all be very easy if he were ever Vicar of Bradley. And so for years he soldiered along, riding in all weathers between these places and his base of operations, coming back in the week after week-end duties as often as he could. He led this ill-paid life not so much because he liked it – though I feel that in a deep sense he would be content if he knew he was doing his priestly work well – but because he could not sever his connections with the place he was going so completely to celebrate. He was dedicated and devoted to Selborne. He was also oddly disinclined to sever from Oxford.

It was an impeccable life, and the only thing he ever took beyond a curacy was the small living of Moreton Pinkney, in Northamptonshire; and this, since he could not reside so far away, he incurred a certain amount of ill-feeling over and the charge, by those who chose to think so, of being a pluralist. He got £30 a year from Moreton Pinkney, after paying his curate. It is true he only went there once a year to collect this. He did not consider that his means thus increased justified his giving up his Fellowship, and the ill-feeling against him intensified. But it had been his coming up to assert his right to stand for Proctor some years before this which had started off the row.

* * *

The whole course of White's Oriel proceedings at this time appears to have been as irregular as his college contemporaries complained it was. We must always bear in mind that they did not know of his financial circumstances as we do. Not even Mulso was aware of them. White rode up to Oxford in the first part of this period of his life fairly frequently, and occasionally stayed there. He always, right to the end, paid Oriel one annual visit at least – he had to – but except for the year when he was Junior Proctor, a paid post, he never really lived in Oxford.

Jealous eyes had watched him riding in on these occasional visits since that Proctorial year, 1752. The owners of those eyes felt that White's mind, like his body generally, was elsewhere than in the college forum, and ought not to be engaged with college protocol and politics. They 'knew' that he had a snug patrimony to look forward to. They thought they knew what he was up to, with the Provost ailing and an election of another pending, but they could not understand why he was up to it. The man they had known and liked for years as an amusing companion in the Common-room, devoted to poetry and sport, the dilettante naturalist-philosopher with a good home always to go to – why should this man suddenly turn up and bid fair to cheat their friend Chardin Musgrave out of the Provostship, as he had before over being Proctor?

In every way, it was thought, Musgrave was a suitable choice for Provost. But White, it seems, did not think so. They had once been friends but were now enemies. So strongly did White disapprove of Musgrave that he went so far as to speak against him to Mulso's influential uncle, the Bishop. This might reasonably perhaps be construed as tale-bearing, since there was rivalry, and of course it got back to Musgrave and his supporters. In the event Musgrave became Provost.

It is a sad thing to contemplate – White, so far from the Madding Crowd, embroiled in all this Ignoble Strife. It is hard to see how he could submit himself to it so cheerfully and calmly. And when his father died, and he at once took Faringdon Cure, and when as Senior Fellow he accepted Moreton Pinkney with the condition of residence attached (unfairly, for this was the first time it had been insisted upon) and didn't reside, and wouldn't even then give up his Fellowship, then even Mulso began to look askance at him.

It is necessary for a layman to understand what the offence was. Mulso puts it squarely. First, writing to White about the Oriel election troubles generally, he had said ominously for so open a man:

> 'With regard to this affair of Oriel . . . I believe this subject will do better to talk upon than to write upon; for though we agree in opinion pretty well, a little error of the Pen may make a discordancy——'

(Mulso is referring here only to the question whether Musgrave was going to make a good Provost. He thought he would, and he was right). But, with White presumably an inheritor, when the Moreton Pinkney Fellowship affair came up, Mulso seems, I think very bravely – for he undoubtedly loved and honoured White – to have decided to risk all by speaking out.

> 'Dear Gil, Though I have talked with your brother Benjamin and Mr. Cane (White's cousin), I can form at present no judgement upon what Plea you can keep your Fellowship with your Estate, so that I cannot give advice of any value to your present purposes. I cannot but conclude from my knowledge of you, that the reasons must appear very strong to you, and that you could not be tempted by Interest to do anything contrary to the Statutes of the University, or of your particular Society; and not only so, but that you can never forget that Fellowships are a sort of Temporary Establishments for men of good Learning and small Fortunes, till their merits or some fortunate Turn pushes them into the world, and enables them to relinquish to men under the same predicament.'

This I think puts the case for the vacation as clearly and as squarely as can be, and Mulso goes on:

> 'I have no doubt what you owe to the present Society in this respect; I speak only as to the general intent of your Founders and Benefactors, and as to what you owe to yourself; in which views I daresay

you would be cautious of appealing to a Visitor, unless the affair was absolutely clear and creditable on your side . . . what I now say is a caution which is unnecessary because I have had a long experience of the candour and honesty of your disposition, and can make nothing against the reasons which you must have, *and which are quite unknown to me*. I have a good deal of curiosity to see your Letter to the Society.' (My italics).

The worldly Pluralist Mulso has been laughed at about the serious tone of this letter to one whose way of life was notoriously modest and ungreedy, but I do not see why. Mulso could not be less than serious when the honour of his friend was in question, and he was himself an honest man; playing a game, perhaps, but according to strict rules.

There was no question, of course, of any real jeopardising of their friendship through this honest caution and tender implied rebuke. Mulso did not know. But I think that that long cool look might have a little lacked its amusement here, and the balance, the level-headedness been a little more strongly taxed than usual.

Anyway, what White now did – and I think he must have felt desperately driven – was to inform his friend exactly of his situation, and the new Provost, his very recent enemy, too. What he told them allayed Mulso's fears entirely, and made the Provost react handsomely, if a little ambiguously. Both recipients of White's confidence were quite secret about it. Mulso, anxious naturally to know the outcome (for White not only wrote to Musgrave but went to see him) was very happy, as he told his friend, to have met 'the Provost in St. James's Park lately and just cursorily asked him what he intended to do with you, and he said it was in your own breast to keep or leave your fellowship, for nobody meant to turn you out if you did not choose it yourself; so I suppose that affair is settled.'

'Nobody meant to turn you out.' The point is that White *could* possibly have been turned out; the fine point at issue resting on the interpretation of ancient Statutes, and whether what White had by his, as we know, not impressive patrimony and 'estate' – he was not even to inherit Wakes for a few years yet – and his religious earnings (never usually included) made up a sum in excess of the modern equivalent of the anciently named Statutory 40 marks. White did not consider that it did; he did not choose to vacate; the affair *was* settled. Neither patrimony, nor matrimony, nor fat goose living made him give up his

Fellowship till the end of what might have been the loneliest of dedicated lives. He held on to it like a bulldog. For every time some event occurred which inclined the Oriel watchers to suppose his financial affairs improved they tackled him instantly on the subject. It seemed it was a continuous battle of moral forces, with those who thought of themselves morally in the right always somehow being defeated. The belief at Oriel that something was wrong, that White was in the wrong, must have been very strong indeed; for, one hundred years after White's death, Oriel came at him again with their accusation.

This from *The Colleges of Oxford*, edited by Andrew Clark, 1891, p. 121 (Rashleigh Holt-White).

> Gilbert White, of Selborne, among the fellows of Oriel at this period has left the most lasting name, yet his College history is in curious contrast to the reputation which is popularly attached to him. Instead of being, as is often supposed, the model clergyman residing in his cure, and interested in all concerns of the parish in which his duty lay, he was, from a College point of view, a rich, sinecure, pluralist non-resident. He held his fellowship for fifty years, 1743–1793, during which period he was out of residence, except for the year 1752–3, when the Proctorship fell to the College turn, and he came up to take it. In 1757 he similarly asserted his right to take and hold with his fellowship the small college living of Moreton Pinkney, Northants, with the avowed intention of not residing. Even at that time the conscience of the College was shocked at this proposal and the claim only reluctantly admitted. White continued to enjoy the emoluments of his Fellowship and of his College living while he resided on his patrimonial estate at Selborne, and, although it was much doubted whether his fortune did not exceed the amount allowed by the Statutes, he acted on the maxim that anything can be held by a man who can hold his tongue, and he continued to enjoy his Fellowship and his living till his death.

But we know that White had not held his tongue. What was it that he had had, so reluctantly and to so few, to divulge, and which obviously had been held so secret by Mulso and Musgrave, to whom alone he appears to have told it?

This most severe indictment, coming so enormously long after the death of a man the nation loved and revered and whose centenary it was preparing to celebrate, is an astonishing thing. Its effect on Rashleigh Holt-White, the great-grand-nephew, can be well imagined. It caused him to put before the world the papers on which White's case rests to this day. But these papers and figures had presumably been with the Provost of Oriel almost 150 years before that, and had satisfied him! What is the explanation? Why had the clock been put back?

Whoever wrote this indictment of 1891 must have had full access to the Oriel archives. If anything like the figures supplied by White had been found there, it is unbelievable that the charges would have been repeated. White's figures had established that all he had from all sources of private income was little more than £90 per annum. Now the substance of the charge in the new indictment of 1891, and the feelings in it, are precisely those which existed before White satisfied Musgrave (who satisfied his colleagues sufficiently) in 1759. All must have been gathered from the papers of these outraged, long-dead members of the Oriel Society of that time. This is why I think that White's figures were not in the archives and that his secret had been kept. If it was only this plain statement and figures which converted Musgrave (and Mulso), why were they removed, why the secrecy at all?

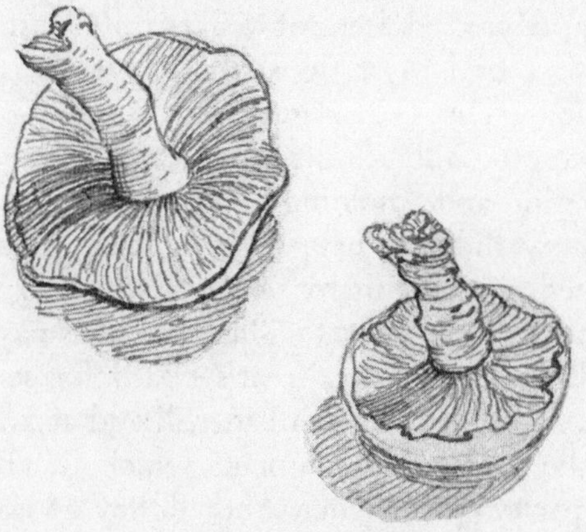

First remember that White did not own Wakes in 1759. He only had to wait for it till 1761, when his uncle Charles died – but that of course neither he nor anyone then knew. We might also bear in mind that ownership of Wakes was not anyway going to make much difference to his financial position. Next we had better see how Wakes did come to him, in a manner which I confess I find in some ways perplexing, though Rashleigh Holt-White's account, drawn from wills and other documents, is simple enough on paper.

Gilbert, senior, left Wakes to his wife, his sole executrix and trustee, for her life absolutely. After that it was to go to Elizabeth, one of their four daughters, to leave to her heirs for ever. Elizabeth White was unmarried when Gilbert, senior, died; she married her cousin Charles soon after, so that this, the inconsiderable Wakes of the time, may be seen as her portion – her provision against old age should she not marry. Elizabeth and Charles White had no children, and at her death in 1753 Wakes came to Charles for the remainder of his life, he continuing to live in his Vicarage at Bradley, of course. His nephew Gilbert, chosen presumably by his Aunt Elizabeth as her heir (or perhaps the direction was given by Rebekah) inherited, on the death of Charles, the house which had been his home for so long. It seems to have been always understood in his family that he was to do so, and he is named in his father's will as 'general heir of the family'. Officially, on paper, in wills or other documents (with the exception of two to be mentioned), John White does not come into the picture of Wakes ownership at all. Indeed he would seem to have been deliberately excluded from it, his father having made his mother his sole executrix and trustee from whom this rather devious descent of Wakes to Gilbert proceeded.

But – and this I find mysterious, though there is probably some simple explanation for it – Charles White, in willing the orchard and garden of Wakes to Gilbert, describes these as being now in his (Gilbert's) possession and adjoining to 'his father's (i.e. John White's) house'. Now, how did this happen in a will? John White's home Wakes had indeed been for many years, first jointly with his mother and latterly alone. In the year 1757 Gilbert records paying him a year's keep for himself and his horse: 'Year's board for self and Mouse to Nov. 5th, £40.0.0' – but this record in will and account-book are the only things in the nature of documents which attach John White to Wakes in the capacity of an owner. And all they do is to bear out what everyone perfectly well 'knew': that John was the owner of Wakes, a property owner, who would bequeath it to his eldest son and heir, and who must himself have had it from *his* father.

John White had no property in Selborne, and little anywhere. He neither owned Wakes nor could have owned it legally. I am going to suggest – tentatively, as you may imagine – that there had been a family conspiracy years before – a kindly conspiracy – made to shield John

White, to save him from unnecessary humiliation and to reassure him as to his future; and that this had never been breathed of outside these few people; (perhaps never to John himself) and I will suppose that such an arrangement might have been made, *if the knowledge of it reached the wrong quarter*, to look like a conspiracy to defeat the purpose of Gilbert, senior's, will, and that anyway disclosure at this advanced date might have had disastrous consequences for John.

Would not this account for White's hesitation to declare his situation until virtually forced to do so? He had to lay bare a family secret, not shameful, not resulting in injury to anyone, it is true, but humiliating certainly to his father and which might cause in him neurotic fear; and he had to disclose it to those whose goodwill he had much reason to doubt. But Mulso had read Musgrave's character better than White: Musgrave acted magnanimously.

* * *

I suggest that the Rev. Gilbert White, Vicar of Selborne, was a stern old man. He looks so in his portrait. I think he did not approve of his son's abandoning his profession, 'doing nothing', living on his wife. It has been suggested that the reason John and Anne left the Vicarage after Gilbert was born was because they feared the strong-minded grandmother and the three young unmarried doting aunts would have undue influence on the child. It might be so, but Whites generally always managed to sort well together, and I only think that the stern old man would have been a tough and ugly proposition to live with if he was disappointed in and disapproving of his son's way of life. I do not imagine any outright quarrel, because we know that they all came back regularly to Selborne each year.

Then we also know that his father considered he had done all he should for John, having paid for his education and launching at the Bar, and paid also for his marriage-settlement. But there was no money paid by John or on his behalf in the marriage-settlement deed. It looks very much as though money was given to John direct for the purchase of some property, and I should think it likely that it was to purchase the house the young people went to live in at Compton.

There is no need to think of the old clergyman as mean. He evidently had not got much to leave, though he would have been comfortably off enough at the Vicarage. He had given property away during his lifetime to his son and presumably to each of his four daughters on marriage, just as he had to Elizabeth. He secured the rest on his wife, and what he had left he left to charity. The whole thing was nicely rounded off. But I suspect that he was glad enough to buy his son out of his house and see him settled not too far away at Compton for his own good, to be independent, and for the development of a weak character, and that the son, through his fear of life, would have been glad enough to stay, and that his mother would have been glad in her turn to have had him with her.

It is generally thought that John White was neurotic, and from what we know of him by now it must be supposed that he was, but to what extent? I surmise that he was extremely nervous, no more than that, but that if pushed past the limit he might seriously have broken down, as he appears to have done at the end, immediately the mother who had stood by him all his life as a barrier and a protector was removed. John was a good kind gentle cultivated man, beloved by all. Hear, inevitably, Mulso (and incidentally White): 'Knowing Mr. White as I do, I can testify the truth of these virtues, which you, with all the warmth of filial piety ascribe to him. No good man can die without being a great loss, and I know in how many respects your excellent father would be so. Amiable family! where the parent is loved for the children's sake, and the children for their father's.'

But John White never did anything to help himself, nor anything much ever but increase his family, whose helplessness his own incapacity might in turn contribute to. The number of children made his wife's property negligible – and we know that it was not so very much anyway. He never really owned anything, and perhaps never really wanted to. If that was so it might be considered something of a virtue in him, but in the circumstances and considering his provenance it does look like the symptom of disease. It seems impossible that he should not have known what his father's financial situation was (but even so it is just as likely that when that will was read it was a shock to him). But is it possible that the truth was kept away or dulled down from one known not to be prone or disposed to see truth clearly, because they knew *he* knew that he would not be able to take it? The mother, Rebekah, would have known he was going to turn to her anyway, and this he did, and lived on her the rest of his life.

While Rebekah lived – and she lived till ninety-one – of course he would always be 'the owner' of Wakes, and of course its effectual owner would be his eldest son, who quickly became his grandmother's informed and able arm. Against this, legal ownership was academic, unreal indeed, until the time of her death precipitated the facing of the truth. Then poor John collapsed, perhaps might have been in danger of becoming unhinged, was never in the event properly to recover. And then Gilbert and all the rest of the kindly worthy family came to his aid, to soothe and reassure him of his safety, and boost more even than they had ever done his sense of the reality and value of his persona.

CHAPTER XVII

After the Battle

WHITE rode back from Oxford at the end of April 1759, happy, relaxed, a little chastened and humbled; for what was he to have tussled with these really rather ruthless men? Of how tough and arrogant a type, some of them – as was too, for that matter, Sir Robert Henley, now become the Lord Keeper, soon to be Lord Chancellor and Lord Northington, with whom, however, it was essential to keep on friendly terms as the patron of the coveted Bradley living.

But Chardin Musgrave had been truly understanding and forgiving, and he was immensely relieved. His thoughts as he rode along the familiar way home, marking the first swallows and all the life flitting among the budding hedgerows, began to turn again to poetry.

'I am glad,' wrote Mulso, 'that you have got back from Oxford with a mind impregnated with poetry, as in former days, and not troubled with Party and Contention. You brought back our old happy feels over Milton' (how that expression reminds one of Keats!) 'by those few words "Now my task is smoothly done,". . . .' White had recently built the Hermitage on the Zigzag, and inscribed over its door these words from *Il Penseroso*:

May at last my weary age
Find out the peaceful Hermitage,
The hairy gown and mossy cell,
Where I may sit and rightly spell
Of every star that heaven doth show,
And every herb that sips the dew;
Till old experience do attain
To something like prophetic strain.

But it was brother Harry who was going to don the hairy gown now busily being stitched for him by loving hands; and, though he was

White riding home

resigned and certainly in need of a little peace, and almost within sight of forty, the merriest and most festal period of White's life was about to begin. But there were many things to be completed before the overture sounded and the curtain went up. He longed to get into the Hermitage and sit there on some pure spring evening soon and look out, with brothers, or some friend. And later, if it got really hot, they would picnic. A great flood of love for Selborne flowed from his heart, and it was then he turned again to his 'Invitation', adding lines:

Oft on some evening, sunny, soft, and still,
The Muse shall lead thee to the beech-grown hill,
To spend in tea the cool, refreshing hour,
Where nods in air the pensile, nest-like bower;
Or where the Hermit hangs the straw-clad cell,
Emerging gently from the leafy dell.

(this last couplet adding to future confusion as to arbours, alcoves and Hermitages on the hill, which I will later attempt to solve).

He took a holiday in October 1759, when the new Vicar, Andrew Etty, took charge. Harry the Hermit had gone to a living at Tidworth, and garden labourings might anyway have to be much suspended in the winter months. White set out for Lyndon, in Rutlandshire, to stay with his brother and sister Barker – Barker who had taken Anne away from Wakes some years before, and who was one of his best nature-correspondents, and whose character and vitality he so much admired – and from Rutland he went to London, to stay with Thomas, returning after an absence of six months. This was 'the only long holiday of his clerical life', says poor Rashleigh Holt-White, feeling it by this time necessary to apologise for any least divergence of his abused great-grand-uncle from the straight and narrow, 'and the last considerable absence from Selborne'.

Still, next year he had to set off again, to Oxford, for his usual annual Easter visit and this, this time, was a little ticklish. It was the necessary statutary appearance for the Fellow, and might be a painful reminder to some still of his recalcitrance in that matter. However, once again Mulso was able to say 'I am glad your Oxford journey ended so much better than it began' (so there evidently had been some animosity) 'and that the Provost and you begin to have your old Feels for one another, such as you had before Competitions divided you.'

No, competition was really at an end there, and all the stress, upheaval, bitterness of that regrettable period had vanished. The College might keep an eye on him, as I have mentioned, until as far ahead as his sixtieth year, but White, content now with that little victory of the small Moreton Pinkney, secure in the knowledge that he had not behaved shabbily, never a great one at ill-feeling, had relinquished all ambitions in that quarter. He knew now he was fixed in Selborne.

Providence, Destiny, the Hand of God – what does it matter what we call it? The fact is that when, many many years later, the Provost's chair became again vacant, and an enthusiast in his family hoped he would go in for it (for he was apparently still eligible) there was not now a ripple of interest in the man completing his *Antiquities* in serenity, and about to hand to the printers his *Natural History of Selborne*.

CHAPTER XVIII

Prelude to Festivity

POOR brother John: it was not he but Harry who had helped to clean-up the Zigzag, his brain-child, and to construct another Hermitage (or Arbour, or Alcove) midway on the Hanger. (Sad though it is, one can only suppose that Gilbert, verging on forty, already found it irksome to ascend to the other; or did he merely want a change?) And he had, John, such a gift for these things; and Gilbert was going at it so tremendously hard now, it seemed – and he for ever sundered, perhaps, here in Gibraltar. Gilbert's affairs were reaching a climax of prosperity, of freedom, whereas *he* was till reaping the fruits of early indiscretion. It may be that their father had left none of them anything, but Gilbert had Wakes – so beautiful – to work upon, and he, John, had only debts.

It was necessary that John should go, though he could not have understood that. He must go and become a naturalist, at White's behest, as keen and as well informed; to be a link with the aged Linnaeus whom he met, with whom he corresponded. But the gallant John, who remembered the making of the Zigzag, and all the future planning he and Gilbert had discussed, as one of the happiest times in his not too fortunate life, must still say to his brother, at the end of a letter which is a tale of woe and personal apprehension: 'I was much pleased with your description of the Hermitage, and hope some time or other to view that delightful spot once more. I beg to hear if you intend to continued the occupier of those beautiful environs of my Father's house (note that); or if the sweet shades and solitudes of Baker's Hill, etc., are to fall a prey to the merciless Hands of the Farmer & Hedger.' And then he adds something Gibraltarian which brings him absolutely into our own moments: 'I flatter myself I could make some pleasing additions to your late improvements in the fortification way. We who maintain ourselves here by Violence and Defiance, breathe nothing but War and Hostilities.'

White, contrary to what some believe, took a considerable interest in his country's affairs abroad. He was much interested in Gibraltar, and not only in its flora and fauna and birds of passage. Later he noted with compassionate objectivity the reactions of some people who had endured the famous siege of the Rock during the four years, 1779–83, just as he noted several of the naval engagements of the period. Only these appear in his letters and journal notes, and not in his natural history, where some have so oddly failed to find them.

John need not have worried about merciless farmers and hedgers and Baker's Hill, for the freedom of sweet shades and solitudes was extended south-eastward from it quite soon, in the following June, with the weakening of farmer John Wells and by the purchase of 'the upper part of Lassam's orchard'. Merciless hedging of a sort there was, though, when Robin Tull and John Lasham were 'busy every day in grubbing, paring, and burning the new purchased garden'. Robin was perhaps the father of 'Tull's naked wench', but Lasham had just become White's regular manservant.

And the next year, 1761, not January itself could hold up the work, wet and raw though it was, for this was the month the ha-ha was built 'of blue rags, so massy that it is supposed to contain double the quantity of stone usual in such walls'. The ditch was dug so deep by mistake as to make the wall 5 feet 8 inches in the centre and 4 feet 6 inches at either end; 'an excellent fence against the mead, and so well fastened into the clay bank that it looks likely to last a long while'. It has lasted to this day and looks everlasting still, though the ditch has become shallower in course of time, necessitating a barbed wire fence to the mead, which rather mocks the ha-ha.

In February he 'Levelled the Terrass and new walks so far that they will want but very small amendments before they are turfed'. In July the fruit-wall was finished, its coping made of stones taken from the Priory ruins, where they had lain unsplit by frost but only 'full of flaws and cracks' (being of a sandy nature), in the little field called stony field still, where the church had stood for some 350 years. This field had been a quarry for the village for more than two centuries. The fruit wall is lightly shown on a tiny scale in the illustration on page 123 after Grimm's 'Haymaking in the Great Mead'. It was of red brick, with stone coping as described, and what remains of it today is only about a third the height of the original. On a plaque inset in the wall is the date, 1761. Already then so much had been achieved of what was planned all those years ago, and Gilbert, the lone operator best fitted, was the one to have survived to do it, it seemed. In his mind, probably, this was by no means obvious. The garden from the first was a co-operative affair. And here, I think, is the place to mention works which are features of its charm today, so harmonious and so old-looking, that they might seem to attach to Gilbert's effort. Trees surviving from his time are few, and cannot with certainty be specified. Many we do see are of Bell's planting in the 1850's. The most imposing tree of all – the tulip tree – was planted long even after Bell, in 1900, as a seedling in a pot, and has grown to its present great state in a mere seventy years.

The beautiful topiary garden of yews surrounding the rose-garden was the brain-child of Mrs. Bibby, the last private owner of the Wakes. There is a one-man struggle, heroically successful, by Mr. William Andrews, to keep these solid shapings trim for us. The original topiarist was Mr. Green.

* * *

Charles White died. White was the absolute owner of Wakes. He owned Wakes as completely as anything can be owned in this world. It remained now to see what was to happen about the living of Bradley and Swarraton. Sir Robert Henley, now the Lord Chancellor, was a friend of the family – it was he who had got Harry his living of Tidworth; would he now put Gilbert in his uncle's place? Gilbert at once applied. He was refused. It appeared that White had inadvertently offended the Lord Chancellor some years before, but he did not know in what way he had offended until Mulso, who had asked his uncle the Bishop to make tactful enquiries, told him in 1763. The Bishop was unable to help White to anything himself, his cup in that direction, as he implied being already overfull, but he wanted to help him as much as he could.

One can see the two bigwigs – the Bishop, now of Winchester, and the Lord Chancellor, now Lord Northington – humming and hawing and warily circling until at last the delicate question was broached. The Bishop discovered that the Lord Chancellor was firmly of the opinion that White had not voted as asked for his nominee in the matter of the election of the new Oxford Chancellor. Oh, yes, said the Bishop, primed by Mulso, oh, yes he *had*. Well, then, said the great man, his expression had belied him. He had seemed extremely disagreeable and reluctant about the whole thing.

It is plain that the patron of the living of Bradley believed that this curate, who sent him cantaloupes occasionally, had had the impudence to disobey him.

This contest for the Chancellorship of the University of Oxford had taken place thirteen years before! It goes to show what careerists were up against in the eighteenth century. White, who had evidently been quite unsuspicious, continued to send Lord Northington melons.

To have been Vicar of Bradley and Swarraton would have perfectly suited him. He need not have lived at either and would have been as safe in Selborne as in his present cure of Faringdon, for which he received only £20 a year. Now he was only £5. 8*s*. 0*d*. a year better off – the money he had for a brief while paid to his uncle in rent. (It will be recalled here that he had paid his father forty, though this was not strictly rent.)

But I think White did not let this last of his disappointments, as it was to be, weigh on him very greatly in the summer of 1763. For it was the marvellous, the festal summer, when in the prepared garden, in the Pensile Bower, at the Hermitage where lurked the sage old-youngster with his cotton whiskers, there were meeting daily the most delightful galaxy of charmers Selborne had ever seen. It was the year the three Miss Batties came to stay with their aunt at the Vicarage.

CHAPTER XIX

The Festal Summer

Many a 'lissom', if not 'printless, clerical toe' had trodden the lawn at Selborne Vicarage since Grandfather White, with God's will, and his muscles, and the help of nature too, had conjured that wide expanse of velvet from the rude field with a stone pit in it. And now, in 1763, toes unclerical but of owners not indisposed towards clergymen, and lissom, and not very heavily printful, trod it with dainty steps, or an occasional few light bounds of romantic joy which told that their owners had not very long left their governesses. And as for their present chaperone, the vicar's wife, Mrs. Etty herself, she too was light, and small, and full of spirit.

Anna, Catherine, Philadelphia Battie. . . .

The eldest was little more than twenty; Kitty was nineteen; and they had just arrived, after hectic weeks in town, to spend a quiet two months in the country. They little knew. They had revelled already in that romantic spot, gazed entranced at that view. It was quite a party, anyway, not likely to be too dull with Mr. Etty – such a gentlemanly parson – and the aunt, Miss Littleton, Mrs. Etty's sister, and her fiancé, the Rev. Dr. Stebbing, who was so amusing. The three Miss Batties were heiresses (more substantial, one suspects, than poor Anne Holt had ever been who now lay so near them in the churchyard). As such it might have been no bad idea to get them out of the way for a little while.

And then came the party from Wakes. There were staying there Mr. and Mrs. Thomas Mulso and his brother Edward (quite young) – what strange fate that it was not brother John, but he had been last year and that this one was to be so special who could have known? Miss Harriot Baker, Mr. White's niece; and Miss Jenny White, another niece; Harry White, his brother, the young vicar over from Fyfield; Mrs. Rebecca Woods, his late-married sister; Mrs. Rebecca Snooke, an aunt – who must once have been astonishingly pretty, and who lived in Sussex, and had a remarkable tortoise; and lastly Mr. White's charming young cousin, Basil Cane. Certainly that house was crowded again, and with only a housekeeper, and a girl, and one manservant – but a few girls were got

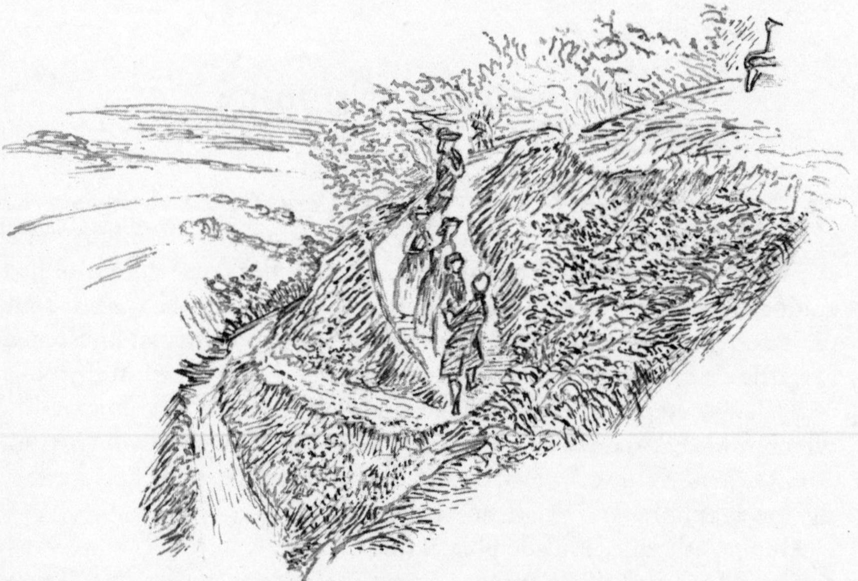

Climbing the zigzag

The Hermitage – waiting

in temporarily from round about to act as ladies'-maids at need; and then, not all of these guests were making very protracted stays. The three young clergymen, Basil, Harry and Ned, were on only quite short leave from their parishes, which were none of them very far off. These two house-parties mingled together as if by nature ordained to form one intoxicating compound for ever, and even now I never approach their haunts without hearing faint echoes of their laughter, catching a glimpse of romping shades, in one of our rare Hesperidean summers.

And this was a wonderful summer; not too good; just enough of showers to bring a little anxiety at times and provoke relieved smiles when they were past; thunder near enough to allow the girls to pretend to be afraid, so as to draw forth the protectiveness in the males; many unclouded days; a good year for the hay. Anna and Catherine and Philadelphia never had half so good a time in London. They would set off for the Zigzag, pretending to wonder what kept Harry away, and climb up quickly with scarcely time now to look and exclaim at the lovely view, and sure enough, after a little wait by the marvellously romantic and exciting old Hermitage half buried in the trees, out he

No one at home

would crawl, looking horridly shaggy and charming, beaming through his beard. And such a gruff voice! How they would shriek and skip away, and the old Hermit would seem half inclined to run after, but check himself just in time, and sit down and tell his beads for a bit, before offering to tell their fortunes. Such fortunes! Sometimes he whispered.

Surprised by the Hermit

Fortune telling

And then, just as everyone was getting a trifle thirsty, to say nothing of hungry, up would come dear Mr. White and his man carrying a hamper, and they would sit to a picnic in that heavenly high-up place, like a platform suspended half-way between heaven and earth. The tea they drank they brewed themselves, boiled a kettle hung from a tripod, just like the gypsies, over a fire they had collected twigs for, themselves; (which gave a good chance of getting out of eyeshot for a moment behind the boughs). Nothing was ever so delicious, so exciting. What happened to Harry while the picnic was going on I have never discovered. Didn't he get any tea? Or did he slip off his 'hairy gown' in the hut and climb out at the back somehow and join them, sauntering nonchalantly in from the wings? We are not told. Pretence, illusion, would be essential to preserve, I imagine. But after all, there might be nothing in the rules against an eremite taking tea and cake for a change, instead of pulse.

It was much roomier in the Hermitage than it looked to be from outside. And outside there were places where you could sit, stumps, and a most elegant romantic rustic seat, and great stones to lean against. And you could dance there, even – if you were careful. Once they sang and danced, and were actually twenty all told up there, with lights and music – fantastic!

The dances the girls danced on the hill were mostly of the nature of eurythmics, inspiring the images of tableaux, swaying, often solo, wrought in a narrow compass. Very other were those they all indulged in at the Vicarage, which would continue all through the night, far into the summer morning.

Dancing on the hill

June 23rd was the Etty's wedding day. On the 22nd, Kitty tells us:

'in the afternoon Mr. White, Mr. Harry White, Mrs. Snooke drank tea here; Mr. H. White & Nancy sung and played at nine O clock Dr. Stebbing and Mr. Airson came (Airson just "a clergyman residing near Winchester": there were many casual supernumeraries dropping in and out of these festivities). Went to bed between twelve & one o clock was very merry after supper the next day being Mr & Mrs Ettys' wedding day we kept it with mirth and jollity. The morn was spent at the harpsichord a Ball at night began minuets at half an hour

Exchanging caps and wigs

after seven then danced country dances till near eleven went to supper after supper sat some time sang laughed talk'd & then went to dancing again danced till 3 in the morn: at half an hour after four the company all went away we danced 30, danced, never had I such a dance in my life before nor ever shall I have such a one again I believe.'

You catch the breathless, ecstatic young girl the better for her style of punctuation, though to present it unedited is scarcely fair on Kitty. The future Mrs. Rashleigh, wife to a rich young squire down in Cornwall, might well have been horrified to think of her artless jottings being published. But how thankful we should be to White's great-grand-nephew, Rashleigh Holt-White, for bringing her diary to light. Thankful too to Oriel College, I suppose, for forcing him to write that great-grand-uncle's *Life* which contains it, so strange a world this is.

But where do you ever catch better the robust spirit in which the century of Reason and Decorum enjoyed itself? On a similar occasion the dancers exchanged caps and wigs. I think you only get its counterpart in that truly marvellous painting – a mere sketch, but of genius – by Hogarth, of dancers dancing much about that date, on such a summer night, with the summer dawn breaking through the mist of performers at hard exercise, the dust rising from the stamped-on floor, in the faint light and fume of candles guttering in the dawn breeze; not very graceful, tall and short, stout and thin, odd-looking, some, and crooked limbed, but dancers dancing earnestly, ghostly in their revelry, with here and there a young creature enjoying itself as never before in a dawn that is breaking for ever.

* * *

Dangerous association of heiresses and unfledged clerics! They ranged from the Tent to the Hermitage, to the Woods and to the Hermitage again, that night when it was all lit up, and never should Kitty forget the happiness of that day, 'which succeeded any I have ever had in all my life'. All nineteen and a half years of it! Kept in by the rain, they all trooped off to be weighed. Somebody slyly put his foot on the scales – 'I weigh 134 lb oh monstrous!', and then, more insidious still, they were measured.

Perhaps the seniors began to be a little apprehensive, for a check was given by a discourse upon 'Natural Phylosophy & Astronomy' (Derham again?) by Mr. T. Mulso. ('I hope I edify'd' says Kitty). Then while the ladies bent over their needlework he read them some of Thomson's *Seasons*, and he went on with the poem next day, after they had gone into the field to toss hay about a little – into the Great Mead beyond the ha-ha, that is, where White had fixed his 'sweet Tent' convenient for relaxation after such exercise. This is almost certainly that pretty pavilion-like tent we see to the right in Grimm's view of Selborne from the top of the Short Lyth. The advantages of tent and summerhouse and alcove within easy reach of the house in uncertain English summers, began to be felt now, for a day or two, when this one seemed to be going wrong. But no, all soon cleared and settled fine, and they were able to ride and walk again and play at being milkmaids with their swains.

Ned, Basil, Harry were all 'bewitched' – you would think in turn and by all the girls together (there is safety in numbers) – by 'the three Sorceresses', Nanny, Kitty and Delphy. Ned Mulso wrote a song about it, and sang it. Harry was delayed four hours in his return to duty by it. These three must have fairly worn their horses out, riding to and fro. And then – perhaps it was the hay-making which put it into their heads – the high note of the holiday was reached when the sorceresses and their victims were changed, as by the waving of a wand, into Strephon, Corydon, and Collin, 'poor bewitched men'. Strephon was Harry, Corydon, Ned, and Collin, Basil Cane. For the girls, we only know that Kitty was called Daphne. Some Phyllis or Chloe, no doubt, served for the others.

Milkmaids and Shepherdesses: 'We were all Shepherdesses' exclaims ecstatic Kitty. One gathers an affair of tucking up the ladies' trains, and changing hats to 'dapper'. So Gilbert tells us in a little set of verses. And one gathers it was his idea, though it was in the air; for isn't poor

Haymakers in the Great Mead (after Grimm)

Marie Antoinette's ghost still sometimes seen in the *Laiterie* at the *Petit Trianon*? It was this kind of frivolity which helped to exacerbate the mob. It seemed the last impertinence – to be playing at peasants. But all that was far off in 1763. But one remembers that almost White's last written words, in his journal, nearly thirty years later, were these: 'The King of France's head cut off in Paris, and his body thrown into a common grave.' Tremendous reticence.

Did he remember then how he had walked among them all through and about his new-made walks and lawns and shrubberies, encouraging all this play; like a sober Silenus, a bowdlerised Priapus; genial but apparently rather aloof; apparently himself untouched by darts pretended fatal? He was a mysterious figure.

Gilbert, a meddling, luckless swain,
  Must alter Ladies dresses
To dapper hats, & tucked-up train,
  And flow'r-enwoven tresses.

But now the Lout with loss of heart
  Must for his rashness pay:
He rues for tamp'ring with a dart
  Too prompt before to slay!

White I think was here deliberately including himself – aged, after all, only just forty-three – among the young ones falling helplessly about him on all sides, for reasons of prudence. For whatever the young ladies may have felt – and Kitty-Daphne in her turban head-dress at the Wakes looking, though perhaps no ravishing beauty, extremely attractive, was evidently a creature of heart and as kind and honest a sweetheart as anyone could want – whatever the girls felt, the young men, two at least, were surely smitten.

Harry even went so far as to commit himself to a poem of nine stanzas, signed 'Strephon', which tries to disguise feelings – very unlike the literary conventional piece his brother contributed. I cannot bear to quote them. They speak of a torn breast, and how stern Reason has bidden him check his woe at Daphne's departure from the happy vale. She herself catches these last words up in her diary, in her farewell:

> Adieu happy Vale, enchanting Hermitage, much-loved stump, beautious Hanger, sweet Lythe: to all I bid adieu with grateful thanks: may the Woods flourish; may no mischievous Boy hurt the little Nest; may all the good inhabitants have as many happy days there as I have had; 'tis the sincere wish of
>
> Daphne.

I think few have ever loved Selborne more sincerely than this young girl.

And I myself do not feel it disagreeable that they should have enjoyed themselves playing at country folk in that period quite lacking in the refinements of class-consciousness we have since evolved. For the

Young squire romping with milkmaids
(after an eighteenth-century print)

desire to be simpler-lived, though impossible for them to realise except so far as in this pretence, as they well knew, was a healthy one, in reaction to rigid conventions and artificialities of their day. It might be nothing now but an amusement, and a little mildly offensive to our democratic taste, but it was spontaneous, and fruitful, since it led to the Romantic idea of brotherhood of Man, Romantic poetry, and incidentally to the great success of White's book.

As for the effects of love in the wonderful and festal season, Mulso as usual has the last word. He was not there, unfortunately, but had been kept well-informed. Ned was his own beloved younger brother, and he had long been attached to Harry. Mulso who wanted everybody to be in love and marry and become as happy as he was – he had waited a more than Old-Testament term of ten years himself for felicity – pondered quite seriously the possible injuries to these evidently stricken lads, resulting from a passion which everyone in the eighteenth century must know would end so from such as they were tangling with heiresses. Lightly enough he wrote to White on July 28th, before proceedings were quite over:

> 'I received a letter last night from my dear brother Ned. If he is still with you I beg you to thank him for it. I gather from it that you find your guests in a variety of entertainments, and keep them constantly employed in gallantry. They are now reduced, by the departure of the *Sorceresses*, to the elegiac strain; and must as least hang verses on the Beeches of the Hanger and the Noar, if they do not serve themselves in the same way.'

On 3 August, bearing a fine cantaloupe for Mr. Battie, the young ladies departed. At the beginning of October Mulso writes again.

> 'As to the consequences to the young gentlemen, it will be no great matter, especially if it purges off in poetry: when passion is fanciful it is not dangerous. Ned requires these brushings, being apt to have torpid and viscous blood, if a love fit now and then did not quicken his pulses.'

What a piteously raw picture of poor Ned's youthful love!

And then Mulso suddenly turns his searchlight onto Gilbert instead. 'It would not do you so much good, unless it was once to the Purpose; for we, my friend, begin to grow into a more serious age, and to mean a little more what we profess. I beg you to get as much this winter as possible into the gay world——.'

And he is back again on this line in December, when he talks of the bustle, talk, and variety of London as being absolutely necessary to White's welfare, adding, strangely:

> 'And if you should have any *farther knowledge* of the Miss B's, it might have rather a salutary than a dangerous effect, for it is my notion that they may be taken either full or fasting.'

Then he switches back: 'How many people did you make happy last summer! Some indeed bear some scars; for even a sweet rose bush has its thorns. I endeavoured to laugh at some of them as mere scratches, but alas poor King Lear (Ned Mulso) was mad in his last letter, the paroxysm was upon him and he complained that he was *cut to the brain*. . . . I hope the poor curates of Ludgershall are come to themselves again.' This refers to Basil Cane, Curate of Ludgershall in Wilts, and Harry very near at Tidworth.

What did Mulso mean by talking nonsense about London being necessary to White, urging him to go there and bustle about and see if he could meet the Miss B's? Ever solicitous for his friend's happiness, was he thinking of one of them for him? I am as sure as one can be in such things that Miss Catherine Battie would have been an ideal mate for White; and I am equally sure that there is none but metaphorical truth in the idea that Selborne was his only love. But of course it could never have been. No White could compete with a Rashleigh of Penquite; an admiral, Sir George Young; a Mr., afterwards Sir, John Call, Bart. The three Miss Batties were booked from the start, and must have known it. Delphy danced, and Anna – who was gentle – sang, and Kitty had a deep wild heart and could express herself in secret; but all were acting a charade in the happy vale that summer, which had its corresponding significance, if anywhere, in some continuum undreamed of then.

* * *

Harry was not the only one who came in while the girls were at breakfast, that last morning, to present Catherine Battie with verses. Mr. White, as she calls him respectfully throughout her diary, came to like purpose. Harry's poem was entitled 'DAPHNE'S DEPARTURE: An Elegy Written At Selborne, 1763': his brother's, 'KITTY'S FAREWELL TO THE STUMP BENEATH THE HERMITAGE.'

This poetical piece, like the other little set I have quoted, is in the same highly artificial style of Shenstone, in the spirit of which, I suppose, White had conceived all this mock arcadian, pastoral, Chloe-and-Cupid's dart business from the beginning. Arcadian in its stiff prim fancy-dress way it undoubtedly was, and saved from downright futility only by the beautiful child-like and immediate response of Miss Kitty; but there is irony in the thought that it was just this kind of thing in a volume of Shenstone which was going to be so nauseating to the young Hudson pining for the true country life of England in the far-off estancia in the Argentine, and from which he would turn with immense relief to the real Gilbert White of the *Natural History*.

But when the fag end of that illustrious summer (and how flat it must have seemed) had passed, and the autumn, when the splendid beechen fires on the Hanger only caused a deeper regret that some were absent who would have loved to see them, and the winter came, when it became a pleasant torture to contrast the ruin with what had been, then White turned to his *Invitation* again and added a few lines which may have special meaning. Now, after the couplets celebrating the Hermit and Hanger before quoted, ending:

> 'Or where the Hermit hangs the straw-clad cell,
> Emerging gently from the leafy dell.'

we get:

> 'By Fancy plann'd; as once th' inventive maid
> Met the hoar sage amid the secret shade.'

The whole section, then, runs thus:

> Oft on some evening, sunny, soft, and still,
> The Muse shall lead thee to the beech-grown hill,
> To spend in tea the cool, refreshing hour,
> Where nods in air the pensile, nest-like bower;
> Or where the Hermit hangs the straw-clad cell,
> Emerging gently from the leafy dell:
> By fancy plann'd; as once th' inventive maid
> Met the hoar sage amid the secret shade.

He was always turning to his *Invitation* again, digging it up, adding or subtracting, when he wanted to fix something considered as truly memorable by this part of his mind and nature. On this occasion he did something else to the poem. Previously it had ended:

'The chilling night-dews fall . . . away, retire,
What time the glow worm lights her amorous fire.'

Now it ended:

'The chilling night-dews fall . . . away, retire;
For see, the glow worm lights her amorous fire!
Thus, e're night's veil had half obscured the sky,
Th' impatient damsel hung her lamp on high:
True to the signal, by love's meteor led,
Leander hasten'd to his Hero's bed.

In the spirit of *The Invitation*, too, he now composed his SELBORNE HANGER. *A Winter Piece. To the Miss Batties.* It demonstrates extremely well the expectable but none the less mournful change of scene since last summer's festal joys: and it seems to me, disregarding the opening rhetorical flourish, to be of a considerably higher order of poetry than usual with him.

'How fall'n the glories of these fading scenes!
The dusky beech resigns his vernal greens;
The yellow maple mourns in sickly hue,
And russet woodlands crowd the dark'ning view.

That is not very extraordinary, perhaps, but now:

Dim clustering fogs invade the country round,
The valley, and the blended mountain-ground
Sink in confusion; but with tempest-wing
Should Boreas from his northern barrier spring,
The rushing woods with deaf'ning clamour roar,
Like the sea tumbling on the pebbly shore.
When spouting rains descend in torrent tides,
See the torn zigzag weeps its channelled sides:
Winter exerts its rage; heavy, and slow,
From the keen east rolls on the treasur'd snow;
Sunk with its weight the bending bows are seen,
And one bright deluge whelms the works of man.
Admist this savage landscape, bleak and bare,
Hangs the chill hermitage in middle air;
Its haunts forsaken, and its feasts forgot,
A leaf-strown, lonely, desolated cot!

These lines, I think, are very much more like Collins than Pope. Indeed they are not like Pope at all, apart from the one obvious lapse, where the bright deluge whelms the works of man (and you will note that this couplet lacks a proper rhyme). The secret is in the rhythm – the movement, which corresponds with real emotion. It is like an underlying current swaying the deliberated thought, influencing without the writer's being exactly aware of it, the self-conscious artist so well-aware of the rules imposed by metre. (It is this that distinguishes poetry from verse.) The lines, many of them, come near to Collins at his best, as in his *Ode to the Popular Superstitions in the Highlands*, which is odd, because White could not have read that poem in 1763. The sea-sound of the woods, the 'treasured' snow, the 'leaf-strown, lonely, desolated cot' mark a great advance of prosody, not only in White's verse, but in the poetic movement of his time. And how well here the exact observation is turned into poetry.

But I am not writing an essay on White's verse. I only want to point out that it is interesting that this result, this change, coincided with the events of that summer; that it was something which had not been before, and was not to be after; that although everything points to Kitty's having been smitten by Harry rather than another – smitten by one of them she certainly was – we should not disregard the possibility of White's having been touched by her. It appears only in this, his nearest approximation to true poetry, and it is quite possible that he was not aware that he was revealing anything of his inner feelings. If he had been, I feel certain that he would have come down on the danger heavily. It was this sort of conflict, I believe, between the intellect and the senses, which drove Collins and the few who were similarly gifted, or afflicted as you might say, 'mad'. White, so otherwise completely of the eighteenth century, was pre-eminently sane.

So he goes on to ask (and who can wonder?),

> 'Is this the scene that late with rapture rang,
> Where Delphy danc'd, and gentle Anna sang;
> With fairy step where Harriot tripp'd so late,
> And on her stump reclined the musing Kitty sate?

White adds his niece Harriot Baker to the rest for prudence's sake, though I think she and her little cousin Jenny White must often have felt out of it, staring big-eyed at these dashing young London fashionables. Jenny, it is true, was not, strictly speaking, a country girl, but what was South Lambeth, even in her prosperous father, Benjamin's, comfortable house, compared with dazzling Great Russell Street.

But you may be asking, what is all this about stumps? Why is one mentioned in Kitty's Farewell, and again here, and why is Kitty's reclining on one so important? The stump was near to and under the Hermitage, and it is Kitty's reclining musing on it in the midst of the other girls' revellings which makes me so sure she was in love.

Everyone who has been in love at the age of nineteen will perfectly know what I mean. But in case anyone has never had that wonderful (and terrible) experience, I will explain that the impulse to withdraw and make yourself conspicuous in that quiet way is irresistible. And Gilbert was very well aware of that fact. But what it was that Kitty mused about I leave to more inventive pens.

Musing Kitty

CHAPTER XX

The Inevitable Question

I SHOULD be counted unworthy of my generation if I turned no eye on White's sex-life. But I am no specialist in such matters and can discover very little and invent still less.

It seems unlikely that the man was over-sexed. There are some, I know, who would find a suspicion of turpitude in 'Tull's naked wench', but I think that if whatever it was he gave her was not intended to buy clothing with, he would scarcely have recorded this, and such a thing would be unlikely to have remained solitary, and that as a clergyman in a small village he could never have got away with it to become the harmless man of legend.

When he was grounding his nephew Jack in Latin he suddenly began to find embarrassment as they were going through Horace's Odes together, and discontinued them. Jack was a fine lusty growing lad who had just entered the stage of puberty. At about the same time White quotes the final quatrain of Ode 5, Book 2 of Horace, 'Nondum Subacta', in *Letter VI* to Barrington. He has been considering sexual changes in birds, and how quickly maturity comes to animals in general, including our own species – beards and stronger features, etc. – but adds that in Man 'this sexual diversity does not take place in earlier life; for a beautiful youth shall be so like a beautiful girl that the difference shall not be discernible'. Then follows the quotation:

> Quem si puellarum insereres choro,
> Mirè sagaces falleret hospites
> Discrimen obscurum, solutis
> Crinibus, ambiguoque vultu.

which the late Edward Marsh has beautifully translated (I give the last line of the preceding quatrain to make sense):

Or Cnidian Corydon,
Who if you showed him dancing with the girls
Would set a stranger guessing, in the grace
Of his soft slender limbs and flowing curls
And sweet ambiguous face.

(All Horace has been saying is that a certain girl is too young for love yet – 'Your heifer is too young . . . to bear the onset of an amorous bull' – but that in time she will be ready 'to woo with butting horns her lusty mate', and that then it will be far better than some practised coquette like Pholoe or Chloris, or a boy like Cnidian Corydon.) One can see embarrassment arising out of this sort of thing, however exquisitely and wittily expressed, between the ageing clergyman and his pupil, but whether White felt it for himself or for the lad most, and what exactly it discovers of himself, are other matters.

Then again, cricket-lovers may be dismayed to know that White disapproved of Jack's going too much to Hambledon (to Broad-Halfpenny Down where the sport had begun),* and where, one gathers, there were junketings bordering on debauchery, possibly leading to immorality and dissipation of worse kinds in the future. White had evidently had trouble with the youngsters at Hambledon when he was curate near by at Durley. And he felt a great responsibility for his nephew, a bright youth, tall grown, whom he much loved, and to his brother John, the lad's father. Still, it might indicate a certain squeamishness.

But what can be made of the squeamishness of one who took such a lifelong benevolent and enthusiastic interest in fecundity, in the ingenuity and concupiscence of Timothy Turner's bantam sow, for instance ('her belly swept the ground'), and who could pleasantly report at about the same time that one of his many expecting relatives was 'in the straw', thus simply and naturally linking beastly and human function in this natural crisis of the sex; who took such interest in the seasonal tiptoe questings of his tortoise after a mate – which would perhaps have been greater had he known that 'Timothy' was in fact a female. In short, this man who never shows the slightest shyness (though a certain 'period' archness) with regard to sex, but only the usual robust eighteenth-century recognition of the facts of life, must surely offer singularly little resistance to the future hero or heroine who,

* So 'Hampshire Hogs' say. Others claim it for Kent.

on Freudian lines, will be very likely to attempt successfully to rehabilitate him within the ranks of the unorthodox.

* * *

On the other hand there are one or two things I should like to note. Clinging to the tortoise – I wonder whether White knew what a distinguished naturalist, the late Malcolm Burr, D.S.C., told me: that among all copulators the ostrich and the tortoise, or turtle, were the most spectacular – his interest in its futile expeditions is not without significance. The tortoise roved, once as far as the Pound-Field. It is not so much in the rather famous set-piece in the first person which White wrote for the amusement of John Mulso's daughter (called confusingly Hecky, like her aunt) though it is a happy example of his archness in the matter, as in something else he wrote about that particular exhibition of amorousness in the reptile. It has unaccountable sympathy, and occurs in a letter to his favourite niece, Molly.

> 'After Timothy had been lost eight days, he was found in the little field short of the Pound-Field. He had conceived a notion of much satisfaction to be found in the range of the meadow, and Baker's hill; and that beautiful females might inhabit those vast spaces, which appeared boundless in his eye. But having wandered 'til he was tired, and having met with nothing but weeds and coarse grass, and solitude, he was glad to return to the poppies and lettuces, and the other luxuries of the garden.'

Here is longing, I think, and dream. And the humble reptile's case is not whimsically linked with his own: both are victims of accident, and space, and the juggling of providence which deprived of satisfaction.

We might also note that when Mulso wrote '... they (Samuel Barker and John White, White's nephews) put me in mind of the Times in which we used to take our Airings together, and seek for every high Hill & every green Tree; but thank God without Fornication or Adultery.' White changed the latter word to idolatry but did nothing about fornication, which does not of course mean that he went in for that to any great extent in youth, but that, as a clergyman, he very understandably abhorred adultery.

I feel sure that it was some laxness of this sort which White raised against Musgrave with the bishop, as priest to priest, professionally; because nothing else whatever is shown against Musgrave in the capacity of Provost, in which in fact he excelled. (I move this in case anyone could have supposed White capable of telling a tale against a rival to benefit himself.)

Again we should take care not to read a man or woman out of the context of their time: such scrupulous sense of duty in this direction may be displeasing to many of us now, and some, we know, have been repelled by Jane Austen's congratulating herself upon having spotted an adulteress at a ball, and have otherwise failed to understand her distress at another's running off from a husband soon after taking the sacrament side by side with her. The point is one of feeling. It distressed such as Jane Austen and Gilbert White, each deeply and simply religious without making a parade about it, because they felt it outraged humanity in wounding religion, and by it they felt spiritually diminished. Of course an insensitive person – or one insensitive in this way – even if a great novelist, or a great naturalist – would not have stayed a moment from their tasks to notice the offence about which their society so beautifully compromised, but this particular pair were in this as in other things somewhat in advance of their age.

'You was so grave with me' writes Mulso to White once, about Miss Jenny Crooke, of Oxford, in whose company he (White) had just travelled from Selborne to Oxford in a Hackney coach, that Mulso had had to drop the friendly teasing at once, one gathers. That, I think, would have been less for White's own reputation than for the young lady's. Her mother was some well-to-do trades-woman in Oxford – with a haberdasher's or milliner's business, it is believed – who seems with her daughter to have kept an eye on the family property in Oxford for White in his absence. Jenny Crooke is one of the two girls whose name has been speculatively linked with his, as to matrimony, the other being Hecky Mulso, but that once plausible rumour Rashleigh Holt-White sufficiently did away with.

White gave Jenny a very large tureen as a present after that journey, she having refused to be remunerated as to the fare.

CHAPTER XXI

Temperament and Physique

THERE was another coach journey taken in female company in which, overtaken with a bout of his grievous coach-sickness, poor White had been compelled to vomit, one understands, copiously: had this journey with Jenny Crooke had similar disastrous consequences, and was the gift of the tureen meant as a ruefully humorous reminder? Well, he gave just such an enormous one to Mulso himself when he married.

Children, notoriously, suffer from car-sickness; White suffered from coach-sickness. It seems to be due purely to the swaying and rolling on loose springs, but few adults are affected, and I should like to know if it indicates some particular nervous condition of tension, affecting the stomach, which White never grew out of. Obviously it does, but why should it have kept with him? Which brings me to examine some indications of his high-strung temperament which he perhaps too well kept concealed – a man (said Mulso) 'so very much Master of your Passions, & so guarded in your Behaviour & even in your Expressions.' He was not always so guarded and repressed, as we see in the matter of voting against his conscience for Lord Chancellor Henley's nominee – at least his face must have betrayed him, which suggests a mobile, nervous countenance. (And in returning to that rather sad happening, I will add that White to me is only the more human by its light, not being able to prevent himself from doing wrong for his own future good perhaps – for we know nothing of the exact circumstances of the objection, nor even absolutely that he did vote that way at all (although he never, it seems, denied it) it is simply, as I said before, that he would be incapable of doing wrong to another's harm and to benefit himself.

But when everyone remarks on White's habitual control, his coolness, his reticence, it would be folly to suggest he was generally otherwise. It must have been some emotion very deep and very truly felt, such as the above, which could move him for a moment out of countenance. It is simply that on paper, in his journal chiefly, and in a few of what might be termed his less guarded literary moments, he seems to me to give himself away. But we know, anyway, that his senses were abnormally acute. One year the scent of the jasmine by his study window almost made him faint. (Samuel Pepys likewise, who seldom found himself by flowering shrubs and trees, was moved almost to nausea in the theatre by the sound of hautboys). When he heard tunes played by his nieces while on a visit to him, on the harpsichord, White could not afterwards get them out of his head for weeks, though it inconvenienced him, disturbing rational thought. The difference here is the measure between the rational and sensual in the two centuries, and in these individuals a great difference indeed, since thus far White could always curb his sensations.

We know him for a creature who passionately loved the summer, who flinched from winter as from a penance; and we know this even by so small a token as his recording, one February day, that he had taken tea again by daylight. Then, with his senses stretched and eager, he would be on watch for the harbingers of spring. And this he might do by routine; but there are the telltale marks of exclamation with which he welcomes each, spring after spring. 'April 5. Luscinia! April 13. Hirundo domestica!!!' (swallows ever dearest – three times as dear, it seems, as the nightingale). But the bird he most of all loves to listen to, it seems, is the wood lark, or titlark, as he says (we should call it tree-pipit): he has heard it in the winter: 'Jan. 17. Wood-lark whistles. Hogs carry straw.' 'April 9. The titlark, *Alauda pratorum*, first sings. It is a delicate songster; flying from tree to tree, & spreading out its wings it chants in its descent.'

* * *

Some of White's journal-entries bring us, as it were, quite next to him in his lonely bed-chamber, where he lies awake, listening for the migrants in the dark: 'March 7. Last night I heard that short quick note of birds flying in the dark.' They were stone curlews. There is indeed something particularly poignant about passage-birds on travel through the night. And yet, in what I take to be a paroxysm of emotion revealed – the best example I have to give; when the balloon carrying Blanchard and, as White supposed, a friend, came flying like a tea-urn 'between the Maypole and the weather-cock on the tower', just as he had brilliantly foretold, and White stood tiptoe and ecstatic with fear for the intensely imagined plight of the intrepid occupants, how beautifully does he solace himself, bring himself back into the realm of the imaginable from that of the hostile unknown, by likening those aeronauts to birds. Great birds. But this I will quote from fully.

First he writes to his niece, Molly, about it: 'O Molly! you don't tell us of the baloon, and the ascension of Mr. Lunardi: did it not affect you, to see a poor human creature entering upon so strange and hazardous an exploit?' That was on 24 September. It is not White's usual voice. Then on 19 October he writes to his sister Anne Barker. He had had time to prepare himself, was already a little cooler. He had for years had his eye and his nose on the 'blue stinking haze' which a N.N.E. wind brought at times to Selborne, and which local superstition attributed to London smoke, and now he felt certain that if the wind prevailed in that quarter on the day of the proposed launching of Blanchard in his balloon, the balloon would be bound to be carried in their direction; more than that, right over Selborne.

This prophecy he broadcast widely, and one can feel his excitement, even as it was being told after the event.

> 'The next day proving also bright, and the wind continuing as before, I became more sanguine than ever; and issuing forth in the morning exhorted all those that had any curiosity to look sharp from about one o'clock to three towards London, as they would stand a good chance of being entertained with a very extraordinary sight.'

It is well known how two farmers in Alton were commiserating over poor Mr. White's having gone clean off his head, when they saw a large assemblage of people on the Butts, gazing into the sky, expecting a balloon: Mr. Pink nudged his companion and said 'Seems to me, neighbour, Mr. White aint so far gone as it seemed.'

> 'That day I was not content to call at the houses only; but I went out to the plow-men and labourers in the fields. . . . I wrote also to Mr. Pink of Faringdon to desire him to look about him . . . about one o'clock there came up such a haze that I could not see the Hanger. However, not long after the mist cleared away in some degree, and people began to mount the hill (Baker's hill, in White's garden – hardly a hill at all, a mound). I was busy in and out 'til a quarter after two; and took my last walk along the top of the pound-field, from whence I could discern a long cloud of London smoke, hanging to the N. and N.N.E.'

The tension was mounting within him, but he went inside for his dinner

> 'knowing how many were on the watch: but laid my hat and surout ready in a chair, in case of an alarm. At twenty minutes before three there was a cry that the baloon was come.'

We sit in our easy chairs before the television set and see the most amazing, incredible things happen on a ghostly square which cannot convey actuality. Besides, we have been long accustomed to men riding the dangerous air in flying machines – though it is not, strictly speaking, flying at all. Whereas there in the remote countryside, it had been the news only recently received in a newspaper that had carried no conviction – of how men had allowed themselves to be taken swinging up in a basket at the caprice of winds and the mercy of a frail silk bubble. Something that had never happened before was now going to happen, was happening before their eyes.

> 'We ran into the orchard, where we found twenty or thirty neighbours assembled; and from the green bank at the S.W. end of my house saw a dark blue speck at a most prodigious height, dropping as it were from the sky, and hanging amidst the regions of the upper air, between the weather-cock of the tower and the top of the may-pole. At first, coming towards us, it did not seem to make any way; but we soon discovered that its velocity was very considerable. For in a few minutes it was over the may-pole; and then over the Fox on my great parlour chimney; and in ten minutes more behind my great walnut tree. The machine looked mostly of a dark blue colour; but some times reflected the rays of the sun, and appeared of a bright yellow. With a telescope I could discern the boat, and the ropes that supported it. To my eye this vast balloon appeared no bigger than a large tea-urn.'

What a singular chance that this thing most worth observing in all the world that day should have appeared before him most capable of observing it! The naturalist's practiced eyes had to function perfectly; and the homely features which help to fix it – the maypole, the weather-cock, the Fox above the chimney, the *large* tea-urn – which gives the touch of most primitives painting – the walnut tree: all contribute to making it the marvel it was, even to our marvel-sated minds. I can see that weather-cock by only stirring a little in my chair, and might have seen the maypole too, had that not long ago been removed.

But now comes the part which reveals White as more than a great observer, as one of unusual imagination and heart and sympathetic comprehension.

'I was wonderfully struck at first by the phenomenon' he says, being now the man of some days later, who had had time to consider and compare and think of literature. 'And like Milton's "belated peasant", felt my heart rebound with fear and joy at the same time. After a while I surveyed the machine with more composure, without that awe and concern for two of my fellow-creatures,* lost, in appearance, in the boundless depths of the atmosphere. . . . At last, seeing with what steady composure they moved, I began to consider them as secure as a group of Storks or Cranes intent on the business of emigration, and who had

> '. . . set forth
> Their airy caravan, high over seas
> Flying, and over lands, with mutual wing
> Easing their flight . . .'

This touches me – the easing himself back to earth from which his imagination and sympathy at the sight had lifted him, by means of his old loved familiar birds in the course of their ever-to-him-mysterious practice of migration.

* * *

As counter to the above I give something which, if it is not exactly indicative of a certain lacking in humane compassion, is at least extremely puzzling in White. In his letter published in *The Gentleman's Magazine* in 1781 about Collins (a memoir of whom had been included the same year in Johnson's *Lives of the Poets*), there is an element of detachment from suffering which seems to want explaining. Many years ago Mr. Edmund Blunden drew my attention to this.

White – I think it must have been in the spring of the year 1754, when Collins was also in Oxford and in so weak a condition, according to Tom Warton, that he could not walk unassisted from his lodgings to the latter's rooms in Trinity – chanced on the poet-friend of former days in a most terrible situation. He saw Collins in a fit of madness, as he supposed, struggling in the hands of some men who were conveying him by force to 'a house that took in such unhappy objects'. He appears to have done nothing at all about it. He merely adds in this

* White thought there were two, but only Blanchard was in the balloon.

letter to a magazine: 'I have always understood that not long after he died in confinement, but when, or where, he was buried I never knew.'

Now this is coolness and detachment carried to abnormality, and its being written by an old man a quarter of a century after the event does not do much to help, considering that White chose to publish this piece of fruity gossip in the year of a noble tribute to Collins just paid by Johnson. To leave it like this, of course, would be most unfair to White, who is elsewhere kind and as just as he could be to Collins's memory. He did not after all know much about Collins after Collins had suddenly left the university in 1744, except what he had gleaned from Mulso and a few other contemporaries; and some of his gossip is valuable and borne out by what Johnson says, and is at least gossip which contains a grain or more of truth, so precious where little is known. But it is a letter which any dabbler in literature for magazines might have written and published for the sake of gaining a little importance, and I think that the mystery here is that it was so written and published by a man like Gilbert White. I think this is more extraordinary than the apparent casual coolness.

It is not my job to defend White if he was really guilty of the cold spirit his words here imply. I do think already that he was a trifle peculiar in the matter of his so formally addressing Mulso; but this is something vastly different, and I shall try to do it away.

To begin with, we do not know that White did do nothing. We do know that Collins was not long in the place to which he had been conducted, that someone, it is believed Warton, had him removed and sent for his sister Anne who fetched him away to Chichester. I suppose that White instantly hurried away to Warton and told him what had happened. How could he not have done so, from all else we know about him? He could not have said that that is what he did in this letter – it would not have been pertinent; of what general interest was it? – and I don't believe that he would have mentioned it either in a private letter to a friend.

White published his account of the balloon in a local paper. I believe he liked seeing himself in print and felt the lack of outlets. This letter on Collins is in some way the opposite of that on Blanchard's balloon, but in it the same forces were operating. White saw something unimaginably strange and outside of his experience. He saw it as he had seen the balloon, with his unmatched powers of objectivity, but he saw it – strong men pouncing on a weak victim – as he would have seen a hawk tearing at a partridge. It was recorded like a nature note, and left like that because it was so terrible. I ask for it to be remembered that the habit of so observing and coolly recording had become a reflex with the naturalist.

But I will not hide my belief that White had always in secret been jealous of Collins and that there was probably some, perhaps less secret, satisfaction – since the best of us cannot always control such things – in a rival's collapse.

Collins died five years after this happening under Merton Wall. He died in care of his sister in Chichester and was buried there. He was then thirty-nine, a year younger than White. Since all the evidence points to his illness not being manic, one wonders how he came to be struggling in Oxford that day. Collins may have momentarily panicked, being in so weak a state of body and in advanced neurosis. He may have become weak and bewildered, suffered a temporary fit of amnesia, been questioned, given way to fears of detention. Failing to explain himself, perhaps he had grown angry – an 'upset'. Then, if his manner grew strange and wild, his fears would have been communicated to those who first had tried to help him. These would have sent for sterner authority; Collins might have tried to escape.

We never hear anything more about poor Collins being violent. We hear of weakness – extreme weakness after an hour or two of the old brilliance in the company of the kind brothers Warton, who had gone to Chichester to see him. We hear of his listening to a maidservant reading from the Bible to him long and patiently, under frequent correction; we hear of his giving pennies to children and being scolded for it by his sister; more lamentably we hear of his howling sometimes in the cloisters of the Cathedral, pulling at his hair, at the great sound of the bells.

CHAPTER XXII

The Book that Died

CAN a man of not exorbitant sexual appetite, of moderate means, circumscribed in his habitat and limited in his conversation with his kind, be happy in a small village and without a mate? Obviously, when the man is Gilbert White and the village Selborne. As the high summer of his life began, the way being clear for implementing his schemes for the writing of the natural history of his native place, with no pains and agitations beyond what usually accompany human growth, the image of White as the easy-going cheerful old country naturalist parson begins to seem a little more acceptable. In spite of all distractions he had stationed himself firmly and stood poised. He knew what he was going to do.

First he had to arrange and condense all his notes for years past jotted into a notebook not too large to be slipped into the pocket – the Journal which had gone wherever he had gone. And brother Thomas, in whose hospitable house he had met Pennant and Barrington, had given him just the opportunity to do this expeditiously, and no doubt to gain new knowledge. And he had his network of helpers all over the country, too. Brother Benjamin was ready at hand to publish. As the high summer turned into a cloudless autumn promising golden harvest, White must often have congratulated himself on his cooperative family, and friends not so much chosen as brought into his way.

Thomas Barker, his brother-in-law, with his energy and scientific tastes, had long been a great stay, and had produced in Sam Barker a nephew who was a really valuable addition. Sam was already a naturalist, a bright lively character like his uncle and sharing so many of his enthusiasms besides, such as poetry. Even quite unlikely people had begun to take real interest, to observe. Even poor old Mulso had come up with something about jackdaws, very interesting, seeming to prove that they can smell food hidden in paper bags. Aunt

Rebecca was beginning to share his enthusiasm for the habits of her pet tortoise, and each year told of the arrival of crossbills in her firs. The great joy, however, was undoubtedly his brother John, who was coming home from Gibraltar soon.

John came home in July 1772, shaken in health but with his future assured. He was to have the living of Blackburn in Lancashire. He was joined by his wife and son, also called John, and they spent the first winter at Wakes. He had been sending specimens from Gibraltar now for some time past, which Pennant in particular had much appreciated and was arranging to have drawings made of; but when all his papers were laid before Gilbert, when the full extent of what he had done was seen, then it became clear that it was essential to make a book of the Fauna of Gibraltar out of this material. It would be called the *Fauna Calpensis*. A natural history of Gibraltar it could not be, since it was lacking in plants.

What had happened to John was this. He had arrived on the Rock knowing nothing of natural history, he says, but with instructions from Gilbert to keep a particular eye on the arrivals and departures of swallows. He found that there was one kind of swallow, apparently like a bank-martin (as they called sand-martins then) which spent all the winter there in Gibraltar, and went off up into the mountains of Spain every spring to breed; that is to say, only about twenty miles, and this was all it did by way of migration. This aroused John's curiosity; he began to investigate, and the investigation turned him into a first-class naturalist. 'It is wonderful what he has achieved,' said Gilbert. In fact John had here discovered a new species, which he called – 'with great propriety', White said – *Hirundo hyemalis*.

But now, in preparing to print this and other new findings, there seems to have arisen some confusion over this new martin, and White urged that Linnaeus be consulted before it was too late. 'The old Arch-naturalist writes with spirit still', he observed when the reply came. But Linnaeus will not have it that *Hirundo hyemalis* is a new kind of swallow, only a variety. Instantly White flies to defend John and to attack Linnaeus!

'... pray what does he mean by saying that your *Hirundo hyemalis* (for so I shall still call it) is *varietas apus?* for the *apus* and *melba* only perhaps have omnibus *quatuor* digitis anticus; while your swallow has a back-toe like other birds; besides the bill of your *apus* and *melba* are much *bent*, but that of the *Hirundo hyemalis* is *straight*.' Again you see there can be no question of false respect of persons where science is concerned. White reverenced Linnaeus above all living naturalists (but it seems he really preferred Ray's classification method, which he always used in private communications, much as he personally held Dryden above Pope), but there could be no reason to hold back truth, and it would be to insult a great man to do so. It is a pleasure to see how White himself is constantly exhorting his correspondents to spy out any faults of his and correct them.

The fact that there was some strong animus against the Linnaean method existing at this time must be left to naturalists to explain. Certainly White was aware of it, and it was one of the chief things brought into question in the presentation of John's book. Yet in the beginning John had been advised to follow Linnaeus, as assuredly in the main White had done himself. But – 'it is the fashion now to despise Linn. yet many languish privately to understand his method.' I take this to mean that though he understood it himself, together with other experts, the generalty did not. That, in fact, it was too new. This, then, was Benjamin's objection, as proposed publisher, and in a measure it was Gilbert's, too, who wanted books read widely.

We know about John and these birds because his remarks on them are almost the only part of his proposed *Fauna Calpensis* to have survived. (The other is an Introduction descriptive merely of the Rock.) At the end of Gilbert's life, long after John was dead, he quoted some of the account in a letter to Marsham. The entire MS. was still in his keeping then, and it is believed to have been in the Wakes many years later, when the house was put up for sale. Then it was lost sight of, apparently for ever. It was not White's fault that this MS., which all who knew agreed to be so valuable for its observation and anecdote, was never published. It was rather due to John's own peculiar temperament.

Some account has been given already of the genesis of the *Natural History of Selborne* – hazards and delays enough to make one gasp with apprehension if one had not known that all would be well at last. The struggle over John's abortive book, though something similar, is shorter and more violent and more obscure.

* * *

Everything seemed to be going well at first. John went up to his new home and settled down and composed a full-scale work, full of meat, for which Pennant's artists were unaccountably delaying the illustrations, so that John began to quarrel with Pennant. Still, the thing at last was completed. The result was more than fulfilling the promise of the rough notes. While the book was progressing its parts were sent to White, whose few criticisms – he could not be uncritical – were of a useful kind, quietly stressing certain weaknesses (not of facts) and incidentally throwing light on his own methods.

> 'Your journal incidents will be the most entertaining part of it . . . you should moreover, I think, have *some letters of dissertations* for the *unsystematic part of your readers*, who will not so well relish a Fauna alone.'

He would like a comparison of climate: 'you have by you an abundance of your own letters.'

John's face lacks grace in the miniature we have. It is a more combative countenance than that of most of the other Whites whose portraits we know. There is something of an aggrieved expression, perhaps of stubbornness and aggression, a certain petulance in it. His mother's portrait, allowing for a not very skilful painter, though she was evidently very graceful and with pretentions to beauty, has this same petulant look. One suspects that John took after her, and that he may not have had much humour to mix with his erudition; that his book was too learned and too dry. But he was not at all well. His health in fact was beginning to fail. He shrank from the job of transcribing his Fauna, and Gilbert suggested he make use of his son, whom they nicknamed Gibraltar Jack. While Jack was staying at Wakes, Gilbert did put him to just this task on his own behalf.

But the time comes soon when Gilbert is to tell his brother, to encourage him, that he considers the publication of the *Fauna Calpensis* to be a sure thing. He advises quarto. He has the drawings from Pennant and will send them as soon as he safely can, and he would like John to make it up with Pennant – who shows willing – *if only for Ben's sake*. (Gilbert knew much about not quarrelling with Pennant.) Three years have now gone by since the return from Gibraltar, and now John takes umbrage at what he thinks is reserve on the part of Benjamin. John had not taken Gilbert's advice as to Pennant, and now, though he is told that the naturalist world is looking forward to his book, he falls out with the best publisher for the purpose in it. It is with a sinking of the heart that one now understands, from remarks of Gilbert's, that John proposes to publish himself.

Alarmed, Gilbert sends his brother his precious account of the great 'Cobweb Shower' to make use of in his book – it looks like a desperate injection, or blood-transfusion. But well, if John is resolved not to publish with Ben, let him at least try for another publisher and not just have it printed for himself.

He tries to make John see that his work is a valuable property, in his opinion worth at least £100. He wants, he says, to see John 'the first of Faunists'.

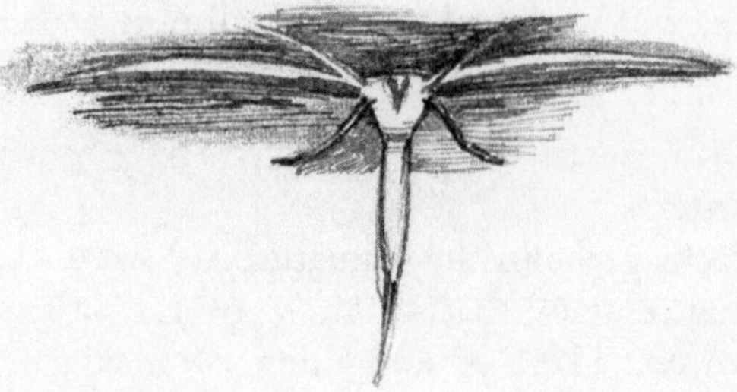

What a worker John must have been! He was already unwell when he returned from Gibraltar, and had stayed with him over the first winter, to try and reacclimatise; and then off up to the north to get settled in to his new vicarage; and now here he was already with a big book written (too big – and no index), disputing with publishers! Gilbert who knew his younger brother so well began to fear, even as he admired. Gilbert didn't think it likely that John would get on with any publisher if not with brother Ben. And he was right; the wonderful manuscript of the *Fauna Calpensis*, the favoured of Savants, which had so well fulfilled the golden expectations aroused by its original notes, suddenly became no more than a bulky, leaden collection of papers travelling from one place to another, unwanted. Naturally, said poor John: if the superior publisher, Ben, had turned it down, that was hardly a good selling-point, was it? But Ben had not turned it down. Or not flatly, that is to say. He offered 'the usual terms' but was not any longer, it seems, prepared to give John a sum down. It was proposed they share the risk.

It was this change evidently that had offended their brother, and testy as he was he was now going to be crazy enough to print it himself! Gilbert again advised most strongly against this. And for the first time he leaves the neutral sideline and ranges himself with Ben: 'We wish to see your papers, and to correct here and there, not out of vanity and a meddling temper; but because little errors unavoidably befall and escape every author.'

Ominous terms – 'vanity, and meddling temper'. White could not have used them unless John had prompted. Things had grown, then, very bad indeed. Proud, testy and suspicious was John; let us hope it was ill-health and no more. He knew that in spite of the Cobweb Shower (which he was meant to make use of but not actually to transcribe), Gilbert's own publishing affairs were thrusting along simultaneously. If John was the least bit jealous, it would be on family grounds – Ben, he may have thought, was sucking up to Gil., as usual, and he was as good, perhaps a better naturalist than Gil. My belief is that Ben knew better than any of them what was afoot. And there is no reason to suppose the terms accepted by Gilbert ten years later were other than those 'usual' ones offered now to John.

It took a long time for Gilbert to give the *Fauna Calpensis* up. But the sad day came when he asked for his precious Cobweb Shower to be returned. 'Do not forestall me with my cobweb shower' he writes. That meant not only that he had given up hope of John's book, but that he had finally determined to publish his own.

Gilbert was busy coming to an arrangement with Grimm, his chosen artist – since Benjamin had said that many plates were good for a nature book – when brother Tom, just retired, rather unthoughtfully I think in view of Gilbert's ideas of what should be a single author's scope, began to involve him in his plan to write a *Natural History & Antiquities* of the whole of Hampshire. White appears to have fallen in with this with his usual complacency and enthusiasm. Luckily it was a mere flash in the pan. What Ben thought of this project is not known. But this did not mean that the *Fauna Calpensis* was even yet quite done with. White had the MS. now in a cupboard at Wakes, and when the learned Dr. Chandler, friend of his later years, came to stay with him, though Chandler was not a naturalist, he asked his opinion on it as a book. This opinion he sent to John. *Was* it Chandler's opinion, or was this in reality a last attempt on White's part to make his awkward brother do the things necessary to convert an unwieldly and dry work into one acceptable to the public?

The result must have been crushing; it amounted to the taking to pieces and reassembling of the whole book; it meant the final disintegration of hope; but Gilbert must have hoped that his brother would take the advice of so distinguished a person as this, who must be considered completely unbiased. Dr. Richard Chandler, of Winchester and Queen's College, Oxford, was a still young, noted antiquary and historian who had just published two successful books of travel. By a happy chance he had become Vicar of West Worldham, near by, and he was to be of great help to White over his *Antiquities*. But it must have been the last straw, in September 1777, for the now mortally sickening John to receive the following courteously phrased and reasonable judgement, as delivered by his elder brother. First of all, 'Dr. Chandler the traveller in Greece' is 'no naturalist and has no partiality for the Linn. system; but avers that it will prevent your book from becoming popular.' (The Linnaean system was the very life-breath of John's book.) 'He asserts roundly that he is *sure* that if he could perswade yourself to divest it of its quaint garb (i.e. the MS.) that he is certain it would be worth £200 of any body's money. He advises – no he does not, for he spoke with great modesty on the occasion – he hints, I should say, that if you could prevail on yourself to exchange *Classes* and *Ordines* for *Chapters*, and to throw all your tables back into the appendix. . . .' But why go on. Any writer who has had the experience of devoting himself to many months of personal involvement with a full-scale work, in which he had supposed he had done justice to the subject, will know what poor John felt. John lay back on the pillows and died.

* * *

That is not exactly true: it was the book that died. John did not die till November 1780. It must have seemed to Mulso by then that no book was ever going to be achieved by any of these marvellous Whites after all. 'That work,' he said, alluding to the luckless *Fauna*, 'is not, I hope, to be secreted, like a certain person's, whose false modesty will not trust forth a Piece really good for fear it should not be absolutely perfect. . . .' But John, stranded up there in Blackburn in his icy vicarage, was to all intents and purposes dead. He had 'long been a sufferer from a serious rheumatic complaint'. Gilbert was in the delights of painting and decorating his Great Parlour, possibly thinking in a wistful way of how nice it would have been to have danced in it in 1763, instead of at the Vicarage, but John was ever in his thoughts, as all these family exiles were. On the 2nd of the month in which his brother died, having giving lately some signs of recovery, Gilbert wrote a letter to Mrs. John White of renewed hope, and even referred to the MS., with faint suggestions *à la* Chandler; and he adds in a postscript: 'When you see or consult your physician at Manchester, should he not be asked whether he has any opinion of electrical applications? My brother formerly used to amuse himself with electricity.'

Thus perished, doomed by providence, a presumably excellent work of natural history. What would have happened if John had gone ahead and printed it himself? What if Ben had been allowed to publish it on 'usual' terms? Gilbert would surely have given it his whole support – even to a Cobweb Shower forestalled, and other anecdotes; and so would Benjamin, and so would Tom; and all their friends would have rallied round. It might well have been that success would have come to John's *Fauna* more quickly and more resoundingly at first than to Gilbert's *Natural History*, still many years away from publication. There is no reason to doubt that the natural history world, as White had said, was waiting hungrily for John's book, or that John's natural science was not of at least equal order with Gilbert's. Possibly he was a better naturalist. Gilbert would have rejoiced at the *Fauna*'s success; it would have contented him; and since he never seems to have felt himself to be essential to the production of great nature books, and since John as a naturalist was in a sense his child, perhaps he would no longer have cared to make the last supreme effort. For if Gilbert had ever looked for fame anywhere, it was not in natural history but in poetry; and though I have suggested that he was (unconsciously) jealous of Collins, he would never have been so of any fellow scientist, let alone one who was his brother.

I think that if we had had the *Fauna Calpensis*, we should not have had the *Natural History of Selborne*, and that it is possible that Ben had understood this – that he knew, as Tom assuredly did not, who carelessly threw his absurdly ambitious Hampshire book across the path, and as the gifted John could not be expected to know, that there was only one White capable of writing the book which was to be famous the world over. I suppose the astute Ben would only have understood this sub-consciously, since he probably forewent certain quick gains in letting John's book go. If so, he too was an instrument of providence. The natural history content of a *Fauna Calpensis* would, like Gilbert's, have been embalmed or superseded in time; but that which made the *Natural History of Selborne* precious and unique – the humanity, the all-embracing love of species – that could only have come from Gilbert among the Whites.

CHAPTER XXIII

'The Sun Declining . . .'

EVERY autumn the tortoise tilted its shell against the fruit-wall to catch the sun's rays at their strongest, and White watched it, and maybe drew a parallel. John's had been a sunless season. No member of his family, it seems, attended his funeral, when he was buried that winter day under the Communion table of the parish church at Blackburn.

Certainly Gilbert was not there. He never had gone up to see his unfortunate brother, though it had often been proposed. The fact was, that it was now too far for him. But it is evident that he had loved John's company. So happy had he been that first Christmas after the return from Gibraltar, when they had all come to stay with him at Wakes, that he went so far next Christmas as to think for once of himself before another: he asked them to come to him again for the season, instead of his going up north, as he had promised. The recent loss of their sister, Mrs. Woods, of Chilgrove, not very far off, near South Harting, had no doubt left him feeling particularly cut off from his family. For this sister, Rebecca, he had had a special regard, dropping in on her on his annual way along the Downs to Mrs. Snooke at Ringmer.

The brother with whom, when they were together, he never seems to have fallen out, resented this request, when he had only just got settled in at his new living, and was not feeling well, yet required to come all the way down again, it seemed, because Gilbert was too lazy, or perhaps didn't think it worth coming merely to see *him*. And Gilbert, of course, would have understood all this, being so calm and rational. He hadn't given poor John the chance of showing off his own proud state of vicardom, and all the improvements *he* had made. Yet for a short while Gilbert too took umbrage at his well-meant scheme being interpreted so wrongly. He had been forced, as so rarely, to defend his conduct; was sorry to have 'surprised and distressed' John, but really he couldn't come. There were visits to be made anyway beforehand, to Oxford, and Mrs. Snooke. And it was *not* easy, as John seemed to suppose, for him to throw up his church and come down, 'which I ought to do, and fully intend: but then when I once relinquish my employ, I cannot reassume it when I please, even though I find myself ever so much becalmed for want of something to call me forth, and employ my body and mind.'

That last little sarcasm, and calling to attention the fact that after all he had something to do worth doing, Gilbert most probably regretted, and also how he had rather tartly ended up: 'Pray write *single* on your letters: for the last, tho' only half a sheet, was charged double postage.' Unusual irritability, and one might conclude that he really had pined for John and was very disappointed. If he reflected sadly now that all was too late, and how lonely John must have been, and perhaps bitter. He had lost his one really valuable neighbour in Mr. Lever, on the latter's suddenly moving himself and his whole wonderful natural history collection to London where, as John knew, Gilbert quite often went to stay with Tom or Ben, and so would see it in the absence of John, who had so wanted to show it to him himself – if Gilbert reflected thus, it would no doubt not have been for long.

It was all over with John. No helping him any more, who had been so difficult to help – so proud; so absolutely honest and uncompromising a Linnaean . . . Gilbert would now help John's widow. He would ask that good-natured and practical and long-suffering dame, who was used to living with a naturalist, to come and house-keep for him at Wakes; thus helping him as he had helped with Gibraltar Jack, their boy, who was a fine young fellow whom he had given a home to for the last five years, and was about to launch on the career of a surgeon. Mrs. John White would be someone to talk to in the long dreary winter evenings ahead, when he sat by the hearth 'putting wood on' as Mulso used to say. Who knew how few of such winters remained to him now, before he too was out of it, like John.

* * *

There were in fact to be thirteen winters, counting the one he was enduring now, and Mrs. John did indeed look after him well to the sudden unforeseen end. That Gilbert hated winters, possibly feared them, as all country dwellers then must, is clear from his Journal records kept for near thirty years. During those years some terrible

View of Hanger, Fardown and Bush Down

winters came, and many formidable springs and summers too, of harsh winds, cold and hot droughts, prolonged rains which 'glutted' fields and pastures.

We country dwellers have commodities readily available; our only comparative disadvantage is that we have pipes to freeze. Against his winters White brewed strong ale, he got in supplies of brandy, of which one thinks he drank little, and made cordials from fruits. He got in a stock of dried fish. He had smoked hams and bacon. The wood for his great fires, which had to be kept perpetually alight, (hazel-wood bavins being laid each day on the still red-hot embers under the ashes, in at least one or two rooms, in that cold, damp house where the sun rarely came in winter), was 'housed' by the end of August. Fortunately there was no dearth of wood in Selborne, and like so many others he had 'rights of fuel' on the hill. It must have been then, in the winter, that he perfected his notes, but it tried even his eyes which lasted right to the end, though his hearing, to his great sorrow, began to fail when he was still in his fifties. Imagine White not hearing the dawn chorus! To write, even in his fine bold hand, by candle-light was murder to the eyes.

But even in winter White was constantly abroad. He lived always up against the weather, defying the weather, revelling in it, foreseeing its moods, interested in it for ever. He was writing the natural history of Selborne, every article of which depended on weather. Success depended, too, on his patrolling his little chosen kingdom unremittingly, spying on it covertly from all angles, on the high hill or in the green recess. His original intention had been to write the complete record of a year: he ended by making it an abstract of all the years of his mature undeflected, steady confrontation.

The Garden Kalender and the Naturalist's Journal form one continuous collection, almost day to day, of routine jottings, nature and gardening notes made for selecting from, or by which to support theories, to aid conclusions. They were never made with a thought of publishing, though a few were extended and almost ready for use as they stood, like the wonderful record of the balloon. These notes are often like the thumbnail sketches of a Turner or a Constable. The need to be exact and then get on quickly gives them often a sort of poetry which we get nowhere else in White: 'Vast, swagging, rock-like clouds', 'Flisky clouds', 'High, rumbling wind.' And suddenly: 'Green woodpecker laughs at all the world.' Why that, for a mere nature note? I gave one summer in particular, 1763, the quality of festal, but of course every summer, and almost all of every year was festal for White. Each had its exciting, dramatic, and above all beautiful adventures and discoveries. Many people even today do not realise what it could mean of delight, to live continually, intimately in touch with nature, to a White, dedicated to it, in love with the study of all things alive. For one year is never the same as another; there is always anticipation of something new, joyful recognition of the known. When White wrote that about the woodpecker laughing at all the world, it was done in an instant of joy, a response to his own feeling. It was just a supremely happy example of what in the same way made him put three exclamation marks after *Hirundo domestica*, when he saw the first swallow.

Yes, certainly White was a happy man: these life-notes were a hymn to nature which never stopped.

And beauty: it besets him all sides. And the whole thing becomes a Te Deum, a Magnificat: Ye Valleys and Hills, praise ye the Lord. And what hills but Selborne Hill, what Vales but Dorton and the Lythe. To what but those green pastures will the Shepherd lead, to water his flock? And yet: the sheep rot dreadfully down there. Only on the down, that is, the south-east top of the hill, do sheep do well. But there is always beauty to cover against assaults. 'Crocuss in high beauty.' 'Crocus in great splendour.' 'Venus sheds her silvery light on the walls of my chamber.' 'Wonderful and lovely to the Imagination are the colourings of our woodland scapes at this time of year.' And later: 'Beautiful rimes all day on the Hanger.' Autumn, winter, spring; it did not matter: 'Light effect at noon on the Hanger beeches in Spring inexpressable.' 'Fields finely diversified.'

But still you could turn aside and see how the cat plays with the fallen leaves. 'Cold dew, hot sun, soft even'; and the swifts fly as they won't do when it is 'rough rugged weather', though swallows and house martins will. The swift lays only two eggs at a time, like the nightjar . . . January is called by country folk the Wolf-month. 'Rugged, Siberian weather. The narrow lanes are full of snow, which is driven into most romantic & grotesque shapes.' Good. But in February he drinks tea again at last by daylight. And then a long cold spring: 'Birds are never joyous in dry springs: showery seasons are their delight for obvious reasons.' And the crocus blows again, and the chiff-chaff returns – the 'chirper'; and very soon again 'men open their fields'. It goes on and on until the last: 'Men wash their sheep. Mr. John Mulso left us.' And the entries cease before the cucumbers that have been cut a day or so before have been eaten. A spasm of malaise, weakness, a 'wandering gout', a week's illness, when the new young surgeon, John's son, hurried to be with him but arrived too late. There lay quiet in the once so lively house he who had seen most, and seen it most acutely.

* * *

There had not really been any winter to that long golden continuum nor scarcely an autumn, or summer, or spring: all had been one season of surprise, delight and wonder. But was White a happy man? No feeling person can be happy, that is sure, this side the grave. And a naturalist-poet, as he feels joy, must feel the corresponding sadness as he sees the fate of individuals, and sees his own in theirs. There is a certain melancholy in 'Chaffers fall from the hedges; they have served their generation, & will be seen but little longer.' Something more than a nature note here. And those wistful recordings of Venus in his letters to Mollie, his favourite niece. He takes pains to make them scientific – do I imagine self-consciously? 'Venus shadows.' 'Venus sheds her silvery light on the walls' of his cold chamber. Soon Mollie White, Tom's only daughter, would marry her cousin, Ben's son. A blessed vent of communication would be closed to him. He would leave no progeny when he 'fell from the hedges to be seen no more' but had his nephews and nieces (to the number of whom these did not add) to be solaced with, much as Jane Austen had been with hers. In this case

Church Meadow from Sparrow's Hanger

the final addition was brought by the marrying of 'Gibraltar' Jack with a charming girl who came and played on the violin to Gilbert the last piece of music, presumably, he was to hear. 'Which brings the number of my nephews & nieces to 62.' he wrote. What a vicarious parenthood it reveals!

It would be easy, then, to round off White's life on earthy simple Virgilian *Georgic* lines. But while he remained on earth there was always the old family White alive and able to communicate with others of that business-like, clever breed. Fortunately for Selborne and for us. A nephew wrote – not a particular one, but who became a soldier afterwards – that a scoundrelly attorney he was acquainted with was up to presenting a bill for Selborne's enclosure to Parliament. It was a regular racket about that time. Gilbert had a document which showed that this could not be, so the lawyer had given it up in this case, but intended, warned the nephew, to call on White to see it. If he could find anything at all contrary to what his uncle asserted in this document, he would return to the charge. Therefore, counselled the nephew, it might be better, from what he knew of this gentleman, to show him nothing.

I will quote a little from the letter of this nephew, James White, one of Benjamin's sons, received right at the end of Gilbert's life, in February of 1793. It is addressed from Fleet Street, and this James, three years later, was to die a Captain in the 82nd Regiment, at Port-au-Prince, S. Domingo. 'Mr. Fisher,' he says, 'told me that the scheme was his own and not dictated to him by Magdalen College. That it was undertaken by him under an idea that they were more interested in it than has since turned out.' For White had told Mr. Fisher in the previous summer, 'That you had in your possession a copy of a Decree in the Court of Chancery, made in your grandfather's time, which decreed that the Wood and Commons and other Waste Land in the Manor belonged to the Tenants and not the Lords of the Manor.'*

That is why the dastardly Mr. Fisher had given up his scheme: 'because, if this is a fact, the benefit which the College will receive from an inclosure will not be sufficient to engage them in expense and trouble which an act of this nature always occasions.' In fact the College never heard a word of the matter. There is no reason to suppose they would have listened if they had. They never heard because, 'Mr. F. told me that, upon enquiry, he finds that the majority of the copyholders at Selborne are very poor, which alone would make him very cautious. This sufficiently convinces me of his Motive.'

What light all this throws on the Enclosures, the system against which Cobbett was about to hurl his denunciations: by what threads the fate of villages hung. Looking down the Tithe Rent Charge Roll one finds many properties against which are written 'With rights of Common on Selborne hill'. Rights of grazing, and rights of wooding, that is, and perhaps others. And all this might have been lost but for the vigilance of Gilbert White, the astuteness of his nephew! Well may we believe that it was providence that fixed that family here. As it is, the Copyholders held their rights until 1925 or a little after, then being bought out for the sum of £50 apiece, but only when the College had decided to give the property to the National Trust.

Ceaselessly vigilant was Gilbert White: he was the watch-dog for the village. A year or two before this Enclosure scare he had entered in the Selborne Church Register the following:

> 'Be it remembered that there had been from time immemorial an undisputed bridle road from the east corner of the north field, across Bushy plot and along the south end of Norton mead and the north

* 1718–19, 19 Feb. 5 George I.

end of Yfre-mead, and across the seven acres into the hollow stony lane leading to Norton farm – till about the year 1770, when Sir Simeon Stuart, at the instance of farmer Young, then his tenant at Norton farm, ordered the abovesaid road to be shut up and so deprived the neighbourhood of the advantage of that way: but now, in 1787, Mr Hammond senior, aged 81 of Newton great farm, but till late of Little Ward-le-ham, demanded a passage for himself and horse, of which he and others have made use the summer through: nor has farmer Richard Knight, the present tenant of Norton farm, made any objection to what has been done. The Stuart family always used to put up the wicket gates of this road, and keep them in repair. This account was written by Gilbert White, an ancient inhabitant and native of Selborne, on Sept. 22nd, 1789.'

* * *

Let nobody think that this kind of thing makes for easy old age. And we should reflect that it was all going on right up to the end. Nor should we think of White as the least of a Radical, either, of course. 'I was born a gentleman, and hope to remain one. I am no Jacobin.' Naturally. But he was not going to let his neighbours be choused out of their ancient rights by any scoundrelly jobbing lawyer, and he had set down in the safest place what a bigwig had arbitrarily done in closing a road, so as to have it put right as soon as possible. It would no doubt have been more satisfactory if he had been able to prevent Sir Simeon Stuart altogether in the first place, but he could not with profit to himself or the community oppose him with the means he had (though I suspect he remonstrated), so he waited and watched and saw to it that nothing was forgotten. It is interesting to know that his action on enclosure did not mean that he approved of the way certain copyholders behaved in abusing their ancient rights. They took too much wood, as he had warned them, and so they did at Alice Holt, in exercise of what were claimed to be almost equally ancient rights, so that the landlord, Lord Stawell came to issue with them. It is plain that White hated such abuses as much on the one side as the other. Immense loads of wood were carried away; immense quantities of peat from Wolmer; the situation was being exploited. What had been devised to help the poor and assist them to a sturdy independence was being exploited by a greedy and acquisitive few who would turn as soon as they could into tyrannical landlords themselves.

The state of affairs in France was enough to disturb anybody. Why, it seemed we were suddenly at war, and raids were being made along the coast, just as in the time of Queen Anne! We nowadays are not unduly aware of there having been any raids on the south coast in Anne's reign, but so it had been, and now the twenty odd miles between Selborne and Portsmouth and Southampton had suddenly become quite small again. . . .

Without turning White into a Mr. Woodhouse it is easy to see that he was worried. He took several weekly newspapers, which, according to general custom, he would read or cause to be read to the illiterate, but just now I suspect he edited the news for them pretty carefully: those goings on at Alice Holt had been downright Jacobinical. But as a general rule, he thought, agricultural communities were not promotive of agitators. In Selborne, it seems, they were more inclined to listen to White, for 'My neighbours' he writes to Benjamin, 'have at last agreed to stint their beechen wood, and to come to one cord for each copy.' And it is then that he goes on to talk of the crews of French privateers having been landed to plunder.

Lord Stawell no doubt found in White a useful neighbour. He called, about this time, and remained talking for several hours. The cynical might be inclined to think that White had good reason to keep in with Lord Stawell, but by now he had long ceased to be a sportsman, and the chief link between them was natural history. It was Lord Stawell who sent the wonderful hybrid pheasant-grouse and many another strange and exciting specimen as it came to hand.

I think that Gilbert White looked at the society he was born into with an impartial eye, steadily and wholly, taking in rich and poor alike. He took it all absolutely for granted. And if one senses that he didn't altogether approve of Sir Simeon Stuart it would have been as a man, not as a baronet. I do not know that he did disapprove, beyond what is implied by the entry in the church register. Or that he ever thought, as Mulso had, apparently, that Sir Simeon, because he was their Member of Parliament, had a duty to repair the roads of Selborne, and might be bribed to do so by withholding the vote at the forthcoming election!

That had been many years before. Mulso had died in 1791 (the John whose departure is the last thing the Journal records was his son). Yes – 'The chearfull, the enlivening Companion, the Charitable, ye generous, the friendly Man, the tender affectionate' was gone. Mulso had written this of his brother Edward, but how well it suited himself! Sad, but amusing at the same time to recall that warm, florid, confident voice, so often wide of the mark, which would never be heard, as always in the letters, again – as in that one, which ended with a typical final twist:

> 'If you lose this opportunity, I shall think that you love your Rosamund's Bower, *because* the Access is inscrutable.'

What a fuss old Mulso had made about getting here that last time: instructions about being met in Alton with a guide to get them through the hollow lanes. But Mulso had advanced towards old age with open arms, in his usual impulsive manner. He had become neurotic about such things long before the end; and had made almost as great a to-do about White's own arrivals when visiting at East Meon.

Could there have been any truth in what Mulso had said as to his old friend's really preferring Selborne inaccessible? It is not impossible; but as to Sir Simeon Stuart's part in the business, I think that White already suspected that that family was more capable of closing than maintaining roads. Many years had passed since in 1735 Sir Nicholas, the grandfather of the present baronet, had had the three untuneful bells of Selborne church taken down and recast, adding a fourth to them which he touchingly had 'christened' Mary, after a favourite daughter. And on that day there had been junketings, with the treble bell fixed bottom upwards in the ground and filled with punch. Everyone drank the health of the Stuarts of Hartley Mauditt that day. But now, in less than fifty years they were gone. Perhaps they were an extravagant family, going downhill already when that road was closed. They certainly ripened pineapples under glass – an expensive thing to do. The great Tudor house at Hartley was regrettably pulled down eventually, but not for a long time on into the next century. Because of the strange name Mauditt it was locally believed that it was cursed, but this had nothing to do with England, Hampshire or the Hartley Stuarts. Where this house stood can be faintly traced in mounds and ridges of the turf, and in the placing of certain groups of trees. It was close to Hartley church and pond. And the period lodge, once at gates leading to it, is today's 'Round house' on the Alton road, and a period horseman in costume of a cavalier is believed to leap those (to him) phantom hedgerows at night at a certain unspecified time of the year. I have been told these Stuarts had property at Newton Valence, and that the avenue of

The Peak and Dell Field, Coneycroft Bottom

Scots Firs leading to the old Vicarage from Selborne Common – an avenue in White's day grand, but now sadly in tatters – had some connection with them. When Hartley house was pulled down, the stable clock was carried to Selborne church tower, where it still is.

The guardian, the perpetual watchdog: everywhere about Selborne that small figure would be seen, and welcomed, and no wonder. In Dell Field, the Peak, the Ewell, the Pound-Field; in Hanger and highwood, in Maiden Dance; on Far Down, on Bush Down; in Dorton and Lyth, Lyth Meadow, Combe Wood, Long Copse, the Plains; on Sparrow's Hanger, Mill Bottom, at the waterfall by the water mill, and right down to another Mill Mead and the ruins of another mill – the mill of priory, and the ruins of the Priory itself. Then up to Wick Hill, or up Rode or Rood Lane, to Honey Lane, and by the once famous copse or wood called Losels (where the raven died), where oaks were choice enough for the timbers of the Old Navy, or for a 'new' Hampton Court bridge, and so to Temple and Burhunt – but first to glance down and back on to Priory, and the woods beyond, down that strange haunted valley still called New Barn, where once had been monkish waterworks, and a penstock whose remains can still be seen. Now up, now down, with a change of spirit at every elevation or dell; he went everywhere, and we shall be trying soon to follow him. White inspected every permanent spring, every lavant as it broke out in winter, and when it began to fail; and the wells of the village, how *they* failed or when brimmed over. And it was not just for natural history purposes that he noted these: future harvests could be told by such happenings. He always kept his feet on the ground; a husbandman, in a way a small farmer himself, as well as a scientist. But very often, of course, a perfect blend of both, as when studying earthworms. He would go out at night with a lantern to observe them. His notes betray his intense interest in the doings of these lowest and loathliest, which most people despised. He was the first to show how vital to soil worms are. Darwin followed him here. But beyond that his notes show how interesting in fact they are. How almost, in some respects, you surprisedly feel, enviable they are. But in point of fact he was not any more interested in earthworms than in other living things; it was simply that no one had really looked at them *as* living sentient creatures before. The love-life of worms before excited laughter, would have excited laughter still but for the handling of White. But such love is cosmic love, and without understanding it we cannot understand our own.

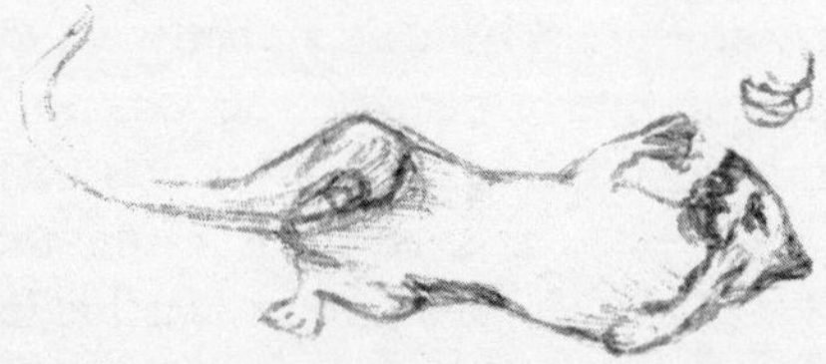

CHAPTER XXIV

The Brief Sunset

THE death of brother John, of Rebecca, the sudden death of Henry, the death of Mrs. Snooke, in old age, and of Mulso, and of Richard Yalden, and Andrew Etty – these deaths each in their different ways naturally affected Gilbert, but we should not think of him as deeply afflicted by them – or only transiently, fleetingly from time to time. For he was rational and long familiar with death as with life, and calmly watchful of decline in himself as well as others. He also had something of Dr. Johnson's faculty of attaching new young friends. Such was the learned and lively Churton – the Rev. Ralph Churton, Fellow of Brasenose College, and only twenty-five when their correspondence began. He was introduced through Dr. Chandler, who has been mentioned as being so helpful with the *Antiquities*. While he held the living of West Worldham (Little Ward-le-ham) Chandler saw plenty of White, and some years later he actually came to be a neighbour at Selborne Vicarage, but in between he was a long time absent in Europe (all the while corresponding) and it was then that Churton so admirably supplied his place as friend. He came and spent Christmasses with White. This, at a time when he was beginning to be less and less able to get about visiting his friends, was a great boon. Even the well-known track on the annual visit to Oxford was becoming too much, but it was not till the spring of the year he died that he gave that up – with his Fellowship.

But the author of the truly delightful letters to his family seems so absolutely to give himself to his correspondent, to draw him or her so into his own orbit, that it is difficult to think him every really alone. The letters to young Sam Barker are very much like one young man's to another. White always seemed to understand young people, to be able effortlessly to share their interests, to interest them. When he writes to his sister Anne, as he does not often, it is as though he has opened a door and gone into her society after a few moments absence. In his letters to Mollie White especially, you feel a tender consciousness of her youthful worth, her valuable femininity, her good sound head. And in all these home-to-the-family letters it seems tacit that they are somehow exiles for whom Selborne is the real home, and the smallest doings up and down its street will be assured a welcome.

This is how we know the grief White felt when Etty died so suddenly, in a week, through the grief, as he tells, of the little light and spirited widow, who had already been sorrowing for their eldest son, Andrew, and just been very ill herself. But mostly it was intimate, trivial at times, not solemn things. Mr. Burbey has had a guest staying with him who let himself down out of a first-floor window and found himself standing in the cartway in his nightshirt – all in his sleep, and only a graze. Unfortunate Miss Berriman has now lost *all* her clothes, two girls having run away after the soldiers, dressed up to the nines in them. Young Bridger, 'our sailor-boy', went all the way to Gravesend, with the blessings of the village, and a watch – 'he insisted on a watch' – to try to get aboard the ship young Charles Etty was an officer in, only to be turned away and have to come home again. A cow fell from the top of the Short Lyth to the bottom without injury. Robert Berriman has lost two horses recently: 'and now his cow; which by some strange neglect got into the barn's floor in the night, and gorged herself so at an heap of thrashed wheat, that she died what they call *sprang*, being blown up to a vast size'. A poor paralytic strangles himself in his bed. All the news: all the horrors. Thomas Hoare seizes hold too vigorously of the tub of salt cod, so it comes adrift and sends a whole cataract of fish down the cellar steps. Brandy of last year's bottling has turned purple. Cobb's well runs over. Prodigious floods in Gracious Street.

White knew that Mollie, who had spent long periods at Selborne as a child and young woman, both with him and at Mrs. Etty's, would relish every titbit; knew as soon as she married she would have other things to think about, so that correspondence, as it was bound to do, a little languishes, or changes character. White is very conscious he addresses now the young wife and mother. There were other nieces less fortunate than Mollie, who was strong and well-made: Nanny Woods and Nanny White were both 'consumptive'; Nanny Woods for a while only. She came to Selborne and soon grew strong and brown. She survived. Nanny White was not so lucky. At Newton she lay sinking, she was at death's door; she began to make an astounding recovery. She went back to London and soon he was burying her in Selborne. Andrew Etty, junior, too. Was White quite impassive as he performed these melancholy functions as curate-in-charge? No. But I think he felt it right that they should lie all together, family, friends, neighbours, young and old. He knew where he was going to lie when the time came. *Not* in the church: it was too unhygienic.

Meanwhile Henry had died almost young, and left a large family in somewhat embarrassed circumstances. It was not Harry's fault, yet with that short neck and the energetic life he led he might have been better prepared. Gilbert bestirred himself to act like the providential uncle he was. Fortunately, being Whites, the children were all pretty bright. But one of the youngsters had a cruel piece of luck: the solicitor he was articled to died insolvent just before the three years were up. The money that had been paid, then, for the articles was lost. The three years had all to be served over again. However, making the best of it, White got the lad another master, near by in Petersfield, and only a small proportion of premium had this time to be paid. White paid it. This was not the only case of generosity of the kind. He had always taken the greatest interest in Gibraltar Jack, and he helped him too, and was gratified by his progress as a country doctor. John's son rode about everywhere conscientiously treating the sick poor; he had the post of surgeon at the Poorhouse Infirmary. But Alton's district was small; Jack could get a reputation, but money would probably be very slow in coming. He reluctantly went to Salisbury, where there was more scope.

Jack did well. He married the charming violinist and increased his uncle's nephews and nieces to sixty-two, as we have seen; and he came hurrying home, too late, very soon afterwards, to say goodbye to one who had so cared for and, better, so obviously loved him. He should have survived into a Trollopian successful, whiskered Salisbury medical, but did not. He had none of his naturalist father's 'vice' but he may have had some of that oddness, his difference, because instead of settling down and flourishing in the cathedral city, he switched off somehow to the East Indies, where his wife died in 1802. They had no children. He then married his cousin Elizabeth, one of Harry's girls. He himself died in Northants in 1821, and his monument says that, leaving Salisbury for the East, 'his life was afterwards varied by many trying scenes and circumstances in different countries'. Perhaps his first wife's early death unsettled him. Perhaps it was merely an un-Whiteian desire to get rich quickly.

* * *

Nothing slumberous, nothing humdrum; nothing to account for that 'certain look of complacency' imagined by someone many years after his death. But a ripeness; that I am willing at last to concede, such as might come to one of his treasured *Orleans* plums, or peaches, or nectarines, his *swans egg* or *burgamot* pears, his *dearling*, *nonpareil* or *nobbed* or *royal* russett apples, dunged and nursed and protected against the perpetual assaults of wasps and other marauders. And this ripeness comes in spite of very vile weathers, when it is mysteriously often more complete, the flavour richer, than if the sun had shone continuously.

Still it is not exactly a case of dropping from twig to palm. We are sorry to note that the weather of this last spring, was one of prolonged cold drought, though the winter preceding was rainy and mild. Merciful that he did not know, when he began for the last time that heroic Journal, how half its pages were to remain a blank. 'Rain, rain, gleams. Venus is very resplendant.' So the first entry runs. And I picture White at a lattice window in that silent bedroom which had once been the family parlour buzzing with happy talk and laughter, looking across at the great dark mass of the Hanger, above whose ragged crest clear cut, the resplendent planet shone. John and Francis and Rebecca with baby Harry in her arms – these four of the merry bunch who had pressed against the wooden palings all those years ago, waiting for the great brother's return from school; who had sat round the fire in that room telling stories, cracking nuts, were gone. Anne was far off in Rutland – it was far now; once it had been not very far. Only Thomas and Ben had come nearer to home again, and Ben had just left Tom at Lambeth and moved to Bentley to be nearer him. But of course they had never, any of them, really been away. He had heard it was a fine place, Marelands – a place of numerous streams; one of Lord Stawell's properties. In the spring he would visit it. But after all Benjamin might not be there long: Gilbert had left him Wakes. Was that because Tom had already a fine estate to leave his children; or was it because he hoped Ben Junior would come with Mollie to live in it one day, and liked to think that she who was his favourite should be there, remembering happy associations of times spent in his company?

That he had owed most to Ben I hold incontestable. The book so well written had been well made, well equipped and well launched. Tom had puffed it, and puffed him; but then Ben had done that last too, and provided as priceless introductions (and customers), and cautioned him all along how to make the most of them. Without

Ben's business head how should they have done? Ben really was the Master, who piloted the book which was slowly but steadily making way. Gilbert might indeed have afforded to look a little complacent at its success – even when they didn't attach to the word then anything unpleasant, but just a solid look of conscious well-being and kind intent. But Gilbert, we may be sure, was still keeping his fingers crossed, and only feeling a little easier every day that it seemed he was to escape the ridicule he had – though rationally and cheerfully enough – dreaded.

The book had brought White new correspondents, chief among them the Norfolk naturalist, Robert Marsham. This time the new friend was older than he, and by a surely happy coincidence had been launched as a naturalist by old Stephen Hales. Gilbert, when he heard this, wrote a little sketch of his one-time old mentor and vicar – a character sketch very much happier than that he had done of Collins. He dwelt on the old man's quaintnesses rather than on his extremely formidable qualities as the scientist who had upset the gentle-hearted Pope by his vigorous and bloody experiments on live dogs and horses, in furtherance of Hervey's work on the circulation of the blood. I have wondered whether White, too, might not have been squeamish about this, and so preferred to present merely a dear old soul anxious about old ladies' tea kettles and their furry-ness, and the consequence to the insides of his younger parishioners – they seem more like patients – of drinking their tea too hot, and dwelling on his extremely ingenious, practical, inventive turn.

It was too late in the day for White to go to Norfolk when this new connection began, though in 1790 there was little apparent weakness beyond ordinary old age to prevent it. There was always of course the old trouble of coach-sickness. And Marsham himself, although a much tougher old man (he outlasted White some years), was twelve years older than he. It would seem they never met, yet a kind of intimacy sprang up between them and flourished. The last letter White was to write to anyone was to Robert Marsham. This correspondence is varied and at times almost chatty, and covers affairs of a general nature as well as scientific. It is here one sees how concerned White was at the way the world was going – a concern greater, I think, than can be attributed to old age in the ordinary way. And we learn how very late it was that he became aware of the existence of the remarkable writer Arthur Young, the practical agriculturalist, traveller and writer on politics, whose

Travels Through France he had just read. As agricultural experts in practice and theory one would have thought they would have found each other before. As it was, it was Young who opened White's eyes to the perils over the water, and who made him sit up with the following sentence: 'One did not find among them (the French clergy) poachers or fox-hunters who having spent the morning in scampering after hounds, dedicate the evening to the bottle, and reel from inebriety to the pulpit.'

This severe indictment must have filled White with mixed feelings. To be sure he himself had written disapproval of fox-hunting clergymen (and tried to suppress it), but he did not want mere laymen butting in. 'Now, pray, who is Mr. Young; is he a man of fortune, or one who writes for a livelihood? He seems to reside in Suffolk, near Bury St Edmunds; so probably you can tell me somewhat about him.' Young had been a Fellow of the Royal Society, too, for nearly twenty years. But what was Young and his pungent style, and his influence to be felt by the agricultural people of England for years to come (because he meant much to Cobbett), compared with wood-peckers and their effect on timber-trees – 'not those, I imagine, of your own planting, but only those tending to decay.' Compared to the *caprimulgus*, the 'goatsucker' or 'puckerridge', unjustly accused (through superstition, without doubt) of sucking the milk of cows.

Trees were perhaps the chief thing the two old naturalists had to discuss. It is rather pathetic how White hurries to tell Marsham of the trees he had planted under his father's supervision when he was barely eleven. But Marsham is even more in a hurry to beg that when White prints his second edition ('which the merit of your book will certainly demand') he will mention, when he comes to Alice Holt, the enormous, the prodigious, the mammoth oak, which he believes the greatest in all England. It grew there out of the clay the Romans had used for pottery, and some now think it not impossible that this 'Grindstone Oak' had been planted an acorn by the Romans themselves. 'I went from London on purpose to see it in 1759,' says Marsham. And no wonder: ' 'Tis at 7 feet full 34 feet in circumference.'

This wonderful oak had a companion not far off in the 'Buck's Horn Oak', nearly as big. The Grindstone Oak was not hollow, so far as Marsham could tell when he had last seen it in 1778, and it lasted until somewhere near the middle of the next century. Then it fell like all such giants when their fortifications have been breached enough to afford hospitality to boys – it perished, that is to say, by fire.

That White should have left the 'Grindstone' out of his letter dealing with the Holt is indeed odd, for of course he knew it very well. It grew near Lord Stawell's Lodge. The truth is that Marsham had alerted an interest in trees previously somewhat lacking. Trees are so abounding in Selborne, of so many different kinds, so obviously yet so quietly flourishing and above all so beautiful in spring and autumn, when they never failed to move him to ecstasies, that they had appealed chiefly as a spectacle, and a mere frame-work forming the habitat of minute but more interesting (because less accessible) species. White took the hint which held a suspicion of rebuke in good part, of course. 'Myself and visitors have often paid due attention to the oak in the Holt which ought indeed to have been noticed in my book.' After this he is a much more assiduous hunter after trees.

But a native of Selborne can never be very enthusiastic about oaks, even monster ones. Oaks grow freely on our sidelands, but grown to great size in their freestone beds they are apt to be 'cup-shaky', like Spanish Chestnuts, and so useless for building purposes (though a great deal of it was once passed off to the naval yards as oak), and are only what they should be in the clays down Oak-hanger way; and no one in his senses would use oak for burning when they can get beech and ash. But beech – ah, beech! And one feels how the flexuous loveliness of this tree has entered into his being from his very earliest years. This is the Selborne tree of trees. 'Beeches with us, the most lovely of all forest trees, thrive wonderfully on steep, sloping grounds, whether they be chalk or freestone.' Yet there are mighty oaks in Selborne on which White's eyes have rested many times with reverence, awe and joy. One or two are still grand in Church Meadow; another stands lonely near the Priory, and might make him weep for its decrepitude, the last of a grove I hold was planted by monks.

* * *

Something quick and slim and bright; something alive between the leaves, fragile and transient as sunlight itself: this must take precedence of the noblest tree though its autumn tint will ravish him to the last. Birds had always been the ruling passion. And most mercifully, though his hearing was dulled, his sight remained to him. But, 'Pray, good Sir, procure better ink; your's is so pale, that it often renders your neat hand scarcely legible!' Was it the ink? Certainly no one who visited him in those last months discerned what the pages of the Journal makes us so dismally aware of. White is dropping out of the sky like one of his beloved tree-pipits, tweeting no faintlier than when it flew up. Still he is out on his old pursuits. Still he is on hand to watch how Timothy emerges, rumpling up the earth of his *hibernaculum* and then to stagger round for a bit till he has become adjusted to the world of his rebirth. White watches this always with curiosity and sympathy, as if congratulating the humble and amusing fellow-creature, as in the autumn

The ancient oak

he watched for its tilting against the fruit-wall to get the last rays of a summer-life sun. This is the last time he will witness the emergence. Who could guess that? And in a couple of years both will be gone; White into the earth of Selborne from which, *he* knows, this *body* will not erupt into a joyous if bemused spring state; and Mrs. Snooke's long-loved, long-tended pet eventually to the Natural History Museum, where they instantly diagnosed its sex by its shell, that sort of thing being their *métier*.

'I don't,' Mulso had once said, thirty years before, when White had injured his knee. 'I don't know anybody who would have felt the severity of being a cripple more livelily than yourself, for if you once come to confinement you are gone.' Again prophetic, and by the same token we can count White fortunate in being ill so short a time, even though he suffered. On the 10th June he was reading the burial service over a young girl. 'Gleams. Cold air.' the Journal says. And the next day, which was a grey one, a man came to the door with a basket of strawberries, which were not nearly ripe. Still, strawberries. The little children of his relative, Mrs. Clements, ate them happily before they all left that day, when there was a 'golden even', and many swifts – those sooty, screaming meteors – playing at roof-level and among the chimney pots their daemonic games of follow-my-leader. 'Many swifts' he wrote down, large and clear. Only one bird perhaps was as agile: the fern-owl. It seemed proved now, by the way, at least to his satisfaction, that the fern-owl also only laid two eggs at a time . . . and arrived about the same time . . . and left. . . . There was that pain again, lower down.

But all was just as usual next morning. He took his last free glimpses and essences: Provence roses blowing against the wall, violets at the turn of the path. Then, 'Cut four cucumbers, Mr. John Mulso came.' Next day, as soon as young Mulso was sped, they sent for the doctor.

There is a curiosity which is not morbid always felt by all who ever followed the careers of the great. How will they meet their ends, and what are they going to die of. These are the mighty questions which make us equal with them. We have always looked to them and must know.

What is 'a wandering gout'? The pain of gout is very severe; a burning and a shooting. But gout was gout in the eighteenth century, when 'none but a fool would cure it'; a thing to be borne till is passed off with abstinence, and not to be feared too much. White had written to Mollie a year or so before that perhaps he had taken too much wine with his friends one evening and in consequence his feet had raged in the night. But he also suffered the pain of gall-stones recently – was glad that there had been no recurrence of it through the journey home from South Lambeth. Then, twice, when he was just on forty – about the time, incidentally, when the Oriel troubles began – he had gone to take the waters at Bristol Hot Springs, to cure what he termed an inward heat. One could conclude that for a long time he had grown accustomed to some measure of burning discomfort inside him, which had come and gone, and that on this last and fatal bout he had decided to say nothing, as usual, and things had been left till too late. Probably he thought more of the slight cough which had been with him all that winter. Not to alarm, not to draw attention on one's personal ailments, would always be a prime consideration with him I imagine. The proceedings between the 15th and the 26th must have been exceedingly swift, and he would have only his own people – Mrs. John White, and the anonymous cook, perhaps a maid-servant, and faithful Thomas Hoare who had been with him so long, to tend him. He had 'never had a day's illness in his life', and the Alton doctor, Webb, would be almost a stranger.

So the Journal was put aside, the naturalist suspended. A curate began to meet his crisis with prayer. Prayer, I take it, is not a thing you can pick up and put down – not to be effective. It is an affair of a life's discipline; of concentration greater, he had always recognised, than anything research demanded. But sometimes this old body insisted too obviously, in its blind witless way; and then laudanum, at first in small doses. But it required more than just an anodyne – thank God. On the 25th there were two visits by Dr. Webb. The worst of it was, it pinned you in; there was nowhere to look; nowhere, almost, to go. Prayer and laudanum, laudanum and prayer. Confinement then might seem infinite. Thomas must not neglect the rain-gauge – *when* it should rain again. Thank you, Thomas Hoare, and goodbye.

What prayer should a good man mutter at last, trained up in God and in Latin well? 'Nunc dimittis, Domine——', with a very English sound. And he lost consciousness at last, knowing that they had sent for John from Salisbury, who would soon put him to rights.

Then I wish I could tell for a fact what I believe would happen: that into that cold grey moment that had pinched him, as a boy will pinch the thorax of a butterfly, light entered, as so often to the child standing on the terrace and facing east. Sunlight flooding up over the Lyth, into Kimbers, firing the fringes of southward-facing beeches; and across the Lyth-hill meadow like a tide; touching, warming, small crooked cattle with the wornils in their hide; lapping up the bank where the field-crickets sat like little men in their doorways, making their summer sound.

CHAPTER XXV

A Special Place

PROVIDENCE brought Gilbert White and Selborne together – happily for us all – and almost miraculously it has remained as he knew it. Selborne is a very special place. And yet it is not obvious why this is so. Selborne's beauties do not arrange themselves into pictures (with one or two exceptions), and on the whole tend to defy artists. The scale is so small, you cannot get far enough away from things. But in among it all it is not so much as if you are viewing, as experiencing something by means of all the senses at once. There may be a sixth sense at work too. Something special there is, certainly, to account for its general appreciation and its survival.

For consider: all the great nature writers of the modern world – Thoreau, Hudson, Jefferies, Ruskin too in certain magnificent passages – all of their 'habitats' where they conversed with nature, and enabled us to share their conversation, have been almost, if not quite, obliterated. But Selborne, where it began, has so far been saved. Ruskin's fair springs of Wandell are clouded or shut away in a drain; Hudson's House of the Twenty-seven Ombus at Quilmes is embedded in the suburbs of Buenos Aires; what is Walden Pond with its pleasure beach to a Thoreau of today, or Coate reservoir to a Bevis boy Jefferies? Only Selborne has been saved.

I will tell you a strange quality Selborne possesses. It seems it reminds almost everyone of his or her favourite country place of childhood, and it doesn't seem to matter in what land it was. It reminds them of where they were first made supremely happy in response to nature. Obviously Selborne is not very like Hungary, Killarney, Switzerland, India and Ceylon, nor North and South America, nor Japan – though that is a little more understandable; yet people from all these and other countries have made something like this observation. I wonder if this strange fact (a fact by my own limited experience) could throw additional light on the popularity of White's book.

But this has little to do, probably, with the saving of Selborne. In the day of the railway it was saved by its peculiar geography. The nearest station was at tiny East Tisted, the two next nearest at Alton and Liss, four and a half miles away to either side of it. The East Tisted station was only about two and a half miles away, but few came to Selborne by it, because it meant a long walk and you approached it from the back of Selborne Hill, which was the least satisfactory direction. It could not in those days have been foreseen that people would want to come in great numbers, anyway. Then came the bicycle, most innocent of all modern predators of time and space, and when the great nature writers of the nineteenth century, particularly Hudson and Jefferies, had implemented the work White had long before set on foot, filling people with the simple desire to travel afield in search of new sources of enjoyment and wonder, Selborne for the first time became a recognised shrine.

The arrival of the motor car at first did not much affect matters. The numbers who began to adventure were still mostly in the tradition of those who walked to get their country pleasure – who would have thought that pleasure much diminished in the absence of such exercise. (Hudson himself at first fought shy even of the bicycle.) It was not until just before the Second World War that Selborne was seriously threatened.

In the middle thirties a by-pass was proposed. It was to run right across the still open fields between the Street and the Hanger – in fact across Wakes' park, so long and happily fought for by Gilbert White and his family. There was opposition; the Selborne Defence League was formed, and the threat passed (though the scheme was never officially dropped, as some Selbornians today remember), but it is still not quite plain whether this was due to the very formidable objecting group available in those days or to the start of the war. It is now apparent to most of us that if there was a need for a by-pass then it is enormously more needed now. Wherever it should go in Selborne it must be offensive to scenery and repose, and the means to effect such a calamity is infinitely improved. I believe, however, that it will not come, and here will pause.

In what has so far, I hope, been a happy book, it will not do to introduce a record of relatively trivial damage sustained by Selborne over recent years. When one considers how undisturbed it has been through the centuries, that would be ungrateful. We have indeed reached the concluding part of a century of absolutely prodigious and cataclysmic change – *sudden* change – which makes, say, the decade of the sixties, now completing, not only to equal but far exceed the eight or nine preceding centuries. With regard to what might happen to affect environment during the following ten years I shudder, but my susceptibilities are probably advanced. As I say, I believe, I have faith, I more than hope that since the all-powerful of our time, who are so apt to rule things out on a map and proceed as though no other dimension existed – Authority, that is to say, without a sense of other than collective responsibility for what it does, and with a clinical mind – since this is composed of individuals, and since we are all human beings, there is reason to believe that Selborne will continue to be preserved as it always somehow has been.

But this must not prevent us from recognising clearly that now and for the first time with the motor car become a god, with earth-removers of gigantic scale, with lethal sprays, with new needs invented almost daily and new social fashions arbitrarily decreed, with economic problems generally, and the population problem with its consequent preposterous increase in the paper-value of property and land, Selborne, with the rest of the world, stands absolutely up against it.

* * *

Now to take a closer look at Selborne. Gilbert White begins his *Natural History* with an admirable general description of the place. He pin-points it on the map, naming its surrounding towns, villages and hamlets. He gives its whole geographical situation, with its main features, Hanger and sheep-down, streams, trees of what kinds, and the very varied soils which play such a big part in making it matchless as a working ground for a field-naturalist. Elsewhere throughout the book he mentions casually other local features by name, and sometimes, as in the case of the Short Lyth where the colony of field-crickets was, gives a tiny detail of description, so that we should know in this particular case, even without Grimm, that this part of the Lyth was then bare of trees. But it was not his business, of course, in a natural history book, to give much minute detail of what most of his readers would never see. Now, thanks to the fame of himself and his book – and the motor car, and motor coach – the case is altered. People are coming increasingly who are not naturalists and probably never will be, but they are all nature lovers, and they want to know where to go to see the sights of Selborne which are not altogether obvious from the Street which, in some cases they never leave, not knowing how to get up to the top of that great wooded hill, or how to discover where exactly the streams are to be found, and the many other joys for which the rumour of the particular pre-eminence of the village as a place to be visited may have prepared them.

For Selborne's sake too some more detailed information is desirable. It must not be trampled under foot. The sympathy of its farmers who after all are a kind of guardians as well as the promotors of its pastoral character must not be abused. The first thing is to know where to park the car: the proper place to park your car in Selborne is in the newly-made public car park behind the Selborne Arms. It took us a long time to get that car park, and it has involved us in having signs erected which are not in themselves beautiful, but necessary and deserving to be looked for. An imaginary visitor coming in from the south-east will easily find the place, but if from the other end of the village he will at once, unfortunately, see what at first sight is indistinguishable from a car park, namely the Plestor, and this has led too often to that space being abused, to the comparative destruction of peace and the confusion of the inhabitants living round it. For the Plestor or Plaistowe or play-place, like a little village green, is not rightly a public parking place at all, though a gravelled space on the street side has been made for people to leave cars while visiting the Selborne Stores, and to accommodate residents living around it.

The village street is too narrow, and through-traffic, much increased since the enlarging of Basingstoke, is in itself a great danger and nuisance, which of course becomes much more so when visitors' cars are added to those of the residents at the kerbside. There have been prolonged traffic jams. All this, we know, is only what has been happening in villages everywhere in the south: we ourselves, probably, do not behave very sensibly or considerately when visiting them.

The Plestor (after Grimm)

CHAPTER XXVI

The Plestor

THE Street is timeless and unchanging. Anything which has happened in it only serves to emphasise that fact. It is still White's 'cartway of the village' – the 'long straggling street' which leads from the Lion's Mouth Fountain to the Grange. Half-way along is the Plestor – the Piccadilly Circus of Selborne, hub of all its life. We will start from there.

Grimm's picture of the Plestor is the one drawing he did for White in 1776 which is at all familiar to visitors, because it is in the *Selborne Handbook*.* The great panoramic view of Selborne from the north-east, such a feature of the first edition of the *Natural History*, does not reappear beyond the earliest future editions, and even if it had been made more available nobody would know where the view was taken from, or what exactly the people on the hill there were looking at, apart from what might be a very denuded Selborne Hanger.

But the Plestor – every one can recognise that. It is White's Plestor, and it is ours. The village stocks are gone. When they were thrown rebelliously downhill into the stream in White's time they were put back, but I suppose that they were permanently removed in 1832, after Fisher's Buildings, ransacked by the 'Selborne Mob', ceased to be the village Poorhouse. And that picturesque ruinous old cottage called Elliot's has gone; and no longer is the narrow passage between Plestor cottages, on the right, and what is now called Plestor House (unchanged too, but aggrandised somewhat) boarded up. Those boards were in a shockingly collapsed condition. Grimm's uncompromisingly honest pencil was never so scrupulously employed as here. If we had only a little more space afforded us on the left of the picture we should see

* On sale in the village.

Burbey's shop where the Selborne Stores is now, only with a fine bow window. Still, those incorrigibly rustic and shabby old eighteenth-century out-buildings we can see are just on the spot of structures of about 1850 which are essentially similar. The entrance to the shop's yard and the entrance to the Vicarage forecourt are in the same places.

We can see the church porch, we can see the church tower, and part of the gable of the old Vicarage: none can we see now because of trees. And my strong suspicion is, that Grimm deliberately curtailed the great churchyard yew so as to allow of these things being seen. The actual tree bears no sign of having been polled. The magnificent horse-chestnut which is such a feature today was not there then, nor the trees which now hide the new vicarage, which anyway may have been set a little further back. That tree we see in the middle is not, I fancy, the one that is there now. I conceive it to be the one Mr. John Carpenter made so many wooden utensils out of in 1786, when he took over the shop, and that the bent and aged sycamore of the present day was planted by Gilbert's brother Tom a few years later than this drawing. Carpenter, a cooper, replaced White's friend Burbey (it was Burbey who had the tame wood owl which first bathed, then drowned itself in a tub of water). White delivered Carpenter's prospectus to his family and friends when the shop was opened. The following card was lately put into my hand. *Jn. Carpenter, carpenter, cooper, bent-ware maker and iron-monger . . . takes this method of acquainting the public that he sells all kinds of bent-ware goods, and all sorts of cooperage, chests of drawers, bedsteads and tables, nails, locks, joints,* etc., etc.

In 1832 this shop came into the hands of a family called Maxwell, who had it until 1948 as a grocery and general store. Anyone over forty thinks of it as 'Maxwell's' still, and feels quite aggrieved when misunderstood.

The Maypole which can just be seen like a telegraph pole between the stocks and the central tree has also long been gone, (but in exchange we have a hundred similar poles elsewhere). You will see in Grimm's Plestor two lads playing cricket, a boy bowling a hoop, two elderly men chatting, and a fine upstanding young woman in front listening to them with a baby in her arms – could this perhaps be Tull's no longer naked wench? and one of those simple, hound-like dogs which are always getting into Grimm's pictures, joining in the conversation in a detached, semi-human way.

CHAPTER XXVII

The Street and Some Characters

If this is a first visit you have probably only got an hour or two, when it requires at least a whole day to visit points of prime interest – the Hanger, the Lyth, and Dorton down to Priory. Here, off the Plestor, lie the church and churchyard, White's grave and the famous yew tree. All these, and a brief excursion into Church Meadow afford an easy first experience of Selborne's quality, and we will go to these things soon; but meanwhile first to the Street.

The Street begins at the Fountain, down at the south-east end. In a cast-iron plate let into a wall by the side of the road, an embossed lion's head lets the well-head stream pour into a horse-trough beneath. This is the stream which never fails. The Fountain must not be confused with Well Head, the spring itself, where White would often be to see how it bubbled into the sunlight and to muse how it would find its way into the North Sea, as that stream on the other side of Noar Hill would into the Channel. I will not further describe the Fountain, since it can so easily be inspected from the roadside, but only say that it was presented in 1891 by a Mr. Lyon (hence, in the punning way, that handsome lion's head). What looks like the door of a safe, let into the wall beside it, is the door to a ram which formerly pumped water for the village. This ram was subscribed for by others, principally, I believe, by the Selborne Society. Well Head itself you cannot see at all, though there is a public footpath running alongside the stream to it, for, already quite deeply entrenched, it runs down between hedges much overgrown. I wish that this could be remedied as it easily might, I think, without causing inconvenience to the farmer through whose field it runs. You could walk then by the rivulet on the inside of the eastern hedgerow, if cleared of weeds and brambles, to this certain haunt or station of Gilbert White.

At this end of the village cottages grow sparser and more widely spaced, but very recently some new bungalows have been added there.

'Gunner's' – a lost cottage which the stream runs under

The stream from the Fountain goes under the road, by a culvert; and it used, until the mid-twenties, to pass right under part of the interesting old cottage illustrated, until that fell a victim to Selborne's first road widening. The stream goes on down between ever-steepening banks to the mill and the waterfall. It goes twice underground here within a few yards, for Honey Lane – 'the road to the forest ' – is carried over it by a little bridge.

The older cottages are mostly of stone, slate-roofed and rather grim, though if the thatch were restored White would recognise most of them. He got Grimm to draw this quarter too, from somewhere above in Bridge Field, so it was evidently dear to him. But by this bridge are one or two cottages (resembling in austerity several other but more complicated and important buildings further up the Street), which are small and box-like, and it is this which makes some people who have arrived at this end feel that Selborne is like a Welsh or Cornish mining village. The man of the past I hold chiefly responsible for this appearance was a very remarkable person indeed, and it is true that the West Country played a part in it.

* * *

Henry, the second Maxwell to own the shop on the Plestor (and remember how grim that looks too – Henry rebuilt it), used to go down to Taunton with a wagon every year to buy his cheese in bulk. And it was probably more than a matter of cheese; slates he ordered too, I suspect; and he brought back men and their families and employed them at a time when work was so scarce. It may account, too, for the strong Evangelical spirit in Selborne.

Henry Maxwell was the genius of the family. He died in 1916, not in Selborne, but at Southsea. His grand-daughter told me that he had made a clear £1,000 profit annually out of the shop for twenty years. In addition he owned house-property and acquired land in and around the centre of Selborne. You might say he owned almost everything of the kind that was not already owned by Magdalen College. He owned – he may have built – a windmill there used to be in his time, thus becoming independent of the old water-mill for his flour; but probably the water-mill had by then become obsolete.

Henry Maxwell sold groceries of all kinds; spices, seeds, sweets, butter, cheese and lard and mouse-traps; bacon which he cured on the premises, and hams. This strong but benevolent man practically clothed and shod the village, too. And he sold hardware and ironmongery – pots, pans, kettles and jugs. Was there anything he did not sell!

This prodigious shopman did not overcharge to get his profits. It was true he had virtually a monopoly. There were then no buses, no cars, and no cut-price competitors in neighbouring towns. He therefore could have relaxed and taken things easily and still made a comfortable living. Instead he set out to give everyone in the village all he could possibly need. There is a photograph, taken perhaps on the fiftieth anniversary of the shop's opening (1882), showing the proprietor himself and some half-dozen male assistants, all beautifully neat in their white aprons and straw hats, standing before a shop with windows and doorway specially arrayed. It bears a quite remarkable resemblance, with little impression of the smaller scale, to a photograph we have lately seen in a Sunday supplement, of Messrs. Sainsbury's in a similar display of first prosperity. Henry was more than the Sainsbury, he was the Selfridge of Selborne. He was the uncrowned King of it. And every year he took a large party of his friends and employees and their wives to Goodwood, by horse-drawn charabanc. He then gave the impression of fast, stylish living: there was champagne drunk and hampers of good things were provided.

Valiantly against competition today 'Maxwell's' has been carried on as the village grocery since the family left it, under the title of The Selborne Stores. It is difficult for us to imagine now all that such a family business comprised. With its many outbuildings to side and rear – bake-house, bacon-curing house, stables and storehouses, and those much older parts attached to the Victorian building, in which for years the family lived, it was like a little village in itself. It has been broken down as it were into individual units, and by the time you read this, much will have been swept away for the purpose of road widening. But the shop endures – now a tenancy – which to old Selbornians will always be known as 'Maxwell's'.

* * *

Poking out into the Street from several of those old 'good stone or brick cottages, which are glazed, and have chambers above stairs' are other little shops surviving from White's time. They included a saddler's and a shoemaker's, and now as usefully meet our different demands, though some are closed. The old butcher's shop remains as in White's day, but does not function, though it did till 1911. In that pretty, quaint little building between Plestor House and The Limes, joints hanging in the low arcaded porch, half obscured by the lime trees White planted, had a curiously antique effect. The butcher, Mr. Muggeridge, handsome and languid and pale, had heart trouble and retired to Bournemouth to die young. He lies in our churchyard.

White owned this property, and the butcher, then, was his tenant. The shop is opposite the Wakes and slaughtering was carried out on the spot, and blood ran down into the road and there were unsightly

The Blacksmith's Shop

Another view of the The Blacksmith's Shop

messes; so Gilbert planted these lime trees that we see, and one other which has long gone.

Nowadays we have two butchers. One of these – a hero of our time, though not a Selbornian, seems to have imbibed the spirit of White. For when a martin's nest fell from his eaves with young in it, he gathered all up, put them in a dropping tin and secured this in the place they had fallen from: the old birds fed their young happily in this odd cradle, which they built round. It is still there and they still raise broods in it.

The blacksmith's shop is said to be five hundred years old. Until April 1969, when the shutters closed permanently, you could look in at the forge and all the coaly dimness of its workings, and pass at once into another and almost ageless age. And it is all still there behind the shutters, and the pleasant acrid singey smell of it remains, on damp days, but nothing moves, nothing works in there, no flame shoots, the iron is cold. What use is the forge without the blacksmith? What will become of it now?

Doubtless the blacksmith's is as old as those experts from the County Planning Office say, who came recently to inspect our Street, most blessedly under a scheme for its preservation; but of course it has been patched up and its constituent planks renewed countless times; still, heaven knows, it looks ancient enough, and one has not the slightest doubt that so it looked to Gilbert White. He must constantly have been in and about it. Our late blacksmith, Clifford Tarr, would certainly have been a man after his own heart, for though he had not originally wanted to be a blacksmith, having an extremely acute, eminently educable intelligence which the State did not, when he was a boy, cater for beyond the age of twelve, he had a fine deep professional interest in horses, and a tenderness indeed for all domestic animals. 'They come first' he once said, alluding to their care.

Clifford's father, James Tarr, had been one of the many drawn from the west to Selborne. He came from bleak Porlock Hill. The exodus must greatly have impressed him, and his story of it impressed his son: ' 'Twas like a little Klondike,' Clifford whimsically said.

The blacksmith's house looks exactly as it did when Grimm drew it among others on a tiny scale, in aerial perspective from the Hermitage: a small, very taking cottage of two storeys, with a high-pitched, hipped, tiled roof – a house as if stitched on a sampler. Apparently of early Georgian structure, at the back and inside it you can see what is very much older. Its garden has that rich black soil which White discusses at the beginning of his book, raising a question as to its provenance unanswered to this day. In the lovely summer of 1959 Clifford Tarr, activated by the rising cost of tobacco, grew tobacco plants in this soil, some of which attained a height of near ten feet. But that year was unmatched for all things growing and ripening, and the experiment was not repeated. The effect of the blacksmith standing in a forest of these huge stems and leaves was supernatural, not unlike that of a picture by Stanley Spencer or the Douanier Rousseau.

* * *

As White was responsible for the lime trees, so he was for the cobbled path which leads from the old butcher's to the blacksmith's shop. This path has been extended to reach some way beyond this. The original job was done at the cost of £1. The cobbles are pieces of 'blue rag' freestone, obtained, like others found about the Street, from the bed of the stream, and already smoothed by water. Both lime trees and cobbles are cherished and have been fought for occasionally by Selbornians proper. The cobbles have been lost today in front of the Queen's Hotel yard, all path levels having been raised, but formerly it was so low as to offer little obstruction to carts and carriages entering what was very much a stable yard ranged round on two sides by stables, its ground gritty and uneven and full of puddles after rain. Cocks and hens used to peck about in it.

When W. H. Hudson stayed at the Queen's – which he did with reluctance, much preferring to lodge with some villager – his bedroom window overlooked this yard, and in *Hampshire Days* he writes that charming description of martins coming down to collect mud from these puddles and being rushed at again and again by the angry hens. The grace and utter ease with which the martins avoided these attacks, floating up and descending again to their business, rejoiced the heart of the old bearded naturalist from the Argentine, peering down on the scene, as it would have rejoiced White's too had he been present, as no doubt in a sense he was.

From the Queen's Hotel carriages could be sent out to meet you on arrival at Alton or Liss, or could be hired to take you for a ride round the countryside which would be extremely leisurely on account of the many hills. And Mr. Moss, of the cottage now called Lassams, (now beautifully restored after a gutting by fire) also ran this kind of equine taxi-service. He was an old man very bushily bearded, not so old

The Blacksmith at work

possibly as he seemed. When he was up on the box with you you could imagine yourself droshky-driven by a muzhik. It was like being in a Russian tale. In addition to horses, Mr. Moss had a few cows, and when he drove them to and from pasture the little boys would 'tarrify' him, as the saying was – would mob him like small birds a daylight owl. And the poor old man would curse and scold in return, making a sound not unlike the lowing of the beasts he herded. These stables, of course, languished with the increase of the motor car, and finally disappeared.

The Compasses of White's day became the fine hostelry now called the Queen's Hotel. The Compasses was a very different looking building, barn-like, long and low to the Street. This was burned down some time at the beginning of Victoria's reign and almost entirely rebuilt. It is registered in the Tithe Roll of 1842 as the *Queen's Head. An Inn.*

Storming the Poorhouse

The White Hart also is so specified, but the Selborne Arms was not. Apparently that was a private house at that date. It is a relief to think that Selborne had not three inns in its Street, since the population in it – including children – was only 313 in those days (it has not much increased) and many people, of course, brewed their own beer.

The Compasses in its final period under that name was the setting for a number of riotous vestry meetings, when the unfortunate Vicar's Warden, Henry Eade, had to struggle with furious small farmers in rebellion about their tithes. It all came to a head in 1832, with the 'Selborne Mob', and the sad business down Gracious Street, when the Poorhouse, Fisher's Buildings, became our little local Bastille, and they terrified the Rev. William Cobbold ('unfortunately the only gentleman in the place', as he said) and also the poor old lady, last of the Whites at the Wakes. In fact no bodily harm was done to anybody, yet some were hanged and many were transported.

They were probably more discreetly rebellious down at the White Hart, which, as we know, was called the Poacher's Rest. This house carried on as an inn certainly up in to this century, and then and since has been a private dwelling with a little shop dispensing sweets. The seller of these, and of cordials long ago which were left over from the Inn's stock, I suppose, was another remarkable Selborne native: Mrs. George Chiverton, who died a year or so back. What was Mrs. Chiverton remarkable for? When the holders of Common rights were all bought out at £50 apiece in 1925, after the Birkenhead Reforms, and the College gave the property to the National Trust, she alone refused to take the money. Her spirited reaction could do her no good, obviously, yet other Commoners regarded her with a kind of awe and honour her memory. It was nonsensical, what she did, but somehow it was sublime.

* * *

The names of Benham and Berryman link us with White in that Selborne which is a living and continous process, always moving yet ever still. Next along the street from the White Hart is a cottage called Benhams. Though it is old it is not old enough to be the house of 'Benham's Eaves' which White so often paused at to observe the house-martins. But it is on the same spot, and a Benham was in it so late as 1842. Also it is interesting that its neighbour 'Maltby's' is still a favourite haunt of these birds.

Berryman's house was somewhere on the site of Elim Lodge, on the opposite side of the road, where Scrubbs Lane goes up between it and the Selborne Arms. White was evidently very much in this farmer's confidence, a man of some substance but not fortunate at the end, with his daughter robbed of all her clothes, and his cow that died 'sprang'. White helped Berryman in the matter of a female ward who seems to have made a runaway marriage. He was present at an interview with the husband and together in some way obscure they succeeded in thwarting his avarice. And then poor Berryman went to a London hospital to be cured of an internal complaint and was sent home to die. Benham and Berryman, so long dead, are ghosts indeed, but where they once lived is worthy of record, I think, because of their association with White. One senses they were of a distinctive breed. Mr. Maltby, who died some fifteen years ago, was of just that distinction too – as marked and as English as some breed of powerful dog, a mastiff or an Old English sheepdog. Like the saviour of the martins (who came from East Sussex) he was not a Selborne man. He came from Kent, member of a family famous for marine engineering, and he too, despite his profession, seems to me to belong to the eighteenth century, rather than to ours.

Mr. Maltby retired to Selborne with an invalid wife when he was not much more than forty-five. He took over the garage the late Ronald Waterman had established. What a garage man he was! He had been through 'the shops' with Lord Nuffield – William Morris – 'motorman Morris', whose praises he loved to sing. Mr. Maltby could have built you a car with his own hands, would have loved to. Such a man could not long be contented with tinkering about with the odd car or two which presented itself in the twenties, and filling them with petrol from one of those primitive hand-pumps of the day. The motorman turned to making hop-sprayers of his own design. He installed a welding-plant and soon was repairing all the agricultural machinery for miles around. In a flash the old forge became a relic. With the war 'Maltby's' grew into a factory performing valuable tasks, but it was still a small factory, and still in some respects remained just his hobby. Mr. Maltby loved best doing a job well, and loved his machinery: I have seen him standing – tall and vast with hanging hands, relaxed – looking with loving looks at some newly acquired piece, a giant press, say, or a new and better lathe. He trained a whole generation of boys to become engineers like him.

Well, they can never have been made quite like him, for he still belonged to a different world. He absolutely could not understand it when he had to give them holidays with pay. He could not adjust – except spanners, to nuts. Completely individual and independent, he was bewildered and enraged by State interference.

This grand man had much of Dr. Johnson about him. Driving a chassis once fast through Farnham, he perceived a policeman step into the road and put his hand up. Mr. Maltby, exerting all his strength and calling on his vast reserves of skill in control, pulled up just short of the constable's toes. 'You was going a bit fast wasn't you?' (In telling me this the Motorman would rise to his full height – about six-foot four, and a quiet unbragging authority came into his voice; he used emphatic gesture): 'The CAR was UNder MY CONTROL.' It was unanswerable, and he was signalled on.

He left his mark on Selborne, and of a kind that was new indeed. Selborne has a factory: is this a right thing for Selborne? It was change – change according with organic growth – the social and economic life of England. It was effected by an Englishman of the old traditional kind, with whom White would assuredly have felt at home.

CHAPTER XXVIII

The Church and its Environs

LEAVING Gracious Street till a later chapter (for the village street falls naturally into these two parts), go across the Plestor and enter the Church of St. Mary. People who go in take the peace of the place and the sense of space and light immediately, but often do not so quickly understand why that is. The Vicar knows, and would be pleased, I think, if we pause a little before looking at the several interesting things to be seen here. A church should in no sense be looked upon as a museum.

Not that the memorial window to White, representing St. Francis and all the birds mentioned in the *Natural History of Selborne* is likely to remove our thoughts very far from God. Delight in bird-watching and the like seems to me the most hopeful sign about humanity at present;

differentiating us from the Romans, Goths and Huns, and other such practical and successful examples of the race who have preceded us. Formerly only a handful of poets had this.

Apart from the bird window, put up in 1920, there is the very beautiful painting over the altar, representing the adoration of the Magi. This – reputed to be by Jan Mostaert (about 1510) – was given by Benjamin White. There is an engraved slab in the middle of the chancel, which commemorates Gilbert White, but it means his grandfather, which has confused many a visitor. The younger Gilbert's tablet is up in the far corner on the right. He was not buried in the church, as we know, and even this memorial was originally outside on the wall, near where his grave is.

St. Mary's church was devastatingly restored in 1877, when there was a wave of such well-intentioned doings throughout the country. A year or so earlier Thomas Hardy, great poet but mediocre architect, had been restoring the parish church at St. Juliot, in Cornwall (he met his first wife, Emma Lavinia Gifford, while he was doing it) and among the things he threw out was the communion rail and balustrade of the time of Elizabeth 1st. The literary will note this relic with interest.*

The font is exceedingly simple and beautiful, and is said to be Saxon, and possibly it was in the Saxon church which preceded this, which is late twelfth century. But there is an expert and most interesting account of the church in *A Selborne Handbook* easily obtainable, so I will not add to that beyond mentioning something I believe unremarked on before: I mean the strange leaf or petal-like ornaments at the base of two of the pillars on the north side of the aisle. These look to me very like a representation of the two meeting doves which cause the flower Aquilegia to be commonly called Columbine, its petals taking on this appearance. Now the same ornament occurs on the columns of Winchester Cathedral (and I think nowhere else), and as a master-mason from that place is reputed to have worked on the Priory church here, it might be that he was working on our fine sturdy pillars also at that time, and perhaps died before the job had well begun.

And of course, in the north transept of the church lie remains of Adam de Gurdon: the two vast thigh-bones and the immense skull, together, interestingly, with a much smaller skeleton of a youth or a girl. There are so few of his bones no doubt because he is known to

* Presented to Selborne Church in 1942 in memory of J. E. Jefferson Hogg, who died in Selborne.

have died at his other manor, close by at Temple, and I suppose some of him was lost in transit when he was brought here as were some of the Templars' stone coffin-lids when that establishment, like the Priory, crumbled to ruin.

The spirit of that doughty old giant (not as old as White thought he was, because three Adam de Gurdons got rolled into one in his account) is perhaps less in the church than in the earth all around it. I gather that he owned at least all that is now glebe land. Modern research has diminished him by a third, reduced his wives to two (or one of them would have been his mother!) and given him a normal life-span (otherwise he would have seemed to be going strong at above ninety); but legend has a way of laughing at learning, and myth has virtues unknown to truth: good Selbornians know that Selborne had this fighting giant, a de Montfort man in the Barons' war, who when his leader fell became a rebel – an outlaw much like Robin Hood. We know that he was sought out and challenged by the young prince, later Edward 1st, to mortal combat on the top of Selborne Hill – where else? – and defeated by him, and forgiven, and led off to sup cosily with the Queen, Edward's mother, at Guildford. And all the other attributes of a prodigy which science has taken away are his inalienably also.

Church porch and yew tree

The Trumpeter's cottage

Out of the church now, with a side-glance at the great yew – if you did not inspect this before you went in. You will scarcely see such another; near thirty-foot in girth and reputed at least twelve-hundred years old. A single yew, healthy and growing yet, throwing its branches out and around in wild confusion and far extent – a fixed symbol of English history.

It is somewhat hollow at the top, but the process must have begun centuries back, for in Vicar Cobbold's time that poor neurotic man thought it a perfect gun-emplacement, and that he might be shot at from it, for it commands the Vicarage front door. It was all imaginary. If they had shot *at* him they certainly wouldn't have missed him. As far as I know, no one ever did shoot at him, or ever laid a finger on him; yet he squealed and whined away making the very worst of his situation; thinking only of himself when times were so bad.* Others suffered, but not Cobbold, who, I will admit, stuck it out for years (he must have had a hide like six rhinoceroses!), and one of those who suffered (but not the most) lies just here under this tree – the fabled horn-blower of the Selborne rebels, a man called Newland. After the mob had rushed the Vicarage and humiliated Cobbold,

* See Mr. Cobbold's account of his difficulties in *Trouble at Selborne* edited by the Rev. L. Sunderland (2nd ed. 1967).

The Trumpeter's grave

forcing him to sign away part of his tithes – which he had no power to do – they sacked Fisher's Buildings at the cost of life for some and transportation for others. But Newland escaped to the Hanger (he lived handy to it, in Adams Lane – a tiny lane leading up from the street near to the White Hart – in a cottage now known as the Trumpeter's), coming down for nourishment under cover of darkness. This was in summer; in winter he gave himself up and was pardoned, and died years later, to be buried strangely alone in this place.

Local interest in this sad historical episode had never quite died away when, some seventy years later, it was strongly revived by W. H. Hudson. He noticed this one grave under the yew tree, a grave without a name and discovered after a long time whose it was, whose task it had been that stressful time to blow on a horn to summon his mates to action. Hudson tells his story in *Hampshire Days*, and after he had written about him the grave was marked as we see it today, with a short granite post on which are inscribed these bare two words: The Trumpeter.

But Cobbold hung on into the 1840s, ever hoping not to be the 'only gentleman'. An amusing reflection of this ambition appears in the sale advertisement of Wakes in 1840 – the production of an ace estate agent, the celebrated George Robins, surely not unprimed. In a list of the great joys which ownership of Wakes must bring we find this: '*There is a worthy divine who has located in our delightful Village for many a long year (the Rev. W. Cobbold). The Purchaser of this famed Property will find him an invaluable Neighbour.*'

It is with relief that we turn to White's grave. Even though he too claimed to be a gentleman, and hoped to remain one, he did not mean it as Cobbold did, and he was so unpretentious that you may have difficulty in finding his grave at all.

It is simply a very small stone with the initials G.W. and a date 26 June 1793, carved on it. The grave is very long and narrow and grassed over. He lies as he wanted to, outside the church, near the end of the north wall of the chancel. Here what remained of him was carried that day of June '. . . without any pall-bearers, or parade . . . by six honest day-labouring men' who each got ten shillings for his trouble. Why the grave of a man five foot three inches tall should be so exceedingly long has something to do with the realignment of the churchyard boundary on this side, in consequence of some alteration in the wall of the chancel, I have been told. You will see that all the graves in this row have been so elongated.

It surely would have amused Gilbert White to have been given the proportions of Adam de Gurdon!

CHAPTER XXIX

The Castle Mound

High on a mound th' exalted gardens stand;
Beneath, deep valleys scoop'd by Nature's hand!
A Cobham here, exulting in his art,
Might blend the General's with the Gardener's part;
Might fortify with all the martial trade
Of rampart, bastion, fosse and palisade. . . .

So sang White. And then, one imagines, rather shrank from associating the parsonage gardens with those of Stowe, which the warrior-gardener, Richard Temple, 4th Viscount Cobham, friend of Pope, had become famous for laying out. So these lines were removed from the *Invitation*.

But we can see what he meant about ramparts and bastions, etc., if we go out through the churchyard into Church Meadow and stand under the slope, with the stream below us, especially if it is a fine golden evening when the shadows lengthen. He had been indulging again in some boyish vision of Adam de Gurdon's castle when he wrote those lines.

And Adam seems definitely to have had a castle or something of the sort here. It is certain nearly all the land around was his.

Starting from the Plestor, he had owned that, and Elliot's and almost certainly Plestor Cottages too (which are much more ancient than they look). Adam gave the Plestor to the Priory, and from the Priory it came, via Waynefleet I suppose, to the village. Fairs were held on it. But Adam de Gurdon retained a right-of-way across it to the now vanished Elliot's, and yards and probably other buildings behind it. The large walled space, now the Vicarage-owned fruit-garden, was his, and the space now used as a coal yard, with its access to Church Meadow. And all to the right of the present churchyard as we walk down to the wicket-gate at the east end was de Gurdon's also, and became Glebe, when the meadow became so, some fifty years after White's time. When we go through this gate we are presumably on or very near to the site of what White called the Castle Mound.

This would have included all of the northern end of the lately extended burial ground (for the churchyard until 1946 ended at a boundary marked by the three fine fir trees of the cyprus kind, by which the wicket then stood). And here to your left you will see the first part of the hump or mound, on the summit of which, still part of the vicarage garden, now stand the remains of a small plantation of cedars of the various sorts – Lebanon, Deodar and Cedrus Atlanticus – planted, probably, by Cobbold's rich successor, the Rev. Frederick James Parsons (1841–75), who was responsible also for most of the restoration of the church. More romantic then, even than in White's day, when it was the vista'd garden of his musings, as earlier intimated. Here surely as a youth he had dreamed of Adam de Gurdon, who was a man of less purely local fame perhaps than has been suggested; for he or someone like him has got into one of the ancient ballads as Sir Adam O'Gordon – a wretch as it happened, for he murdered a lady together with her babes in 'her castle of Rode' – would not Gilbert have noted this coincidence, studying with the enthusiastic Wartons; for there is a Rode (or Rood) farm close by, between Temple and Priory, which some antiquaries think was once a place of greater extent and importance.

* * *

To this 'castle mound' I would direct your steps if you have only limited time at your disposal, or elderly or infirm people with you, or little ones, for here, as I have said, you get quickly and easily a taste of Selborne's quality, a glimpse of one of her 'boldest beauties'. You are in the church-litten copse of White's time, with church-litten closes all around you, but you do not see the phantom oaks and hazels of the one or the hedges or rail fences which divided the other; yet some can remember the seven or eight great oak trees which survived on the slope where it is steepest, and swept the now smooth rounded bastions of the hillside with their long mighty arms until felled in 1916 by good kind little Vicar Norman* – a man much smaller even than Gilbert

* 1906–28.

White – wishing to help the village over a fuel crisis. A few of the stumps remain.

The ground falls steep away; the mounds are like the brows of elephants; and you look over the 'valley scoop'd by Nature's hand' and out and down on the Lyth and Dorton. And if there are children, as soon as they see that sheer green slope they will want to rush down it – they always do – and you must let them, and wait for that pretty gurgling noise they make, part delight, part fear – a hoo-ooo! with suppressed or half choked laughter in it – as they let themselves go rushing downhill to come safely to the green soft level again – the floor of the meadow. Up here in Sparrow's Hanger – *on* Sparrow's Hanger I should rather say – across the valley, I have heard thousands of such intrepid venturers make this delicious sound as they fly – far nearer to flying than ever they will be by any aeroplane – with open mouths and arms outstretched, in fear of their short legs' overtaking to disaster by their bold impetuous spirit. And did Gilbert and all his brothers and his little sisters rush down here before them? Probably not. The way was not open and clear then, though the path was here. Without the space time has given to the church-litten closes no such inducement to fly would be felt.

Children running down Castle Mound

CHAPTER XXX

Four on a Hilltop

FOUR people on a hilltop: who are they, and where?

Put there by Grimm, in his great view of Selborne from the north-east, they are where we cannot sit now, because of trees planted sometime in the 1830s – high up on the Short Lyth, that is to say, and directly facing the spot where we have just been standing, and the slope down which the children have just rushed and are making for the little stream, from which they will take a great deal of distracting.

We cannot tell exactly who they are, these elegant eighteenth-century people, except that the lady is probably Mary, the second wife of Richard Yalden. She afterwards became the second wife of Benjamin White. Accounts agree here, as they do not about the men. The man coming up the hill with arm outstretched could be Gilbert White but was more probably Richard Yalden himself. He has a bob wig and is the only clergyman present. The upstanding manly figure by the lady could be either the brother of the Rev. Andrew Etty or Mrs. Etty's brother-in-law Dr. Stebbings (but he too was a clergyman); nothing is clear. The fourth figure, the man coming jauntily past the tent, would be Thomas White by common consent, except that Rashleigh Holt-White says that he wasn't in Selborne at all that summer. But he adds that he thinks it is Thomas, all the same, and that Thomas got round Grimm to put these figures into the view at a later stage, before the plate was engraved for the book; and he is certain the tent at least (which, by the way, he seems to accept as the 'sweet' one of Catherine Battie's diary) was never actually there on that July day of 1776. It couldn't have been got up there, he says. But as to that, he is wrong. There would have been no difficulty in getting it there in summer by the carriage which presumably brought Mary Yalden. The men no doubt walked. Two of them have long canes like staves, and Thomas appears to have a thumb-stick.

The carriage would have come up the lane that led from the Grange

Selborne from the north-east (after Grimm)

farm up to Culvercroft and Goslings Croft, and turned down a track midway between these fields to the edge of the Lyth – a track which is on the Tithe map of 1842. And unless I am mistaken they could all have walked down into that green valley; arriving close to where those haymakers are, by another track connecting with this last, which ran aslant down the sideland, parallel with the boundary of the Lyth south-west. It would bring them to the apex of that vee in Kimbers which I mentioned in my ninth chapter; but as this is *not* on the Tithe map I

cannot be absolutely certain it existed then, as it did this century until quite recently. But anyway descent is quite easy between the Short and Long Lyth.

We will for the present leave these charming, stylishly dressed people on their vantage-spot chosen for them by White, and proceed to the great feature they are principally addressing their gaze to; for the Hanger is King of Scenes in Selborne, as the Lyth is Queen. But we shall return here by and by.

CHAPTER XXXI

Selborne Hanger and Hill

WHEN Gilbert and his company went by the Hanger, to climb by the Zigzag he and John had made, they skirted along Baker's Hill to the south-east, and turned sharp right, along the boundary of the Pound Field. This last part was called The Walk, and is still so named on the Ordnance Survey Map. Along the first part of this route White made an avenue of Field Maples and some beeches. The Walk is an avenue of beeches to this day, but I do not know if these were planted after his time. At the end of the Walk was a wicket gate, and the remains of such a gate is there still.

One can see them setting off in a group gay as butterflies, chattering like finches, or soberly, in pairs, with heads inclined in discussion. Or see the single man, dark-clothed, neat, with a short but well-turned leg, his looks inward, steady and grave, or darting like the bird observed, slipping away thus privately to his solitary secular devotions. We, the public, cannot use this route, but as we go up the Punfle path (clearly marked 'To the Zigzag' on a post just outside the car park) we are passing directly alongside the Walk. It is still an avenue, its beeches thinned, with a path of sorts trodden out between the trees through the elders and other bushes which have sprung up. I wish it might be revived, cleared and trimmed up inside, and made available to visitors to the Wakes, who would then get a more extensive view of the park than, as now, from the ha-ha only.

Before the Zigzag was made – a prodigious short-cut – there were only two main or official ways up to the top of the Hanger from the village. One, Scrubbs Lane, went from the street diagonally south-east, into paths or tracks of some sort over King's Field; the other was Wood Lane, running up from Fisher's Buildings, at the bottom of Gracious Street. One can scarcely count what more resembles a slidder or ditch coming down to Scrubbs Lane from near the Wishing Stone, and connecting with meagre Adams Lane; the way by which, probably, the hunted Trumpeter came down from his hiding-place.

No Zigzag, no Bostal, no 'Love Lane' along the foot of the Hanger. That beautiful path is comparatively modern. It lies over Wakes ground, conceded in kindness as a substitute for a very rough equivalent path which ran in the Hanger some way above, and it was only made officially public after the death of the last private owner of Wakes, when the house became *the* Wakes, and a museum in 1955.

As you stand at the top of the Punfle path, facing the hill, the part up which the Zigzag runs, and all to the east of it, is the Scrubbs, and was once so scrubby that it did not resemble the rest of the Hanger at all. So they had marvellous unrestricted views over it. And this, in fact, is Arbour Hill. Just where that arbour was, and what it looked like and how they got to it before the Zigzag was constructed, we shall never know.

You will see at once that the Zigzag is a masterpiece of scientific layout. It is so perfectly graded that even the quite old need not be afraid of climbing the 300 feet from street-level to the summit. You go slowly and the landscape north-east towards Oakhanger, Kingsley and the dark-bright drift of Wolmer Forest generally, jerks away and unfolds and opens out as you turn your head to the left or right. Plumy beech trees lean out and overtop you either side. Think of poor John as you climb, with his brilliance and ingenuity and mind, so unlucky, never quite recovering from that 'imprudent and incautious procedure at my first stepping into the world', and leaving this, and not a great work, for a monument. I am sure that it was Gilbert, the kind elder brother, who, to remedy John's distress, suggested their working on John's plan together on the latter's being sent down from Oxford.

'See the torn Zigzag weeps its channel'd sides' said Gilbert in his *Selborne Hanger. A Winter Piece*. It weeps in winter still, and quite often in summer, but not down those channels specially dug and kept clear to carry off the water, which now runs mainly down the centre – a cause of anxiety to the present guardians of the Zigzag, the Selborne National Trust Committee. Some think it is the youth of Selborne madly careering down the face, scorning to use the path so dexterously cut for them, breaking down the wooden planks containing the path and scoring a channel of their own. It may be so, but I have never seen any so offending, and never heard the shouts which would be sure to accompany such an exercise; whereas the proper channels either side are difficult now to keep clear and deep enough, and consequently in very wet weather, a miniature Niagara of considerable power pours down the Zigzag and could cut this way for itself.

On the other hand it is a painful fact that acts of vandalism have been known to take place. The stout wooden seat at the top, put there by the Gilbert White Fellowship to mark the 100th anniversary of his death, has several times been woefully defaced, the carved tortoises on either arm hacked away. It has had to be entirely renewed and set in concrete. Selborne people believe that it was the work of lads from outside the village. But when 'musing Kitty' Battie, in her valediction, hoped that no mischievous boy would harm the little nest, she was referring to the Hermitage and no bird's nest.

* * *

About two-thirds of the way up the Zigzag there is something of a break in its rhythm, where a strong plain seat of iron affords rest, if not much comfort. This is one of five such seats placed about Selborne, three on the hill and two in the vale, at the instigation of a Mrs. Mackensie, who lived in the cottage called Dowlings at the top of Huckers Lane. She proposed and collected for them in 1898.

As you sit on this seat you will see a path to right and left leading off the Zigzag. The first runs simply straight across the Scrubbs and connects with that ditch-like path to Scrubbs Lane which I have just mentioned, but the other begins shortly to rise a little and leads to a sort of recess cut back in the steep hillside, and this is presumed to be where the Hermitage stood. It accords with its placing in the view of it (on a very tiny scale) in Grimm's panoramic 'Selborne from the North-East', which holds the place of honour among his illustrations.

This hermitage is the one and only, the old original, before and around which they danced and sang and picnicked in 1763, and from which the 'View from the Hermitage' was taken in 1776. But there were in all four structures on the Hanger: the hermitage, the 'pensile, nest-like bower', a 'plain thatched cot', and a New Hermitage on the Bostal, and nothing at all is known as to what these last three looked like, nor even where the bower and the plain cot were exactly. It would not matter now, except that some, like myself, are happier if they can follow White about and see the places as he knew them. I think the 'pensile, nest-like bower' might very likely have been his way of describing the old arbour on Arbour Hill, because in the *Invitation* in which it occurs there is a footnote which says 'A kind of an arbour on the side of a hill.'

But we have two portrayals of the hermitage as it was in 1776; why haven't I preferred the larger one – the vignette which also decorates the 1st edition of the *Natural History*? Unfortunately it is impossible to tell, by that picture, whereabouts on the Hanger it is supposed to be. It looks as though it is at the very top, which evidently it was not. Mulso said he should not have known it for the place he so loved. The Hermit, he said, was quite admirably Harry – he always had been – but where was the Zigzag? where the sense of height?

Now I have extolled Grimm as an honest topographer as well as an artist with a sufficiency of romantic sense. In fairness to him I must add that Mulso (who prided himself on his aesthetic) also found fault with his distance – that blue distance of Wolmer Forest – and this Grimm has touched in most beautifully. I am sure that there is as much of his habitual truthfulness, up to a point, in this as in any other of the twelve pictures whose details are more instantly recognisable. Grimm's hermitage and its environment was as real as he could get it, and Mulso it was who was being unrealistic and over-romantic. Look at that seat, for instance – that fantastic, rococo, impossible, cast-iron garden seat! – I don't believe that White or Mulso, or any of their friends, ever really saw that seat, so completely inappropriate to a hermitage. But it was there all right, and as necessary to them all and to their make-believe as those pitted quaint rocks so laboriously dragged into place, and Grimm saw it there and professionally recorded what he saw, as usual.

But perched as he was on the side of a very steep hill, it was just not possible for Grimm or any artist to get the close-up view *and* give the tall incrowding beeches he crouched among on that Hanger side of the Zigzag, and which came edging into his line of vision; nor to get in proportion the still steeply mounting hill and Zigzag behind the hermitage. He was too close to it all. An impossible view! Honest Heironymous gave what he could. Why didn't he choose the opposite side of the Zigzag? Probably because that other path then hadn't been cut: there was only the thick scrub bushes into which White hoped some house-martins might descend to hibernate.

But in what Grimm gave he makes plain that there was a platform, big enough for the events White and Kitty recorded, which are so difficult to imagine in the actual spot today. Twenty people, remember, at night, with lights and music and refreshments. Here Delphy and Harriet *could* have danced, in a demure, restricted kind of way. One wonders whereabouts Anna stood to sing, and where the stump was, on which Kitty sat. Think of them all about their merry tasks – of their making their fire on picnic occasions, retiring all different ways to

> Cull the dry stick; call forth the seeds of fire;
> Deep fix the kettle's props, a forky row,
> Or give with fanning hat the breeze to blow.

Sometimes on dark summer nights I look across at the Hanger and wonder, could it possibly have been like that? The merest scrape and flicker of a match up there would be as startling now as the blowing of the top of Krakatoa. And twenty of them feasting, with music, lights and song! Fantastic happening! We only know that it was so.

* * *

At the top of the Zigzag is what for many, many years has been called the Wishing Stone. White who placed it there called it an obelisk, conforming to a fancy of his time for putting some conspicuous mark, pillar or tower on the top of an eminence. This large 'wishing stone', which once stood erect, is sunken now and at a slant. It is not of local stone but what is known in Wiltshire as a sarsen – some kind of granite, much like the stones of Stonehenge. The Selborne villagers, creating their own folk tradition, have long been accustomed to trot when little three times round it, in an anti-clockwise direction, eyes shut, forming a wish which must on no account be divulged. It is not cheating to put the fingers of your left hand lightly on the top of the stone to steady yourself. Indeed you had better, if you are over forty.

There used to be no habitation near the Wishing Stone, beyond a very small single storey stone cabin, slate-roofed – a hovel, indeed – and a small Victorian cottage of mediocre appearance a little further up the hill and scarcely to be seen from there. In place of these lately have appeared (rather mysteriously, in view of regulations so strictly applied elsewhere) two quite considerable modern buildings, white, and very conspicuous especially from the road approaching Selborne from Empshott. This is rather regrettable as affecting the seclusion and sense of remoteness of this very sacred and special place in Selborne, but apparently there was no helping it, and quiet lives are led by the inhabitants up here, apart from the inevitable intrusion of visitors bent on sharing the magnificent views.

Bearing easterly between these properties – which are on sites incidently, which never belonged to the National Trust – you will find another gift seat, erected by the Trust on land donated. It is small and

The Wishing Stone or Obelisk

tucked away, and closely fenced round with wire, and so in some respects is not so pleasantly situated as the seat by the stone; but the view is far wider and finer, taking in Blackdown and Hindhead, Wolmer Forest all between, and even on very clear days far south-east to the wealds of Surrey and Sussex. But indeed from many points on this side of the great hill, here 700 feet above sea-level, wonderful views are obtainable. From the same aspect a little further on, and higher, the South Downs may be discerned as a faint line as far as Chanctonbury; and even the Channel, too, through Amberley and Burling gaps. If it were not for Noar Hill, the nearest of the Hangers, to the south (which anyway looks noble of itself) you could see the downs clearly at their highest point of Butser and Wardown – at near 900 feet, almost actually a mountain indeed.

This eastern side of the hill was the sheep down proper, and it was the sheep that kept down tree-growth on the Scrubbs till Gilbert (presumably getting it fenced-off) sent Goody Hammond, his old, mannish weeding-woman, to plant it out with beech-mast, so that in time it resembled, as now, the rest of the Hanger.

The sheep would be driven down from the hill by some of several tracks, the main one running into Scrubbs Lane and the road to Tisted at Gally Hill. They would pass quite close to the gallows in the very old times, for Gally Hill is gallows hill. The Priors of Selborne had the rare power to try and if need be execute offenders – a fearful privilege, ill-met with religion, and doubtless due to the proximity of the Royal Deer Forest. Gally Hill and Kite Hill near by, then (and possibly the King's Field) are names dismally suggestive of past misery and horror.

* * *

The most obvious way to take after climbing the Zigzag goes up on to the plateau of Selborne Common, where are three main well defined tracks leading round and across it. If you keep to the central one for about a mile you will come to Newton Valence, the quietest place, and as lovely as its name. This track, you may tell yourself was, until the Bostal was cut, White's shortest way to get to his close friend Richard Yalden, who lived in the vicarage there. The first of Newton Valence you see is the remains of that avenue of Scots firs which I suspected was associated somehow with the Hartley Stuarts. The left hand track, which goes skirting round the common will bring you to this point also. Take the right hand one, or keep inclined to the west. and you should discover the dew pond – Wood Pond – weedy now, shrunken, well hidden, to search for which may be one of the pleasures of your day on this big wide furzy space too overgrown now for the horse races and cricket matches which used to take place here right into our own century. (I suspect they were unheard of in Gilbert's time.) On this common, among the furze and blackthorns, nightingales sing and breed – almost the only place where they settle in Selborne in any numbers – and it is worth going up in the season (the middle of April to the end of May) to hear them. But at night it is gloomy up here; best then choose full moonlight. It is even possible to get lost on the Hanger in daytime, if not for very long. And this is what one goes for: here lies the excitement of it, and we should not wish for any signpost on it, as some have well-intentionedly suggested from time to time. Surely it is good to lose your way and find it again; to sit and look at things and listen for a short while at peace, disorientated.

But if your time is short, and instead of going to the open common you turn from the Wishing Stone and follow along the Hanger's edge, with that immensely steep beech-grown slope on your right, and the High Wood with its far older trees on your left, you will have an aerial prospect to the village – where swathes have been cut from the hanging woods – which is one of the most satisfying things Selborne offers, and which brings us very close to White. The great charm of Selborne and of any comparable place of ancient human habitation lies in its blend of pastoral and wild, and this blend, so visible here, very much corresponds with the component parts of his nature. Here you look down from the relatively wild to the fields long cultivated, spread out on the level plain below you – that plain which the narrow valleys are cut into, flanked by other woods which seem from here no bigger than hedgerows. You look on to the roof-tops of little houses on the street. It used to be that you saw the blue smoke rising from cottage fires, and on still evenings heard voices, laughter, the ring of the blacksmith's forge. There used to be, besides the bullocks grazing in the park fields of the Wakes, other domestic beasts, commoners' ponies chiefly, up here not far off, to heighten that effect I indicate, of blended wild and tame. And once I saw, to add a pretty refinement to it, Aylesbury ducks in a troop, strayed from the home farm of the Wakes, white amongst the celandines and ivy and dog's mercury, climbing, wriggling, thrusting with their yellow bills.

You may still, if you are lucky, see a little smoke, for some still burn the wood that is so plentiful; and you may hear a casual hail and answer. The forge is silent – very recently vacated – and the traffic by which you profited in getting here is lost in the deeper silence.

As you progress along the ridge the path inclines slightly, dropping till you come to its end near to an enclosure called the Wadden (it seems only to have meant a wood, in this case larches), and then you will see the top of the Bostal, and another of the iron seats (the third is set in the hillside half-way down it). The Bostal leads not too steeply down to the foot of the Zigzag again, where you started, and to the Punfle, and your car. At the top of the Bostal too, a little further on and near the Wadden, is the beginning of Wood Lane. It is quite wide, between high banks in places, but except in the driest weather is likely to be extremely muddy. The surface of Wood Lane was deeply scored about and smashed and rutted at the last assault on the timber of Hanger and High Wood, some ten years ago, when modern tractors proved themselves on the whole less efficient than cart-horses at getting the loads out. This way will lead you back to the bottom of Gracious Street.

To this end of the hill – to the Wadden, the Coneycroft, Coneycroft

Hill and Coneycroft Hanger, the Peak, and surroundings – we shall be returning. Meanwhile let's sit down on this seat and admire a view long favourite and justly famous, which in a way has taken the place of that from Arbour Hill, which delighted the Whites for so many years; which Gilbert himself assured should be hidden 'for ever' when he got Goody Hammond to sow the Scrubbs with beech-mast. Though the beeches took years to grow high enough for that, it was as if he had turned his back on it when he cut the Bostal and built his new look-out here.

Bostal is a West Sussex term. There are bostals running up the wooded slopes on the inland faces of the South Downs, and no doubt White was familiar with these through his long annual rides to see his Aunt Snooke and Timothy at Ringmer. I don't know whether there are other bostals in East Hampshire but I doubt it, though this part of the county – what is called Hanger country – is more like the wooded west of Sussex than any other part of Hampshire. The cutting of what I believe in modern forestry are called wedges in the tree masses on the Hanger in comparatively recent years, towards the end of Magdalen's and at the beginning of the National Trust's regime, have not much changed its distant appearance – as long as the top fringe is retained that is fairly safe – but has resulted in a considerable change in the Bostal itself. The path was over-shadowed from end to end, smooth-carpeted with red dead leaves, and slippery. The beeches either side grew extraordinarily tall and slim from being planted so close together. The Bostal had a cool refreshing gloom at the height of the hottest summer. Its silence was beautifully broken by the long shaken-out trill of the wood warbler, which is like a silver penny spun and reeling to its close. This sort of wood is the favourite habitat of these birds, and when it was disturbed, as in the Lyth too, they forsook Selborne.

Although they are so slender, as the many left standing testify, these Hanger beeches are very old, and many are decayed. In the 1780s the clear-felling of the trees White knew had got well into its stride and that this had been already carried some way by 1776 we know by Grimm. By the time White lay dying they were nearly all gone, but if the melancholy chopping was one of the last sounds he heard, at least he was spared the hellish bowel-searching scream of the power-saw. (Why this noise is tolerated I cannot understand, when motor-cycle engines are forced to be baffled.) White deplored that felling, but typically comforted himself and those of his family who had loved the trees, with the news that the fringe was saved all along. It was then, about the height of the slaughter I suppose, that he saw to the planting of the Scrubbs, and then too, because obstructions were removed, that he cut the Bostal and made his new lookout.

The trees we see, then, were planted after White's death. I knew an old man whose grandfather had told him that he had cut a walking-stick from this new plantation, which I calculate would make about 1810 the date of it. However, beech seems an odd wood to choose for a walking-stick in a place where thorn, holly and ash abound, and if it was of a new-planted sapling, beech it would have had to be, as now, under a rule of the College made centuries ago. Pannage was one of the most valuable rights of the copyhold commoners, which meant letting out their pigs under the beech trees to fatten on the mast. The rule still holds under the terms of the hand-over to the Trust, new plantings must always be of beech, and though pannage may seem very remote nowadays it was resorted to in the last war, when strollers in the Long Lyth, I have been told, were sometimes surprised – and rather alarmed – to find themselves sharing its amenities with rooting hogs.

On the Bostal

The policy of cutting great wedges in the close-regimented old trees of the Hanger cannot be considered happy in the event. The beeches so firmly rooted in the chalk of the steep hill protected each other from the winds, which now swept in and bore them down. In falling they broke down others. Nothing much grows under such trees, but now long buried seeds sprung into the light. White in his journal mentions how after the previous felling masses of wild strawberries had appeared on one of the 'slidders' – cleared spaces or runs down which the felled tree trunks were slid – which has ever afterwards been called 'Strawberry Slidder'. Children gathered them and brought them to his door. Now elder, sycamore and ash sprung up, and grew, as such 'trash' always does, lank and sprawling and unsightly.

The work of clearing and replanting took many years, meanwhile the Bostal itself badly deteriorated in places for lack of the trees whose strong developed roots had absorbed the moisture. People often said that no care was being taken of the Hanger, but this was not at all the case; if they had looked closely they would have seen the little new-planted beeches thrusting up. Directly they have reached a certain stage, of course, they begin to reassert their preventive influence on other growth.

It was bound to be a slow job, because the Trust in Selborne has not the money to employ whole gangs for labour. This work of clearing and replanting was nearly all done by the one permanent professional woodman employed by the committee. He is dead now. His name was Cunninghame, and he was a rare workman apart from his skill, since he did not mind working alone in solitary places. In this he was like a man of the old times. I saw him once when he was taking his midday 'nuncheon' and spell of well-earned rest, curled up on the bare earth beside the fire he had kindled.

Where there is apparent neglect it is scarcely the fault of anybody, but one of the incidental attendant effects of change.

The Hanger and the Lyth are difficult to work, difficult of access for modern machinery. The beeches which were once so valuable in days of horse-drawn vehicles and cheap and plentiful labour cannot now find contractors to bid for them. Dead and decaying trees are no use to them alone, and they must take a proportion of hale ones too, but the struggle – expensive – to get all out of the way here makes it simply not worth it today. What this 'ownership' by National Trust exactly means is I think not fully realised. It is not realised how very greatly the different properties of the Trust vary in value. They vary just as privately owned properties do. Selborne is one of the most beautiful, and therefore in one sense most valuable; but if it is in itself one great show place it is also land of no great agricultural value, and it possesses no display-feature else.

There is here no magnificent house to charge entry to; with grounds that may be turned into a zoo or kind of circus – and if there were it would be absolutely essential to avoid such exploitation in Selborne – nothing which could be a means to raise funds to afford a better working of these woods, fencing, hedging, all the things wanting for the benefit of a happy public flocking here increasingly, innocent of responsibility in such matters. Perhaps it would have been different if the Trust had bought the Wakes, first offered at a very low price to it. But the National Trust has rarely in recent years accepted house property, even as a gift, without endowment for its upkeep. The Wakes must provide a fair income through its visitors, as was possibly not anticipated fifteen or so years back, but it also costs much to maintain and to run. It was made the subject of a separate trust on its own. Some few of the trustees (who all, doubtless, have Selborne's welfare nearest to heart) function on the National Trust Committee also. Still it is a pity all could not have been under one roof, as you might say.

What to do to meet the rising tide and content everyone? So set is the spirit of our times on not denying to anyone the pleasures previously enjoyed privately by right of freakish fortune, that perhaps it is just as well that there are not unlimited funds, or much indeed at all, at our disposal here. We might else have a Hanger plastered with notice boards and signs, to make everything absolutely easy, and wider, asphalt or concrete paths; and really sturdy and capacious litter baskets bolted into concrete bases, like some of the seats; a Hanger made available at last to motor cars and, following them, booths and funfairs (there is nothing wrong with these in themselves, but in our time they are so apt to become permanent) and café-restaurants. Litter baskets were tried, and got squashed out of shape and tossed down the Zigzag, and residents up the hill have a great deal of bother disposing of rubbish left near to the Wishing Stone. Some of it is perishable enough, but not pleasantly so. Meanwhile that wild and lovely common with its gorse sown by Thomas – a flower before which (for it did not exist in his native Sweden) when he first saw it, the great Linnaeus fell worshipping on his knees – is very much as White knew it, and what neglect there is on the whole propitious to wild-life.

Could we keep it so? Could we accept it as a country place, and not mind getting a little lost, or muddying our boots or even our socks and trousers, looking for the Peak, the Money-dells, the dew pond, the Wadden, the Old Coach Road, and Coneycroft Hill and Hanger, and the site of the coneycroft itself?

And think that this great shaggy hill on which, in one or other of his 'pensile nest-like bowers' he could sit lofted and buoyed out, and feel even more akin to the birds that were his constant joy, meant evidently so very much to White. From it he stared on blue distances, or at twilight glimmering, and down at his beloved fields. We can do so still, because of his fame, and because he stopped it being enclosed. And I would point out – though it is so unpleasant to be told what to do, what to think – I would point out that it is up to us to be quiet and decorous on this hill, and to do what we can not to spoil it for others, so that we can experience something of his experience; we who are in need of that peace and the chance of sweet solemn music in the mind far more than he ever was, or could have dreamed of being. And if it is to be objected: 'They had their junketings on the Hanger, so why not we?' I will answer with a variant of some famous words of Shelley: 'We are many, they were few.' So very few. And moreover the occasions of their jollity – the events at the Hermitage – were limited it seems to a single summer.

But in case I may be thought to have leant too heavily towards the 'good old days', here is something to counteract such a tendency. Towards the end of his life, White records the following:

> 'An old hunting mare which ran on the Common, being taken very ill, came down into the village as it were to implore the help of man, and died the night following in the Street.'

I think this could not happen today.

CHAPTER XXXII

The Peak and High Fields West

WHERE were the Money Dells, where was Maiden Dance, Dell Field, the Peak, Coneycroft and the Old Coach Road? It won't do just to scatter these names as Thomas scattered gorse seed on the Common. They are all of places and enclosures on the west side of the hill, and now almost all are forgotten.

They lie under or near the North Field (at the top of Northfield Lane, the road going up to Newton Valence), the Foredown (or Fardown), and Bush or Bushy Down, which is the hill we see on the right of that road, barring the way to Faringdon and across which White had to travel habitually on his way to his duties. Up here on the wide high lands from which those night birds came crying down to the swampy fields below, you get most lovely views and a sense of wildness, freshness and freedom.

Of all the places named, the most curious is the Peak. It is a weirdly-shaped, long field, which comes eating its way into the Hanger like the sea into the wooded coast of South Devon. Even on a map it looks dramatic; an in-curving horn turning sharp on itself, burying in the mass of the beech woods. The extreme tip of this horn is Dell Field and its companion, Acre Below the Wood (also called Coneycroft Bottom), a silent lonely place. You would think the sun seldom shone on it, but it faces south-west, and it has been suggested by a member of a family long seated in Selborne that here might once have been the Money Dells (we must imagine this end of the Peak cut up into small separate enclosures, hence dells), for my informant, Mr. J. Coles, tells me this Peak (as distinct from the Peak Common Field below it) was given over in old times to the very poor.

This seems a likely explanation; and was the name *Money* Dells then just a heartless joke? I don't think so. Almost everyone in Selborne was poor, men farmed the strips nearby in common; the difference here was that no rent was charged for the dells: they were the forerunners of allotments. Incidentally, a Stephen Coles farmed strips in the Northfield and elsewhere nearby in 1677. White once called them Mossy Dells, too, but that might be a slip.

You should on no account miss Dell Field, that lonely, fascinating place – in which, however, I cannot be persuaded that it would be easy to grow much, so enclosed is it on all sides by beech trees. Today this furthest part of the Peak, one long undivided grass-field, is crossed by a footpath between two overgrown hedgerows running from Hanger to Hanger, which separates it from the Peak Common Field below. If you want to get to the Dell easily it is best to make for this point by taking Wood Lane, to the left of Fisher's Buildings at the bottom of Gracious Street, and branching off it to the right and following round the base of the hill. You do not, that is to say, follow Wood Lane up to the top of the Bostal.

But an equally good way, if you are at the Bostal's head, is to go a little way uphill from the iron seat until you reach level, and then take a path to the left of Wood Lane to come down by. The thing is, to be going downhill. It is not possible to be explicit, and even a map does not help much; but after walking some few yards down this well-defined path you should take one on your left *but going downhill.* If presently this begins to go up hill again you will know you are heading for the Highwood and Common on the summit, so retrace your steps and take the next path left-handed, and so on until you get it right. All this while, while you are going down, you will be conscious of a great chasm in the hill before you. You will come eventually to the green narrowed open space of Dell Field, which is unfenced from the Hanger (Corneycroft Hill) at this point. Keeping to the right, hugging the edge under the wood, as I came down it the other evening, I had the Nettle-leaved bell-flowers blooming freely all beside me, lolling their heads, as is their custom, into the rank grass. The path dividing the Peak will bring you over to the south flank of the valley and continuing a short way up into the wood – called here Copse Under Aylesworth – brings you to what remains of the Coach Road, running from Northfield Lane to the top of the Hanger at the Newton Valence end.

Why a coach road in this out of the way place? Where on earth should it be delivering coaches to in tiny Newton? The answer must be that they were not stage-coaches but private coaches – carriages. In other words, this was no more than what we should call a drive, and went perhaps to that 'other house of the Hartley Stuarts' I mentioned.

Part of the Peak Common Field in Coneycroft Bottom, showing vestiges of lynchet strips

It may have had connection with that lane whose closure White recorded in the church register. All is dark, and I don't think we are likely to get it clearer; but I do know that I was once told by that same man whose great-uncle had cut the walking-stick from the new-planted Hanger as a boy, and who had farmed up here long ago, that there was a superstition of there having been a house in the further Peak, reached by a drive. It would seem now to have been impossible, but there it is.

*   *   *

Coming up by the Northfield road to the Newton turning you have a clear view on your left of the Peak Common Field, with its terraced lynchets, token of a medieval agriculture carried on into our own century. Lynchets are also found in several places on the hill, and in the King's Field on the other side of the Hanger. Many other fields were divided into strips in the ordinary way. Nine Acres, for instance, a field more or less level and so not requiring to be terraced, had no less than eleven – but hear an expert on the subject. W. Sidney Scott, in his edition of White's *Antiquities*, says: 'The arable fields were divided into strips, with different owners, some owning few strips, some many; the particular strips owned by any one person being held, not together, but scattered among the various fields. The strips were divided the one from the other either by furrows, or by bands of grass called "balks". They were tilled according to a three-year rotation, two being in cultivation and one left fallow. The strips into which these fields were divided still exist in a large number of cases, some of the fields still being owned by several owners. All the villagers had certain rights in these fields; after the crops had been taken, they were thrown open to common pasture for the beasts of all the inhabitants until seed-time.'

We now know what White meant when he wrote in his journal, 'Men open their fields', and understand more of their comparative poverty and their spirit of interdependence as well as independence towards the outer world. Quarrels must have been frequent under this system. I have heard of a case where a man holding three out of four strips of a field (the owner of the fourth being a near relative), took in a substantial part of a neighbouring strip when ploughing his own, with resultant outcry and reproach. That was about 1910. Imagine what a row there would have been in times less polite!

Maiden Dance is a name to fascinate. One day White noted in his journal: 'Nightingale sang in the hanger beyond Maiden Dance, opposite Coneycroft Hanger.' Where was this strangely-named place? Only two people in our time had heard of it. The late Mr. William Bright, who was born in a cottage down where the Coneycroft House now stands, said it was up the lane at the point where you turn left for Newton Valence (that would be at a sort of cross-roads, if you counted in the footpath or track to Norton, which runs over Bush Down). Mr. Fred Smith had heard of the name, and could remember that it was somewhere up on the North Field. As it was presumably where they held May Day dances, I conclude it was a field, or part of one, and that Maiden Dance is the top corner, now hedged off, of the field anciently called Aylesworth.

In Walter Johnson's admirable edition of White's Journal a field called Preston Close (in 1842) is designated Maiden Dance in a hand-drawn map provided in that book, but this I am sure must be wrong. There are several odd discrepancies in that map, and I prefer to trust living informants who ran about these fields as children. Maiden Dance is not on the Tithe map, of course, since it had nothing to do with property or money.

How comes so extraordinary a name to be almost forgotten? Wonderful that it should be remembered by any. Narrower minds perhaps suppressed it (though they had never heard of the Golden Bough) as associated with pagan rites – orgies – perhaps even human sacrifice. . . .

If you go up to inspect Maiden Dance – just a simple triangular-shaped field – you will pass the entrance to the Coach Road, which an old chalk or lime pit marks for you by the roadside. And at the turning at the top, to your right, a track to Norton along under Bush Down is unsignposted, but exists for you if you are resolute and take the lower of two iron field-gates facing you as you turn at the corner. The way is not obstructed. Follow along the hedge and you will see the gaps as you go, and soon, historic Norton itself. There was an attempt to do away with this public footpath not so long ago, but it was successfully resisted. It should be posted.

CHAPTER XXXIII

Gracious Street, The Grange, Old Roads

LEAVING these wide upland freedoms, to return down Northfield Lane to Gracious Street, we also leave other oddly-named fields and places, such as Snap Grove, Yap Mead, Faringdon Hern (or Heron), and Frenchmare, and the Humlicans, which are outlying farmsteads beyond Bush Down.

There lies unseen in the bottom corner of the Peak as we pass, taking the sharp turn left, to go by modern Coneycroft to the Grange, the source of the Seale stream, under Coneycroft Hill. In all but the wettest summers it dries up – or rather, 'moles' underground, leaving little pools, to reappear in some seasons only in the lowest part of Church Meadow. Of course it is flowing on under the stony bed of the watercourse, all the time. Because of this habit the Seale was dammed at source to produce what White knew as Knight's Ponds, mentioned often in his journal, being, with Combe Wood Pond far below, his chief place for watching the swallows feeding. One thinks the ponds were then more open. They are now in the grounds of Coneycroft House, whose new owners delight in them and appreciate their importance to lovers of White.

The little stream goes on through what has become a beautiful water-garden, running out by the side of Fisher's Buildings and under the roadway, to emerge in front of the Grange Farmhouse – a farm no longer. Here it used to form a pond extending into the farmyard through an opening in the wall (which you still see); one of the two ghost ponds which haunt Gracious Street for old-timers. It was gay with ducks and all the animation of a farm-yard, and it is a pity it was filled-in. The other pond was a little wedge-shaped one, fronting the wheelwright's cottage and forge further up the road. It was once populous with newts – efts, as they are sometimes still called – and had a post-and-rail fence round it, and beside it on one side was stacked brushwood for the forge. On the side opposite the road, between the pond and the Seale, here running deeply entrenched, goes the path connecting with School Lane.

Fisher's Buildings and the Grange Tithe barn and farmhouse almost face each other, and where the great barn comes into view, there the old road to Alton via Norton, Hartley Mauditt, West and East Worldham joins the street. It is one of a pair of which White wrote: 'There are two rocky, hollow lanes, the one to Alton, the other to the forest (Honey Lane) . . . by the traffic of ages and the fretting of water, worn down through the first stratum of our freestone, and partly through the second; so that they look more like watercourses than roads; and are bedded with naked rag for furlongs together. In many places they are reduced sixteen or eighteen feet below the level of the fields; and after floods and in frosts exhibit a very grotesque and wild appearance, from the tangled roots that are twisted among the strata and from the torrents rushing down their broken sides; and especially when these cascades are frozen into icicles, hanging in all the fanciful shapes of frostwork.'

And then he goes on to say how 'These rugged gloomy scenes affright the ladies when they peep down into them from the paths above and make timid horsemen shudder while they ride along them.' This must refer to the truly ravine-like part of the road as it leaves

Wheelwrights and a Ghost pond

Norton and goes up in a northerly direction, to die away in the vast fields between the new road and Long Copse, from which point it disappears for ever. And since White was notoriously a bold horseman I fancy he had in mind, in this passage, the reckless pillion-carriage of some young lady – perhaps a Miss Battie – along that route, for the sake of causing her to clasp his waist more tightly.

At this end the old road is very accessible, and is metalled as far as Nine Acres but no further. Nine Acres is now the site of a private house. We are free to venture up, of course, for it is a right-of-way; but it is not really profitable to use it, for it disappears just as the other did, and we should not know how or where to go. Moreover, if we want to see more exactly what these old lanes looked like (for there was a network of them, most of them connecting with this) there are two other examples very close by. One of these comes out by the tithe barn hand-in-hand with the old road, as it were. It looks like a dried up watercourse, but is the remains of that old hollow rocky lane, also to Norton Farm, which it seems likely was the one White's disputed bridle-path from North Field led into long ago.

Now this old road has been fenced across near its mouth in two places, one of them barbed-wire, which it should not have been, for this is a right of way which can still be made out. A length of it, for some two hundred yards at least, affords a delicious cool quiet example, of ancient interest to the visitor, of a hollow lane unaltered.

The third old specimen is unobstructed to the foot traveller. At the entrance to the Grange stock yard will be seen a sort of style opposite, which will bring you into a lane in excellent condition still. If you go up this you will come into the new road, and across this on the opposite side you will find it continuing but grassed-over. This last part takes you to the top of the 'Rifle Range', a little valley we shall visit presently, when we return to the Lyth. It is by this way that the lady and the tent could have been brought up to sit to Grimm for their hilltop portraits, for of course the road led formerly right across the farm-yard from Gracious Street. The ghost of a monk is said to haunt this lane.

Gracious Street is written down Gratia Street in the seventeenth-century Survey made for Magdalen College, and it most unaccountably has become Grace's Street in the 1909 Ordnance Survey map. An appellation not at all understood, as White said. It must be a name given five or six hundred years ago, handed down by ear, and so written in various ways. There is no reason to suppose it different from

Riding pillion: too near the edge

London's Gracious Street, which is known to have stood for Graziers.

If we want to recover White through Selborne scenes we can as well here as in the village street – better, perhaps, for some of its cottages are surely the oldest in Selborne. Beginning down here at the Grange, at the intersection of so many lanes and footpaths, all so important once to weather-beaten, bent forms, clerical or lay, hurrying to and from their business, we have the great barn which cannot have looked much different in White's day. The Grange farmhouse itself was modern to him. The original Grange stood closer to the road. Its foundations were traced some few years back, and the digging brought to light a Roman coin of gold, with a palm tree and a crocodile on it, which had begun life, one supposes, in Cleopatra's Egypt, and Antony's and Julius Caesar's!

Fisher's Buildings is thought to be at base coaeval with the Grange. It is certainly very, very old. It was owned by a man called Fisher in the 1840s, hence perhaps the apostrophe, but this is misleading, for it was Fishers before that, and seems most likely to have had something to do with the monks' once well-stocked and carefully tended fish-ponds above it. This lowest part of Wood Lane today was once called Fishers Lane. On the opposite side of this little green way leading to haunts of Hanger beauty is an ancient stone cottage called Trimmings, in whose garden hedge White noted that tooth-wort was to be found. It is not to be found there now, this odd parasitical plant which springs at the roots of old decaying or neglected thorns or hazels; nor in that other place where White noticed it – 'in the Church-litten – coppice, under some hazels near the footbridge' – lost with that coppice and Herb Paris which grew higher up in it; but not lost to Selborne, for it grows elsewhere nearby. I am told by a distinguished botanist that all but two of the rare or unusual plants listed by White in Letter XLI to Barrington are to be found still, more or less where he located them.

Trimmings, like nearly all the buildings in Gracious Street, has been well done-up and modernised without injury to its ancient character. One or two of the cottages carry initial-and-date plaques on their frontages – notably 'Wheelwright's,' which is late seventeenth century. Others which look as though his eye might have rested on them as solid and satisfactory, if homely enough, representatives of Georgian architecture, have dates of just after his death. I am told we should be chary of accepting these dates as always indicative of a building's erection, because sometimes it is merely that new owners, moving in, wished to record the event.

The oldest cottage in Selborne, I believe, is the one modernly called Deep Thatch. It is just beyond the turning where the footpath sign is, directing you up the Ewell to 'Love Lane'. This fine cottage has been re-fronted, but upstairs there is a good example of a barrel ceiling, and over the hearth of the sitting room is built-in a large fragment of worked stone, which looks as though it must have been part of the capital of one of the Priory's church columns. White mentions something very like this as having been found and lost in his time.

'Deep Thatch' might better have been called Malters (perhaps it once was), if it was where the village malster lived, as seems likely. Almost next door to it, separated by an early Victorian house, are oasts, now turned into a dwelling; the neighbouring field was called Malders, and the narrow shady lane behind it, by the stream (now School Lane) was called Malters Lane in old days.

Owing to the curious old farming system, the majority of the large number of small-farmers did not live next to their stack-yards, barns, etc., but in houses and cottages at a distance. Farms as we normally view them were few – the Grange and Priory being chief of these. Thus we have Hale's Yard & Barns, etc., and Kimber's ditto, and the yards of many another prosperous denizen of the village, particularly where Gracious Street reaches the top, before the Street and the Plestor, where the Alton Road now branches off it. Then there was still a lane – Webb's Lane – going down in the same direction, but only as far as the wooden bridge I mentioned in Chapter IX. Either side of that lane were the barn-yards of Hale and Kimber, just mentioned. You will see the entrance to the former leading off at the top of Gracious Street, before you get to the corner and the pretty modern cottage called Crossways, just as it used to do, with its farm gate pushed back out of the way against the latter's wall. Inside, much of the yard remains, together with the barn, now transformed into a modern dwelling. Kimber's Yard became the site, about 1850, of a pretty little 'Gothicky' Victorian cottage called Vicarage Cottage, which early in this century used to be nicknamed Cowpen Cottage, but why was not clearly understood.

The barn-yard of the farmers Wells, who for so long withstood the White family's yearning for a park, must long ago have vanished. It would have stood on the south-east side, beyond the high bank opposite Deep Thatch, and have been reached, I suppose, over the site of the very pretty little Early Victorian cottage on the Street, facing the Plestor, and which was built by the naturalist Bell, who took over Wakes when the last White left it, in 1840. The same architect it would seem designed an identical cottage at the top of Gracious Street, which is sure to be admired. The last work of the building-and-vista-planning Whites in the region they had occupied and cherished for so long was undertaken by a nephew of Benjamin, Francis White, a neighbour of Bell's, who had built himself a little house in Wakes' grounds, probably on the site of this barn-yard of farmer Wells. It must have had a perfect view over the park to the Hanger.

Edward Blythe, editor of a valuable edition of the *Natural History* in 1836, stands up for this cottage in his preface, for it had been criticised as Cockneyfied. He said it was 'not seen from the road, or from any place where itself is not the principal object'. It was 'a plain thatched cottage, whitewashed, certainly, as it should be, as it appears among some trees, and having some of its openings very simply ornamented in a sort of half rustic and half Gothic style.'

It is a pity that this evidently pleasing building, with its association with the White family, should so soon have disappeared and become something of a mystery. I take it to have been of the same order as the gothicky cottages described, and of the village school of 1844. Possibly the same architect had a hand in all. It could have been a good example, had it lasted a little longer, to the builders of the rather plain and less happily Victorian houses which in the sixties and seventies appeared here and there in Selborne during the next wave of development, whose still-locally-quarried stones were set haphazard, to a crazy-paving effect to the eye, and whose roofs were of slate. It is a fascinating period, this of the late 1820s and early thirties, when you feel you could almost reach out and touch White; when the Queen's was still the Compasses, and the old road was still in use, and there were still only dame-schools, and Selborne was as yet unthreatened even by the railway. Blythe, coming in by the old road, did not at all approve of it. He failed to appreciate his situation – that in a few short years that road would be replaced, to become almost instantly as obsolete as the aeroplane has made the old silk-route to China across the Gobi desert. But my grandfather, in 1893 – a man incurably romantic in such things – yearning to go by a road Gilbert White had actually travelled on, attempted to take his trap, or whatever it was, up the ancient road, and foundered. Walter Rye was ahead of his time, so far as historical appreciations of the kind were concerned.

Blythe's enthusiasm fell short of this, and he was occupied mainly with the scenery. Just as his carriage was approaching the climax of the journey, everything disappeared. He found himself jolting about in a ravine, with no time to admire the *filices* that so pleased White, ferns jutting from every niche in the rocks, or the way the roots tangled, and how eaten into was the stratum. So the next time he came he walked from Alton, and the route he took by footpath and stile over the intervening fields is what was adopted for the new road some fifteen years later. Where that road now dips to transect the hollow lane by Norton Farm, a picturesque footbridge, illustrated in some old editions, carried the path over. And the traveller then would strike across the low swell of hill concealing, until he had the glory of the Hanger risen full before him; and would begin to descend between Gosling's and Culvercroft, then entering the vision of anyone standing on the Vicarage terrace; would cross the track of the carriage coming up from Grange with a lady and a tent, and the footpath next, which runs along the back of the Lyth. As he went down Webb's hill to Webb's bridge, he would see on his right a house where the Loes lived – Timothy and Elizabeth – old now but full of memories. He would cross the stream, and go up between the barn-yards either side, and would glance down Kimbers valley, where the newly-planted larches shimmered in their fresh young growth on the rough tilting sideland where the field-crickets had lived – insects observed too well, alas. For, sadly, even in White's end-days, the boys he had instructed how to get them to come forth by the insertion of stiff grass-blades had captured and condemned them, every one.

CHAPTER XXXIV

The Lyth and Green Retreats

ALL footpaths come in from the north to the Grange; all go back to the Priory.

The path just described, running along the top of the Short Lyth, dips to where the Long Lyth begins; and the path through the church-yard and Church Meadow, down which the children ran, joins this at the Long Lyth too, and together they become the path to Priory and Oakhanger – one of the most ancient and important of the footpaths of the village. This runs down in the valley all the way henceforth, on the side left of the stream as it goes down. The Seale stream and the Well-head stream have become the Oakhanger stream under the Lyth: let us go down from the Street to where they join.

William Collins described Salisbury as 'the green navel of our isle', and this at Church Meadow foot is the green navel of Selborne. We have been here already once by the steep green path from the church, but have not yet come down Huckers Lane. You enter from the Street between the blacksmith's and the Queen's. It goes level for some way, then suddenly and steeply dips, just past Dowlings, an old, old cottage where the Miller of the Windmill once lived. Here on your right, under an abrupt cliff of what looks like chalk but is centuries-weathered freestone, is a way into a field called Huckers Mead. The cliff has an immense beech growing above it with exposed roots gripping it, and there are two old sycamores doing the same. These trees – at least the beech, for certain – are among the clump Grimm illustrates from across the valley in his north-east view. They appear quite unchanged. Grimm paused in the lane, this cliff on his right above him, and began to draw his 'sweet view of Dorton and the Lyth', as White called it. He was slightly incommoded by the pigs which Pescod was keeping under the cliff and track to Huckers Mead, and he had once to step aside to let that horseman with a led-horse and following colt go by.

Huckers Lane in 1776 (after Grimm). *White's 'Sweet View'*

The same view today

The place is fascinatingly the same. When one has taken in the very different cottage in the foreground – Tudor, infinitely picturesque, L-shaped, with high chimneys, a tiny window peeping like an eye from the shaggy high-pitched thatch – the cottage which White called Pescod's House, and the shock of the Short Lyth Plantation's being quite bare, and the rather scruffy appearance of the Short Lyth itself at this date, the centuries between are as nothing. Some of that drystone walling round Pescod's is still to be seen protecting plain little Huckers Cottages on the site.

Grimm has instructions to do a close-up of that other cottage in the view, staring out at us right below there, confident of being recognised as Dorton's though there is more of it than today, its door is no longer in the middle, and tile has replaced thatch. We will go with him along that small path to a stile on the left, half way down the lane. He will find it somewhat shrunken, and the stile become a narrow 'pinch'. Now we are in the 'North-East View', and watched by the four on the hill. They see a hedge on our left, as we come through the stile, invisible to us; and they do not think we should be progressing diagonally across Church Meadow just at this time, but should have had regard for the hay (as precious to them as petrol) and be going across by that hedge to where it joins the path from the churchyard.

Then we come to what they cannot see, Dorton's – tucked away under the hill they stand on, and I think that I had better bring them down to join us at this point, if we are not to get wholly lost between past and present. We have already been using each other's eyes, and it will amuse us to see some of us avoiding trees no longer there; that thin straggle of church-litten-coppice coming down beside the path to the hazels, past the great oak alone remaining, to a foot-bridge which is merely a plank.

Here is Dorton's, the stone part only, as Grimm saw it that day. It is odd that White had this very humble little abode – not after all so very ancient in his day – included in two of the twelve pictures he commissioned. In the 'Sweet View' it must have been included, but this is a close-up – a portrait, indeed. Dorton's is by tradition a squatter's cottage – i.e., constructed in a hurry between sunset and sunrise. That is plainly improbable in this case, and it has been suggested that there was already the ruin of a building on the site, and that it might have had some connection with the Priory; a rest-house, possibly, or perhaps that 'mill of Dorton' which is referred to in the Charters of

Dorton's in 1776 (after Grimm)

Selborne Priory (but the latter we shall see is unlikely).

Now it would not be unlikely that a squatter could make himself some kind of improvised residence between sunset and sunrise in a ruin, and at the back of Dorton Cottage there is a part of the wall far thicker, rubble-filled, and obviously far older than the rest. The only other reason I can think of for White's having Dorton's in two pictures is that it might possibly have been that cottage to which Vicar Longworth went after he was ousted from the Vicarage by his father-in-law, Jethro Beale, during the Commonwealth. Of Longworth (who was reinstated in 1660) White said 'after he was dispossessed (he) retired from the church, where he earned a small pittance by the practice of physic'.

Jethro Beale would not appear to have been a very nice man; he exulted over his son-in-law's over-throw, preaching, in his first appearance in the pulpit of St. Mary's, on the text: 'They are brought down and fallen; but we are risen and stand upright'.

In 1939, when, with excessive patriotic zeal, the incumbent dug up the Vicarage lawn on the outbreak of war, a very large number of seals from bottles of sack was found buried. I think they were Beale's, conscience having driven him to drink.

Gilbert White, senior, became Vicar of Selborne two years after Longworth, and of course never knew him, but he knew the sons, evidently, and the White family honoured Longworth for not taking the league and covenant and for sticking it out by helping his parishioners in the only way he could; so if this was where he retired to (and the distance is somewhere about right, counting from the churchyard boundary) they might have held it in special regard. Or it would

Dorton's today

be pleasant to think that the cottage had some early romantic associations for Gilbert. But we must get on.

* * *

Down by the footbridge among the hazels which, like the tooth-wort we see, grow, as we know, no more here, we notice that the hedge is on the meadow side of the stream. And also what a wide space, wheel-marked, there is between cottage and Lyth. This space was part of Dorton Common until the late twenties of this century, when it was arranged with the College to be taken in to Dorton's. The Commoners enjoying their rights of wooding in the Lyth used to come with their bundles, and following along the end of Dorton's garden, paddle somehow across the stream to get to Priory Lane. Three wonderful old cottagers – Mrs. Fairminer, Mrs. Warren, and another whose name I never had – I used frequently to see passing so in my youth, under bundles of kindling big as haystacks, laughing and chaffing each other as they went. They were not, probably, as old as they seemed, but thin and struggling with their loads, yet always merry, and I used much to wonder at their spirit and endurance.

This 'wooding way', as you might call it was, I believe, the only exception to the rule that Dorton and Lyth were quite separate. And even then there was no bridge. No bridge into Dorton's from the common, certainly, until the beginning of this century. The only way was across this footbridge from Church Meadow.

But those wheel-marks took a different direction from the wooders, following along the short Lyth west. It was a wagon track used in summer only, I suspect. I cannot say if it then continued to the top by the lost track up Kimbers which I mentioned as certainly existing in our time, but anyway the wagons could return by the way they came, and go up between the Lyths, in the valley known as 'the rifle range', and anciently called the Redden, which we shall come to in a moment. And meanwhile we can go where these wheels direct as far as the hedge between Church Meadow and Kimbers till we stand half way up that valley, with the church and Vicarage garden on our left and the Plantation towering on our right. Cattle have kept the way under the trees trodden into resemblance of the old track thus far.

We are standing at the Vee, where today is the ruin of a penstock, or hatch, which used to keep the Seale back, so forming what must have been the prettiest little pond, with a miniature island in its centre. A post and rail fence was round part of this water (which in summer was fed less from the stream, usually then dried up, than from two small additional springs in Kimbers, a short way up the valley) and a piece of that fence was there on the south side until very recently. You can clearly see where the pent-up water has worn its channel round the islet.

When this penstock was operated and whether it existed in White's time at all, is hard to say. Although the brick wall on the south or church side has firmly held, the wall on the other has long been washed down by winter flooding, and part of it lies in the stream. These bricks are not old, but 'stock bricks', and it has been in this state for at least sixty years. Nobody now knows who built the penstock.

But was this 'modern' wall built on the stone foundations of an ancient one? When White wrote in his poem, 'Swell to a lake the scant penurious rill', was this what he had in mind to do? I hardly think so. The rill is penurious, certainly, but there was never what could be called a lake here. Some think, though, that it was meant as an ornamental feature. There is still the vestige of a path down to it, through a double hedge, from the Vicarage garden, about where the cedars now are. It must indeed have been a charming feature – was so even in its ruin without the damming, when Kimbers was grazed, and before the great trees had fallen. I wish that it could be restored.

But White never once mentions a pond here, which he would surely have done, and my guess is that this was one of the many works of Henry Maxwell, in about the 1860s, for he owned Kimbers. He or his son, George, later made a very good bargain in exchanging it for another field, as we shall see. And there was until recent times another dam, in the valley opposite, trapping the well-head stream, for the purpose of feeding water by ram to the Wakes. Henry was certainly responsible for *this* dam, and he owned the fields either side of that lower part of the mill valley – Huckers Mead and Sparrow's Hanger. This dam was destroyed completely in the prodigious flooding of 1951, but before I speak of that event I shall return for a while to Kimbers.

If you stand there at the ruined penstock on some golden summer evening, or at the time when Kingcups bloom, the scene so beloved of White is still revealed in something of its former glory. But Kimbers is unaccountably neglected, ungrazed, full of what country folk used to call trash – hogweed, nettles, willow herb. And from the terrace now you cannot see anything, because of what, in effect, is a small copse of sycamore and ash, grown up over twenty odd years in the field below, just under the wall. The yew hedge behind this barrier of young trees has shot up to twice its height into what is virtually a line of individual trees; you see it all brown to its original height, at which it was kept well trimmed until the war.

The war . . . how miniscule is this lost terrace in face of the fearful whole! I do not see how such a hedge could have been maintained in

The Wooders of yesterday

present times. And as for Kimbers, it is perhaps not worth while now to graze it – too small to put a number of bullocks into, where in the old days a pair of carthorses were enough to eat it down. It is difficult and dangerous, too, to get stock across the road into it. What is to be done with this once so lovely field?

When every angle, curve and quirk of hedge, every ditch, every culvert, every little copse, is the result of past thought and sometimes jealous contention, and, always, heavy toil, perhaps no apology is needed for dwelling on them with such detail. All these difficult steep sidelands of narrow little valleys leading off the main vale down to Priory – what could we do for them, we who are not farmers? Farmers work hard, often alone with their dangerous appliances – tractors and 'swipers'; do the ancient work of fencing and draining, and otherwise keep them clean and clear, so that they still, in the main, resemble the fields White knew. They alone, the farmers, carry on the ancient country traditions.

In this polite age, will people be found much longer to herd and tend cattle? The first is often a desperate business for a few and mostly unskilled hands. We had recently a regular rodeo through the village in pursuit of a single bullock, startled out of its customary lethargy, which actually careered right through somebody's sitting-room – in at one french window and out at another – scattering furniture as it ran with rolling eyes and saliva dripping from its mouth!

* * *

On a November day in 1951, after some forty-eight hours of continual heavy downpour following a wet summer and autumn, a lady living at Highwood, on the eastern side of Selborne Hill – a house commanding a magnificent view towards Noar Hill – saw break from the sloping land between Noar and Hanger what looked like a pocket handkerchief, white and bright upon the green of the field. It was water burst from its natural reservoir in the chalk, and it came pouring down, overwhelming the usual source of the stream at Well Head, and foaming down that channel, rushed across the road to cover the bottom of Honey Lane, and swept on into the valley. As it passed the old Mill House, I was told, the water was so high that it came close beneath the windows, and when it reached Dorton and came up against the swollen Seale it flooded the cottage there to a depth of eighteen inches, and then drained away almost as quickly as it had come.

This was a most extraordinary happening. Never in living memory had Dorton's been flooded; and had such a thing been ever usual, one would suppose, that ancient squatter's cottage under the Short Lyth would not have been built there. And yet, I don't know: people in the early seventeenth century (or it might have been even earlier) were hardy, and would put up with much when searching for a home; and the water, at least until the last repetition of that flooding, went very quickly away down a hole to the right of the fireplace, which might have been specially contrived for that purpose. All I know is that in 1951, in living memory of oldest inhabitant, such an event was unknown. White never mentions it. He speaks of flooding at the bottom of Gracious Street, and of the wells of several persons running over, quite often, but he does not mention corresponding flooding at the bridge where the well-head stream passes under the road at the bottom of Honey Lane. Selborne Street, if you could look at the land in section, is like a bow, and at these two extremities, Honey Lane bridge and the Grange, flood water collects, to arrive inevitably in a double dose down at Dorton. The event is spectacular and frightening, where at the confluence, all of the bottom of Church Meadow, from Sparrow's Hanger foot to Lythe, is one foaming and swirling lake, and Dorton's stands out lonely and gardenless, with just the tops of the hedges indicating boundaries normally so wholly familiar. Surely if he had ever seen it, White would have recorded it for us; we must therefore conclude that it had never happened before, and that more water is coming down than before – which is a reversal of what is generally found now that it is being drawn off at base so copiously elsewhere. The answer is, of course, that ditches are neglected in the fields, and that even an ordinary downfall of rain on a summer day turns all the ditchless, metalled roads to watercourses. I have indeed seen it pouring down from the high lands into Northfield Lane, and the Empshott road by the Burhunt – Temple turning, in torrents like waterfalls.

Whenever we have a really wet summer and autumn now we must expect these floods. It happened again in August 1954, in 1960 twice within the month of October, in 1968 late in September, devastatingly. It then hung about for many hours. In between it was threatened often, the water creeping up to the door. When it floods, it comes in not only from above but from below. It is frightening and destructive, and now that the sewage pump and sump have been put in the meadow, just above the cottage, it has become dangerous, for the pump is put out of action and sewage effluent comes up through the manhole lids and from the pump itself, and pours out in fountains, and runs into the stream and down the road – and of course into Dorton's.

Nobody seems much to care. In fact hardly anyone has ever seen the valley when it has been thus flooded.

* * *

A Redden, Reading, sometimes Roding, I understand, meant a clearing in dense woodland. All of the valley between Short and Long Lyth – the 'rifle range' – and the large field, too, which backs the Long Lyth, must once have been covered with trees. The rifle-range was still called Reading in 1842. It got the name of rifle-range as long ago as the Second Boer War. There were targets on the north-east side which are marked on the Ordnance Survey Map (1909), and a clump or two of gorse now indicates where these were. This valley is a short one, rising to the great fields between the Alton road and Long Copse and Wick Hill, and at the top, on the left, you find (blocked, but I am not sure to what extent it ever was public) – that green lane I spoke of, leading back to the Grange. On the top of the other slope is Lyth Hill meadow, across which the public path runs from Goslings Croft, and here is the mutilated remnant of a long narrow copse, once very beautiful in what was a most lonely and beautiful spot – a strip of ash, oak, wild cherry trees, with hazel underwood, and bluebells all beneath.

At the bottom of the valley is the Long Lyth footpath to the Priory via Combe Meadow, the monks' fishpond, the Plains, and through Combe Wood. This was the beginning of Gilbert White's 'Summer Evening Walk'. Not far along it is one of Mrs. Mackensie's iron seats. Was this where White stopped and in more relaxed attitudes dreamed of the imaginary lake and waterfall? It is not impossible, for it would be a good place for it, but expensive to do properly, because of those floods. In 1960 the whole wide floor of the valley was awash from side to side.

We will only follow White as far as Priory, first down the Lyth and then through the Dorton. I tried to indicate in a former chapter the probable course of the whole walk from there onwards: up by Temple and Burhunt and somehow by Gally Hill and the Kings Field to the top of the Hanger.

The Long Lyth is not nearly so steep as the Short Lyth. It runs in a long curve for perhaps half a mile, and in the centre, where the bank is shallowest, a sort of bostal used to run down across it, connecting you with a path along the top. The grandest beech trees in all Selborne grew on this Lyth – and some are there still – and under them were drifts of dark green and golden mosses, and brown beech-mast, and low holly bushes. It faces east, and in the evenings, as you stood on that path, the declining sun came down between the great trees, and it was like a cathedral. You would only hear birds, and chiefly the jackdaws which nested high up, and were always chucking and clicking like billiard-balls in collision. Here the wood wren would often be singing.

Below the path, where poplars of some kind are growing now, was all pasture field, with cows which did not stray up under the beeches, though these were not in my time fenced off. There is, of course, a stile at either end. The Long Lyth is still very beautiful. In 1932 very many of the trees were felled, according to time-honoured custom. They were got out with great difficulty, and the footpath was never quite the same. In the end the contractor tried using naval winches – sell-offs left over from the First World War, I suppose – in an attempt to drag the great trunks up to the top, but with little success, and one winch got left behind, where it lay rusting for many years.

What was really more grievous about that felling was, that afterwards a curious plantation was made in the Lyth meadow. Sycamores and larches were planted in two belts, the larches down by the stream. After a few years the Long Lyth became like a thick wood with the path running down its centre. Many people did not know what it had looked like. The sycamores came to nothing, all scabby, and bitten by grey squirrels. The larches did a little better.

Then in 1958, not long before the College sold Grange Farm (with which the Lyth belonged), to the joy of many of us, all these trees on the Lyth meadow were cut down. Once more we could see that long beauteous curve, and beech trees were just closing in again on the slope. But alas the clearing of the meadow was only the preliminary to a renewed Lyth felling, and when that was finished these poplars were planted, not only in Lyth meadow but on the common of Lower Dorton too. It is a catch-crop, I have been told, useful for making matchsticks and white-wood furniture, and should be ready to crop in about ten years from now. I should be surprised if the present owners make much money out of it, however.

The Long Lyth and the Short Lyth were given to the National Trust in 1961, by Mr. R. R. Edgar, of Newton Valence Place, to whom we can never be sufficiently grateful. He gave with them a large sum towards their upkeep. If he had been a younger man, he told me recently, he would have contrived a lake, and perhaps even a waterfall, and thus fulfilled White's dream. Who knows but that may not one day come about.

If you look back towards the end of the Lyth you will see in winter, when the leaves are off those poplars, the Hanger rising up before you. Much depends on the light and clouds, but this is the view which really can support White's claim that the Hanger has a certain mountainous grandeur. It is about the only feature of Selborne that you can get at a proper distance from, to appreciate in the true aesthetic eighteenth century or Gilpin manner.

We leave the Long Lyth by a stile. All before us is haunted Priory ground which it would be easy to see cowled spectres skimming. It is a large irregularly shaped field, sloping down right-handed to the stream as it flows under Dorton Wood. It is very bumpy and swampy in places. In fact the floor of Combe Meadow is a swamp, following the line of what most probably was once an irrigation ditch; and down there in the southernmost corner, nearest the stream, there are grassy embankments which presumably once enclosed ponds. No one knows whether these had anything to do with the Priory.

On our right, then, lies Dorton Wood, on our immediate left is Long Copse. This copse very soon turns left and proceeds up the valley of Milkwood, Milking Hanger, Mill Wood Hanger, or what you will. I call it Milking Hanger because I first saw it named so on a map of 1808 in the County Records. East of this valley is Combe Wood. Down it, under woods at either side, runs a sturdy rivulet, pretty deeply entrenched, and these filled Combe Wood Pond, the 'Monks Fish-pond', which lies straight ahead of us, but there is now no pond, only the broken embankment which for centuries penned it in. My friend the farmer who owns this pond and drained it assures me that he thinks of restoring it; and it would be a good thing, since it is not only where White frequently came to observe birds of all sorts – it is here that he saw the cuckoos hawking for dragon-flies, for instance – but was once the scene of a little miracle which I believe he had never heard of. White himself must be a spectator here a while by our side.

It is perhaps not much of a miracle, and the cynical might think it arranged between two old school chums. What happened was this.

St. Richard of Chichester and John, the first Prior of Selborne had been brought up together at Worcester. John begged Richard to favour the Priory with a visit, and he did so, and blessed the new-founded monastery with his holy presence. But unfortunately there was not enough food of the sort the occasion merited, and Prior John felt this keenly, so he went so far as to ask his old friend, the Blessed Richard, if he would go and stand by the fish-pond: 'My lord, may it please you to go down to the water with us, lest perhaps by a gift of God we may be able to catch some fish when you are by.' I quote from the Life of St. Richard of Chichester, by Ralph Bocking, his Father Confessor. To me, it seems unlikely that the Prior would have been quite so direct.

Anyway, they all went down to the water 'which was not far away', and at first there was a terrible muddle and tangle with the nets, and they couldn't catch anything. Then a relative and friend of Richard's who was present asked him to put out his right hand and give a blessing, Richard did, and immediately a very large pike came splashing over the pond and virtually gave himself up.

This event meant much to the Priory.

In those days the makers of encaustic tiles used to travel round the monasteries manufacturing them on the spot. Usually the monks chose stock kinds, but now and again something was ordered to special requirements. Thus at Selborne Priory a tile was found representing two fish, obviously by intention pikes, and this is not thought to have been found anywhere else.

There is another supernatural happening recorded in association with the Priory, of a very recent date. I find it moving and persuasive of reality of some sort, though I don't suppose it would satisfy the Society for Psychical Research, any more than the behaviour of that pike would have satisfied Gilbert White. (Though it must have aroused his curiosity.)

In 1962, then, a lady who had a shop in a town on the Sussex coast wrote to our vicar to ask if he could give her any information about the Priory – tell her of any books about it, and if the foundations were still there, and when it had ceased to be a Priory. She said that she had found that 'a great many years ago' a relation had been Prior of Selborne. His name had been Sharp.

The vicar handed this lady over to the Rev. G. E. C. Knapp, who was (and is) in control of the archaeological researches at the Priory. To him she revealed a strange story.

She had been sitting in her shop one evening, after business hours, thinking about an acquaintance who, with a wife and children, was in dire straits over housing. He had to vacate his present house and couldn't find another, because people wouldn't let when there were children in the case. There were three, and the wife was expecting another. She – the narrator – had been trying desperately to get friends to accommodate these people, but nothing could be done. She had returned, and was sitting in the shop, when – 'I glanced up to see the following inside the shop by the door. A man about five feet eight inches with very dark hair and large eyes his skin seemed very sallow, and his face small and oval with a long nose and as if the skin was close to the bones (no fat). His head was leaning forward (chin on chest) and I noticed he was thin on top and unshaven with dark growth round the chin – he had beautiful hands – he was dressed in a black monk's habit with cowl pushed off his head and the bottom of his garment was greyish-white with chalky dust as if he had been walking in it.

'His lips did not seem to move but I heard him say – "My child we will help this man together – listen and you will hear what to do – remember – always remember, seek and you shall find."

'He then vanished as quickly as he had arrived but I saw a green field with a hill to the back right hand side and saw white daisies and the kind of grass that when we were children we used to hold in our hands and try to knock the heads off – and could hear bees and running water.'

The narrator never was exactly told what to do, but she got up directly and rang up 'one of our Councillors whom I knew very slightly and I argued with him far more forcibly than I would normally have done'. In short she put it to him that since this man in trouble had a good job in London and was earning a very good wage, they could very easily grant him a hundred per cent mortgage to buy a house with. And they did.

The old Prior Sharpe (as I shall take him to be) returned once more – in a sense – the following day. The lady, not a Roman Catholic, confided in one who was, who suggested he might have been 'someone to do with St. Anthony, who had to do with finding things'. Some unspecified time after this suggestion, she said 'although I didn't see the man again I saw the field exactly as before with the raised hill at the top right hand side and heard the water to the left, it was warm and sunny with the noise of insects and birds – and the same voice said with a laugh – "Oh no, I am nothing to do with St. Anthony, I am only from Selborne – and the kitchen is by the water".' This last remark makes one think that the old Prior had been taking an interest in the diggings, which had been going on for some years. It was only when the name Selborne occurred that the lady remembered her 'ancestor' Prior Sharpe.

John Sharpe, or Sherpe, 'alias Glastonbury' (Charters of Selborne Priory), 1478–84, had been the last Prior but one, and not very efficient, it seems. He had died in 1484, the Priory was dissolved two years later. In 1525 the Priory lands were leased to a John Sharpe. Twenty years after that 'a tenement' (at Priory) was in the occupation of John Sharpe. In fact Sharpes ran the Priory, farming it and living off its ruins, from the dissolution onwards for well over a hundred years. Whatever reasons Prior Sharpe might have had to skim the plains, he made a dear and good old spectre on this, one hopes his last, manifestation.

* * *

At the top of Combe Wood Pond, where the rivulets entered, was a little dell – a few oak trees, bracken, primroses in season – into which you descended to cross by a plank-bridge, and go up and through a gate into what is called the Wells Plantation, and, after a very short way, double back sharp left, and over another gate into the valley of Milking Hanger, at the Plains. From there you went straight up, entering the wood again where it crosses and fills the valley, to come into the open once more, and continue so to the top, at Lower Wick Hill Farm, near the road between Hartley and Oakhanger. You must look in the Ordnance Survey Map, where it is clearly marked, together with another way up through the woods to Upper Wick Hill Farm, also leading to the Oakhanger road.

The map does not mark these ways as footpaths, but they undoubtedly were so, and habitually used by villagers until recent times. They were open enough when the woods – part of the Dutton Estate shooting syndicate – were patrolled by keepers (and browsed by rabbits). They have not been blocked, but the footbridge (marked) has rotted and not been replaced, and the paths are in places densely overgrown with nettles and brambles. Still, resolute wayfarers might penetrate, and perhaps the Footpaths Association, or bands of volunteers under Nature Conservancy, may come to our aid. No Selborne walk is more lovely in a sylvan way than this up Milking Hanger, and even in the days of the keepers it was not disputed, nor your presence much objected to –

provided you did not blunder in in the nesting season. The other way was equally lovely. If you did not wish to turn up towards Upper Wick Hill Farm, you followed it on under that hill, to come out at Candover, on the Oakhanger road also, or you might go left, down by a muddy lane to Priory – a lane down which, as I will later explain, Chaucer himself may have ridden.

And now we will go along the top of the embankment of the Monks' Fishpond, into the fringe of Combe Wood for a little way, over meadow-land next, till we come out on to that very lane. Priory is just below on our right, but still hidden.

But the true road to the Priory is from Dorton, by the Priory Lane. So we will return to Dorton Common and take this through the woods, and on our way find out a little about the three subsidiary valleys on that east side of the vale. Back in Dorton, the first thing I direct your attention to is a signpost to Alton, by bridle-path via West Worldham. It is perfectly true – you can get to Alton this way; but this sign is a replica of one very very old, set here by the County Council again, I suppose, in accordance with some statutory obligation, most quaintly. It refers to that route between Priory and Candover we have just touched upon, but I should be sorry for the visiting stranger who tried to go by it today.

CHAPTER XXXV

'Down Dorton'

At the foot of Huckers Lane Dorton begins. It used to be gated at either end. The gate at the Huckers end is gone. Until about ten years back the gate posts stood for a bounday mark, just beyond the entrance to Sparrow's Hanger. The Priory Lane too began at this gate.

Before we go through to Dorton we should look at the valley running up south-east to the mill. The sidelands here at their broadest part are, Huckers to the south, Sparrow's Hanger to the north. Sparrow's Hanger – more extensive than it is today – was Gilbert White's property, which he left to Benjamin. It was then entirely covered with what he called in his will, 'my beechen grove', and to Marsham he proudly cited 'my tallest beech, at the north-east corner of Sparrow's Hanger', as a fine specimen. In the swampy south-east corner at the foot, then a bog, he and his brother-in-law Barker planted Grass of Parnassus, but it is not there now. Nor are the beech trees, with the exception of one. Within a few years of his death White's 'beechen grove' was felled and the sideland became as bare as Huckers Mead opposite.

The farmhouse that White owned here, and let to a man called Parsons, is long vanished too. It stood not at all where the present house stands, which was built up there in 1900 by R. Bowdler Sharpe, the naturalist, but right up on the level field above, as aerial photographs of late have plainly shown. Exactly how one got up to it is not at present known.

Today's Sparrow's Hanger has to be reached by a little bridge off the lane – which would seem to be not quite where it was in the old days, but just down in the river bank close to it is a spring noticed by White. It was until lately the sole freshwater supply for Huckers Cottages and Sparrow's Hanger, and in times of severe drought people have been known, as in 1921, to descend the mead to get to it. It was tacitly understood in the old days that all springs should be open in such times.

This little valley of the mill is not as interesting or beautiful as its opposite number, since it does not curve as that of Kimbers does, is narrower, and the view is now blocked by trees. You cannot go up Mill Bottom and get a close look at the waterfall. White, with surprising refinement, for him, named this Silkwood Vale, and I must think that he often came up it and sentimentalised, and that it is a pity we can't. It is fortunate indeed that we have Grimm's view, to get which he must literally, I think, have been squatting in the stream. The banks here have closed in and become exceedingly high. (High indeed must the flood have been that day in 1951, for the Mill house is set well back.)

Silkwood, as I have mentioned, is that large black-malm field between the street and this valley, neighbouring the field called Hastards. The Mill is, of course, one of the most ancient of Selborne places, but its present buildings, though charming, are not really old – only eighteenth century – and it is thought the original mill was in a higher place, above the waterfall. The lane down to the mill led from the street through the two famous fields just mentioned. At some remote time there was a skirmish of some sort, either at the mill or in Silkwood Field above. The high bank between is all walled to prevent it falling down on the house, and a few years ago this retaining wall gave way, and some skeletons were exposed, and round-shot of various

Entrance to Dorton Wood

sizes, some of iron, some of stone. Selborne, all through the many wars, has remained so mercifully unafflicted, that perhaps any small forgotten fierce episode is worth recording.

Selborne's windmill is something of a mystery, since no one I could find, however old, could remember it, but one or two knew where it had been, and that it was pulled down. I know that it was not there in 1776, or it would have appeared in the view from the Hermitage. I know that Henry Maxwell once owned it, and I suspect him of building it. It is said to have stood where Stream Cottage stands now, in the north-east corner of Hastards, and that it was pulled down when that house was built in 1870, and yet about 1890 it is shown in a drawing by E. H. New, in the edition of the Natural History which he so ably illustrated. It was a crazy place to have put a windmill in, I think, and quite out of keeping with the Selborne scene, and I will leave it at that. One concludes that by the time it was built, the water mill had become inadequate for the supply of flour Henry needed, and that by the time it was removed flour was easily and cheaply obtainable from outside.

* * *

The Dorton was gated at either end because Commoners used to turn their animals into it, to graze. Lower, or Little Dorton is the part opposite Dorton Cottage, Great Dorton is the wood through which Priory Lane runs on. It is like one of those New Forest 'shades', as they call those clearings in the dense woodlands of that wonderful region.

No animals ever graze the Dorton now. The 'shades' in its wood are largely overgrown with brambles, if not with saplings. And Little Dorton, once smooth and be-flagged – for this is where the golden fleur-de-lis begins, which continues at intervals all the way down as far as Combe Meadow – has nowadays poplars like those in Lyth Meadow planted all over it. Incidentally it was all covered with trees of some sort in 1842, so all this planting was probably traditional and planned.

After you have passed the old cottage, so much modified since Grimm drew it, and with a plank bridge now connecting it with the common, the old lane, rising slightly between high hedges, dips again, then enters the wood. That swift plunge into leafy shadow is dramatic, and the scene at entry so beautiful that a sketch can barely indicate the effect. Immediately short of it is the valley leading up south-east to Honey Lane, and which is opposite to the Rifle Range. It is called Little Combe – pronounced Liddyc'm. The copse on the sideland to the left as you look up is still called Sparrowhanger and was once part of Sparrow's Hanger, the farm. It is a little innocent valley, broken half-way up by a bank across, with hedge and trees, and behind these lies, virtually quite hidden, the sewage disposal works of Selborne. It took a great deal of pains to select the right spot.

Just within the wood to the left and a little below, under a very splendid beech, is the last one of the iron seats, probably more used than any. And yet, from where you sit, you can see now nothing but the hazels of the little 'Copse in Dogs Ford', as the small tilted field beyond it is called. Otherwise you would have a very choice view up to Dorton's and Church Meadow, with the church on top, and with the Hanger looming beyond. Yet it does no harm to be sitting still for a while with your face towards those clean and tasselled bushes, which are nowadays never cut as of course they used periodically to be. The stream lies below us on our right hand, spread wide over the stones, shallow and glimmering under its tent of leaves – a lovely sight. Papers, etc., get rather strewn about before this seat, but may be quickly and easily covered by leaves.

On your right, a little further on after you leave this seat, is an ancient cartway with high mossy banks, inviting up the side of the wood. It leads only to a long solitary field called 'Upper Burchams' – an ancient name; but if there is to be charm in names, a neighbouring field up there was called Plumtree Willow. About half-way along through the wood presently we come upon Lower Burchams, which slopes down to the stream, and across which you see the Long Lyth. This is a beautiful field, full of interest. It was cherished for near a century by the blacksmith Tarrs. My late friend Clifford would come bumping down the lane to it with his pony-cart nearly every day, and only recently mowed it single-handed with a scythe. Gone now are his little hay-stacks, the like of which you won't see today outside some Rembrandt print, and his primitive iron shed which somehow, as *he* constructed it, always seemed perfectly part of the rustic scene. In accordance, perhaps, with simple West Country ideas of fencing inherited from days on Porlock Hill, Clifford was not over particular what he used for that, and I saw him once diligently incorporating an iron bedstead with brass knobs – perhaps the very bed on which he was begotten. Prizers of the antique will find it there still. And a swampy piece in Lower Burchams he laboriously drained, but left the golden kingcups to bloom annually in that spot.

The Priory Lane was metalled throughout by the monks, some five hundred years ago. It must have been one of the first of their necessary works. Mostly lightly buried now under the soft black leaf-mould, those cobbles which made up the metalling are still there. There are weak spots in the wooded length which sometimes make walking difficult.

Horsemen go down here today, as in the past. Did Gilbert White in his youth fancy, as others have done after him, a posse of churchmen trooping this way on jingling quick-treading mules and ambling palfreys? So it must often have been. And I have thought these busy imagined prelates might have been not so very different from many of us in our time – neither so much haloed by devotion nor so utterly devoid of piety as romantic literature would have had us believe. But earnest, thorough, devoted in their way, to the practical ends of God. People who lived in monasteries and busied about between them must, I think, have been exceptional in this, that they were all in escape – from the world of cut-throat warriors, expert with steel as the athletes of today with bat and racket, club and ball; wildly uncertain of temper; half insane with pride. Among those mounted clerics, then, would have been all that were sensitive, intellectual and aesthetic, in revolt. They saw their goal even as the arch of daylight at the end of this long funnel of gloom opening before us, and they knew they would come out, and yet somehow they never did, and it is very sad.

Some three-quarters of the way through the wood, we see on our left a gap and an irregular sort of grassy path leading across an open but brambly space, and down to a bridge across the stream, and eventually to a stile into Combe Meadow. The way over the field to the stile at the end of the Long Lyth opposite has been viable since time immemorial, but the village has only just put in for it to be made a public footpath. Not very many people will use it in winter, for it means crossing the swampy piece, but it links the short walk round Lyth and Dorton.

And now Dorton gate is in front of us. Before we go through we must slip down through the wood to the water where, it is certain, the only Mill at Dorton was. You will see how the stream takes a sharp turn left, and the blocks of stone coming out of the bank – very fine masonry indeed – where the water-gate was, by which it could be closed to hold back and build up a head of water. You are looking at the first of three pools, one above the other. The place is known locally as the Spintop. Spintop or 'spend-top', I suppose. The second pool is deep and bridged over, a second narrow sluice, and there is a fall, and then comes the last pool, much wider, more obviously a millpool.

The spend-top was functioning at the beginning of this century, and when White was alive there was still the remains of the mill, but on which side of the stream he does not say. The mill-bridge connects two long pasture fields, that on the left being known as Mill Meadow, that on the right, stretching right down to the Priory farm, also having that name in the tithe map. My guess is that the mill-house was on the right side – the Priory side of the pools, and that it was reached from Priory Lane above. Neither the mill, then, nor its pools were strictly *in* Dorton, but they were definitely *at* Dorton; and of course we know that there was no ruined mill-house, no pools, where Dorton Cottage stood in White's time.

Close as your view of the Spintop is, you may like a closer one of the

The Spintop or spend-top: Old Mill pools

pools below it. I must say that we cannot go there today without trespassing, but that, since it used to be visited as a curiosity (and some even bathed in the pool lowest down – though it is icy cold) a place in the fence at the far end of Mill Mead, as you come over the bridge before mentioned, has been very kindly left without barbed wire on its rails, on purpose.

This beautiful field was once Maxwell property. Henry's son George it was, who made the way down through the wood to get to it, and the plank bridge, which is marked on the Ordnance Survey Map, 1909. He traded Kimbers for what was always known as 'the fat meadow', into which the bullocks were turned to eat the cream of the grass before slaughter. And when Miss Maxwell told me of this great bargain, a quiet smile played over her lips, and a gleam was in her eyes.

* * *

Where the Priory Lane continues green, with the stones under the sward, it is open to the west but has a hedge and copse at first on the east. Going on down to the Priory (which you cannot see till you are on it, as it lies round the corner) you may spy, through a gap, over a gate, a very old and lonely oak tree. This – now literally only half a short if living stump – is the sole survivor of Butts Wood. It must have been a great tree in the Priory's heyday. Infinite frosts and gales it withstood, and was still a firm structure with its plumes of greep atop, like a wrecked galleon under jury-rig, until some twenty years back one frost and gale too many pulled the half away, and exposed its inner mysteries. Countless generations of barn owls had nested in this oak – I suppose since the days when, standing in the centre of a wood, it had brought them privacy. And they had gone on using it as their castle even when this loneliness betrayed them to the eyes of every marauding, pitiless boy, but they did not even then forsake it, nor did till the storms blew it in two.

But just before this gap and this historic tree, we pass the last of our three pairs of subsidiary valleys opposed to each other down the main vale. It is the valley of New Barn – ancient name – and New Barn Farm is at its top, on Honey Lane.

The fine oak trees once in procession up this valley are mostly felled. It is an open valley, different in character from the rest, down-like and bare, and the life of the Priory somehow clings here more than than anywhere else but on the site itself. Here without the aid of second sight we can see in fancy monastic flittings, for the monks were often at work here. They dammed the valley right across with an earthen bank, as you can still see, for here was penned their fresh water supply. A lovely clear spring gushes from high up on the northern flank, in what I have always thought was, geographically, an odd place, for the hill runs down towards Priory on the other side almost immediately.

This spring fills a little reservoir nowadays, and feeds a ram at the bottom, running out and under Priory Lane to reach the Oakhanger stream as it must have done before the Priory was founded. But the monks brought it by some means to fill the moat which ran round their premises on two sides, south and east, to pass eventually to the stream under the 'rere dorter' (their privies) through an admirable example of plain but finished domestic functional masonry – a drain like a vaulted passage. It was this sort of thing, of course, which gave rise to all those stories of secret passages leading to monasteries. The conducting of this water so far from the valley must have represented a fine feat of engineering. It involved lead piping somewhere along in between, for White records some lengths being dug up and purloined. If you want to see what that piping looked like in the ordinary way, there is in the Wakes a short piece found lately at the Priory itself. The fall from the bottom of New Barn Valley to where the moat began is very slight, and it has been thought that for most of the distance it was led round, across the intervening field of Butts Wood, and over Rode Lane. I think you might with less labour have turned the spring back through the hill, to face the Priory at a much shorter distance, and have a much greater fall; but then you would not have had your great supply on tap, and the place invited a dam, and it was comparatively easy to build. The modern ram distributes water to fields far away on top, and until recently, I believe, supplied Priory Farm as ever. For washing their dishes, however, the monks seem to have used the stream, for remember, 'The kitchen is by the water.'

There is no right-of-way up the New Barn Valley, despite that inviting cart track going along its southern side, from which so lovely an English view over 'the forest' can be obtained. The gates at top and bottom are kept closed and heavily wired. All the same there is a stile of sorts at the side of this one, and I myself have often gone up and down this valley. Only the ownership of Priory Farm has just lately changed, and I should not think of doing so again until I had permission. We should not like unlimited trespassing ourselves, with the likelihood of a right-of-way being established, if it were our own property.

But I hope I may go again and stand and listen to the old ram in the bottom there once or twice before I die. Its quiet 'clunk-clunk' in that lonely open place is the very voice of time eternal, but I think it has not yet been heard here a hundred years. But the water is the same – or if not, then the streamlet which motivates the ram is the same the old monks so long ago were patient and cunning to control. (What a pity those who manipulated their souls were not as patient and as cunning!) The fact that a hundred or six hundred years are equally insignificant means nothing at all as we listen. Keep this sound of eternity in our ears in going the last yards of the green lane, through the last of its gates (generally left wide), and round the corner to Priory – or all that is now to be seen of it; a plain Georgian farmhouse, walls, cart sheds and barns – nothing more above ground of what was a precious consortium of souls and a harmony of well-hewn stones.

The old oak in Butts Wood

CHAPTER XXXVI

The Priory

THE Priory of Augustinian Canons was founded in Selborne in the year 1233 by Peter des Roches, Bishop of Winchester. It 'ran' until 1484. Its dissolution therefore had nothing to do with Henry VIII. It had just petered out, after many earnest attempts to keep it going; rather like a petrol engine baulked of feed, but in this case a very special spirit.

In 1484 Waynefleet was Bishop of Winchester. He had recently founded Magdalen College, Oxford. Waynefleet acquired for his College Selborne Priory and all the lands in Selborne it had owned. It appears to have been all 'above board', for those trying times.

Selborne Priory was extensive, and its church must have been very beautiful, as fragments of its carved stone-work preserved now at the Wakes show. Almost everything in the way of solid structure was pulled down in the years that followed, stones being used to build the farmhouse almost on the site, and probably several other houses in or about the village. Some stone was even used to mend roads. The field where the Priory had stood was, in White's day, known as the Stony Field, and I believe it still is. As everything visible was gone or buried by the time White was born, and as modern scientific investigation was then unthought of (though the romantic curiosity was about to bud) he not unnaturally concluded that there was nothing left of the Priory, and said so. The field was just a pasture field like another, only considerably rougher. In 1900 Dr. R. Bowdler-Sharpe did a little digging for a short while, unearthing a few encaustic tiles and exposing some of the buried foundations. He found some of these tiles on the floor of a summer-house. There was an empty stone coffin above ground, used as a trough.

But in the early 1950s Dr. Sidney Scott began a much more determined and informed attempt, with results highly promising, after which the Rev. George Knapp, still more expert, took over with his trained aides and teams of students, all archaeologically-minded enthusiasts. All this would have delighted Gilbert White.

He was the first to tell the modern world of the sad decline of our Priory. He was helped by Chandler. Together they grappled with documents which had lain in the Founder's Tower at Magdalen College ever since Bishop Waynefleet had removed them from Selborne. I find White, then an old man, boyishly keen and excited over their 'discoveries'. He begins to use ancient ways of spelling familiar local names, in his letters to Mollie and Sam Barker and others, while research is going on. However, I gather from some that he failed to make the most of his opportunities.

Of course, present day scientific methods have enabled us to learn infinitely more about the Priory and its past generally. For about fifteen years the archaeologists have been delving and discovering, and we have an admirably concise report from the Selborne Priory Excavations Committee easily obtainable, and I don't doubt that a complete one will soon be forthcoming, when matters are brought to an end and the team turns, as I hope, to the 'Castle Mound'. All the same, White the eighteenth-century curate – the Romantic White, moved however superficially at first, does manage to get to the hub of the matter; does seem to appreciate largely the extent of the Priory tragedy. We get it in the dismal details he excavates and translates, showing the decline and fall of these holy men; but particularly we feel his understanding break out in words with which he describes the wonderful spirit of true religion which led people of all kinds to back the enterprise.

> No sooner had a monastic institution got a footing, but the neighbourhood began to be touched with a secret and religious awe. Every person round was desirous to promote so good a work. . . . Thus did the more opulent monasteries add house to house, and field to field; and by degrees manor to manor; till at last 'there was no place left'; but every district around became appropriated to the purpose of their founders, and every precinct was drawn into the vortex.

Selborne's was a very opulent monastery; the founder was a very magnificent man. He was Bishop of Winchester, yes, and he was also Justicar of England under King John – ruled England – a regular power-house of a man, and like all such he loved building – large buildings. He lived richly, splendidly. He went to the Holy Land and 'lived it up', as we say, and built monasteries galore. When he returned he built Tichfield Abbey, and evidently employed the same architect here, or his plans, for the Priory church turns out to have been almost identical.

It is unfortunate that it is only this kind of man, it seems, who has enough energy to spare, of the right kind, to found anything. And his chief aides, in the beginning, were very much of the same kind – Jacobus de Achangre (Oakhanger), Jacobus de Nortun, John de Venuz, and, for that matter, Adam de Gurdon, and Ela Longspee, Countess of Warwick. These people had only one idea with regard to religion, and that was to use it to buy themselves off in the hereafter, in which all implicitly believed. Ela appears to have been obsessed with the idea – or was she in graver doubt? – since she arranged with the Prior to have someone say a special mass for her every day, dead or alive, and paid an extra sum of 100 silver marks to have it done in her special chantry in the church too. She appears particularly keen that her name should not be forgotten, either. And it has not been, yet, though she is not the famous Ela Longspee who had founded Lacock Abbey; that was her mother. The first-named benefactors, by the way, did not exactly give their lands away. Peter des Roches seems to have had to pay their debts first: other properties came upon reversion.

If one thinks that it was not after all such a very good start, one should reflect that they *all* began like that, and that these, the promoters, were the ones most likely to be sinful, because they alone had the means. They were all right: ordinary humans of frailty magnified. It was just unfortunate. But the *idea* did not begin like that. White was right; people in general were 'touched with a secret and religious awe', 'desirous to promote so good a work'. And it all came to rather worse than nothing. The day arrived when a shrunken handful of Canons and their Prior had to read this dreadful reproach from the visitor sent by William of Wykeham:

> – we came down to visit your Priory, as our office required: and every time we repeated our visitation we found something still not only contrary to regular rules but also repugnant to religion and good reputation.

And after that we can all relax, and say 'how typical!' I don't believe it was typical at all. I think it was an exceptional and particular calamity, and which seems to have happened quite soon – for Prior John is agreed to have been the ablest of them, and what a flair *he* had, it seems, for wrong values! After that dubious miracle he got hold of a piece of St. Richard's skeleton – a 'joint-bone' – and his comb, and his chafing-dish, to draw crowds with. This was the very worst kind of prestige, in contrast to that great spirit which had been abroad at the start.

What had happened then was a rebirth. It is fascinating to think that they were much further from Christ in 1230 than we are from them. The spirit had, and has, remained the same, but seldom has it been so vividly apparent. And they pawned the plate and relics, let in women at night, refused to wear their habits and affected smart clothes; they had eaten and drunk away their money and neglected their fine lands. There was hardly a book in the place. They liked hunting better, and there, I think, is where the root of the evil lay.

There are depths which it would be unwise to peer into unless one is very indifferent to the spiritual; and if one is not indifferent, then impossible to look at at all without compassion, self-humbleness and fear. *What* a catastrophe! One glances round; everything is peaceful and ordinary and old; a tumbled field with its filled-in excavation and bits of old stone; an old-new farm-house. Here we are in the ruins, and it takes some time to realise that it wasn't always like this, with the little stream between its broken banks, and silted; the sound of the water, the humming of the bees, the daisies and the nodding tasselled sedge-grass; the crowding leafy copses overspreading narrowed paths – a place forgotten in a hollow of small hills. But that there was a church here, big and new, and people doing all about – pushing barrows, wielding heavy spades, digging, planting, tending; and making roads, clearing thickets, ventilating everywhere. Those many generations of honestly devout, simple lay-monks, let alone their masters, the Prior and the thirteen Canons; it is difficult not to think of them as one fixed group in decline, always the same, like a group of delinquent dolls at a child's tea-party. But it took generations of men, a quarter of a millenium.

What killed the Priory stone dead at the start was the proximity of the royal deer forest. Visitations of royalties drained it of wealth and filled it with court fashion, follies and frivolities. But much more deadly were the powers it had of life and death. Henry III gave powers and privileges to the Priory – rights of every kind: of Soc and Sac, Thol and Them, Ingfangenethef and Utfangenethef, Hamsoc and

Blodwite, and finally of *Furcas* – the right to try, condemn and hang. It was something that surely could not have been except for the proximity of that forest. It did little to encourage the free exchange of spirit, and people under such a threat would be unlikely to cavil at goings on down at Priory. You cannot double the roles of gamekeeper and man of God.

The Official Gamekeeper – the Warden of the royal game forest – lived at Great Ward-le-Ham, which today we call East Worldham. About the climax of the Priory's fiasco he was Thomas, son of Geoffrey Chaucer, who as we know was severe on priestcraft. It has been suggested that Chaucer may have had Selborne canons in mind when he wrote his Prologue to the Canterbury Tales. His wife is buried at East Worldham Church, and her nephew, Cardinal Beaufort, was Bishop of Winchester and patron of Selborne Priory. It seems unlikely that Chaucer should not have visited East Worldham; likely that scandal from Selborne should have reached his all-receptive ear. So that by one of those three ways down through the wood behind us he may well have wound to see for himself – by Lower or Upper Wyck, or the Candovers, all good secondary thoroughfares of his day, as the Oakhanger-Hartley-Worldham road was undoubtedly a main road; and that thus we have the monk that

> – did not rate that text as a plucked hen
> Which says that hunters are not holy men –;

who said

> Let Austin have his swinke* to him reserved,

and who

> – was therefore a good man to horse;
> Grayhounds he had, as swift as birds to course.
> Hunting the hare or riding at a fence
> Was all his fun, he spared for no expense.
> I saw his sleeves were garnished at the hand
> With fine grey fur, the finest in the land.

Which, for those who love poetry and England, a good deal does away, in some roundabout manner, with the sadness of what happened here at Priory.

* Swinke=labour.

Chaucer and a monk

The faintest of religious breaths – enough to stir a feather or mist a glass – inhabited the Priory for some while after its close. For a priest continued, at least for some years, to read masses in a corner of the already crumbling church, for the souls of Jacobus de Nortun, de Achangre, John de Venuz and the rest.

Like the bedesman in Keats's 'Eve of St. Agnes', sole among the wreckage, he would sometimes steal about, and I imagine that villagers at dusk, coming down the Plains or out of Combe Wood, and passing on towards the Lyth, with backward looks would spy a tiny light, shudder and press on.

Then secular rule took over the property again, and the lay grip tightened; Sharp was the word, and stones of fairest promise were re-ordered to suit a mundane need. All was over at last for the Priory.

But I think that the spirit which had moved to that strange passion in the Middle Ages is only waiting; and I am not sure but that it has not already begun to show itself in a rebirth, in the antics of some of our young people remonstrating all across the world – unpleasant and offensive in some ways though some of these are. It is possible that we are seeing an old desire putting out in a new effort towards the freedom which can't be bought with money; towards a kinder way of life and a better understanding of all things living; against the tyranny of possessions; and that this time it may not want to be shut in behind expensive walls, and fulfil itself in close rituals, vulnerable to power and so to corruption, but it will be walking in the sunlight, through the countryside.

I count the amenity societies in this, and all the land-owners trying to work-in with each other for the benefit of strangers who cannot do them or their property much good; and all the givers to the various Trusts, and Nature Conservancy, and those bands of young people coming unpaid to help in its activities. There is some spirit in this, and very great – a spirit which, if not exactly touched with religious awe, has certainly resulted in divers persons getting together in the desire to further a good work. It may be that I am being 'starry-eyed': well, better starry eyes than eyes like dead oysters. So though I don't know how Selborne will develop – or be developed – whether into a park or reservation, or merely something like Hampstead Heath – I am pretty sure it will not be bricked and concrete-slabbed out of identity, nor become a hedgeless waste, its trees cut down, its soil and living creatures poisoned; nor be delivered to the horrors of the factory farm.

But I believe that it will continue under Providence as when it was sent its Gilbert White, to be a place of joy to us as to him, and a reminder of his excellence for ever.

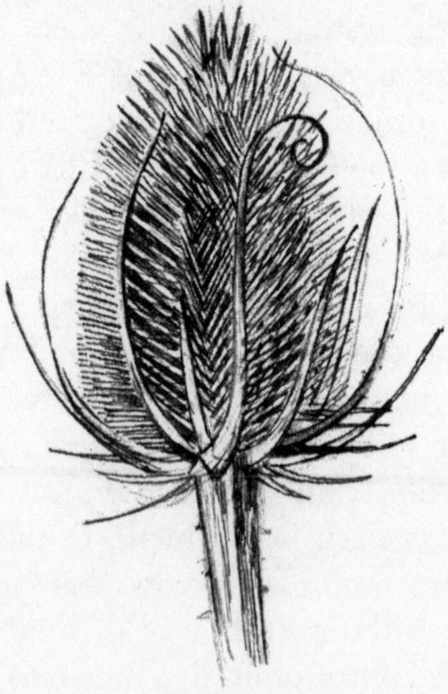

A Short Bibliography

NOTE: Out of some dozens of published editions of *The Natural History of Selborne*, this list only includes those which the author has found it useful to consult.

CLAY, ROTHA MARY, *Samuel Hieronymus Grimm*, Faber & Faber 1941

HOLT-WHITE, RASHLEIGH, *The Life and Letters of Gilbert White of Selborne*, John Murray 1901

HOLT-WHITE, RASHLEIGH, *The Letters to Gilbert White of Selborne from his Intimate Friend and Contemporary The Rev. John Mulso*, R. H. Porter 1960

HUDSON, W. H., *Hampshire Days*, Longmans Green 1903

JOHNSON, CLIFTON, *Among English Hedgerows*, The Macmillan Co., New York 1899

LOCKLEY, R. M., *Gilbert White*, H. F. & G. Witherby 1954

MACRAY, W. D., *The Charters of Selborne Priory*, Simpkin 1891

TOMKINS, HERBERT W., *Selborne*, Dent 1905

SCOTT, WALTER S., *White of Selborne*, The Falcon Press 1950

WHITE, GILBERT, ed. Walter S. Scott, *The Antiquities of Selborne in the County of Southampton*, illus. S. H. Grimm, Falcon Press 1950

WHITE, GILBERT, ed. Walter Johnson, *The Journals of Gilbert White*, Routledge 1931

WHITE, GILBERT, ed. Edward Blyth, *The Natural History of Selborne*, Orr & Smith 1836

WHITE, GILBERT, ed. Sir William Jardine, *The Natural History of Selborne*, Routledge 1880

WHITE, GILBERT, ed. Grant Allen, *The Natural History of Selborne*. Illus. E. H. New, John Lane 1900

WHITE, GILBERT, ed. R. B. Sharpe, *The Natural History of Selborne*, Fremantle 1900–1901

WHITE, GILBERT, ed. Richard Kearton, *The Natural History of Selborne*, Cassell 1911

WHITE, GILBERT, ed. N. J. Massingham, *The Natural History of Selborne*, Nonesuch Press 1938

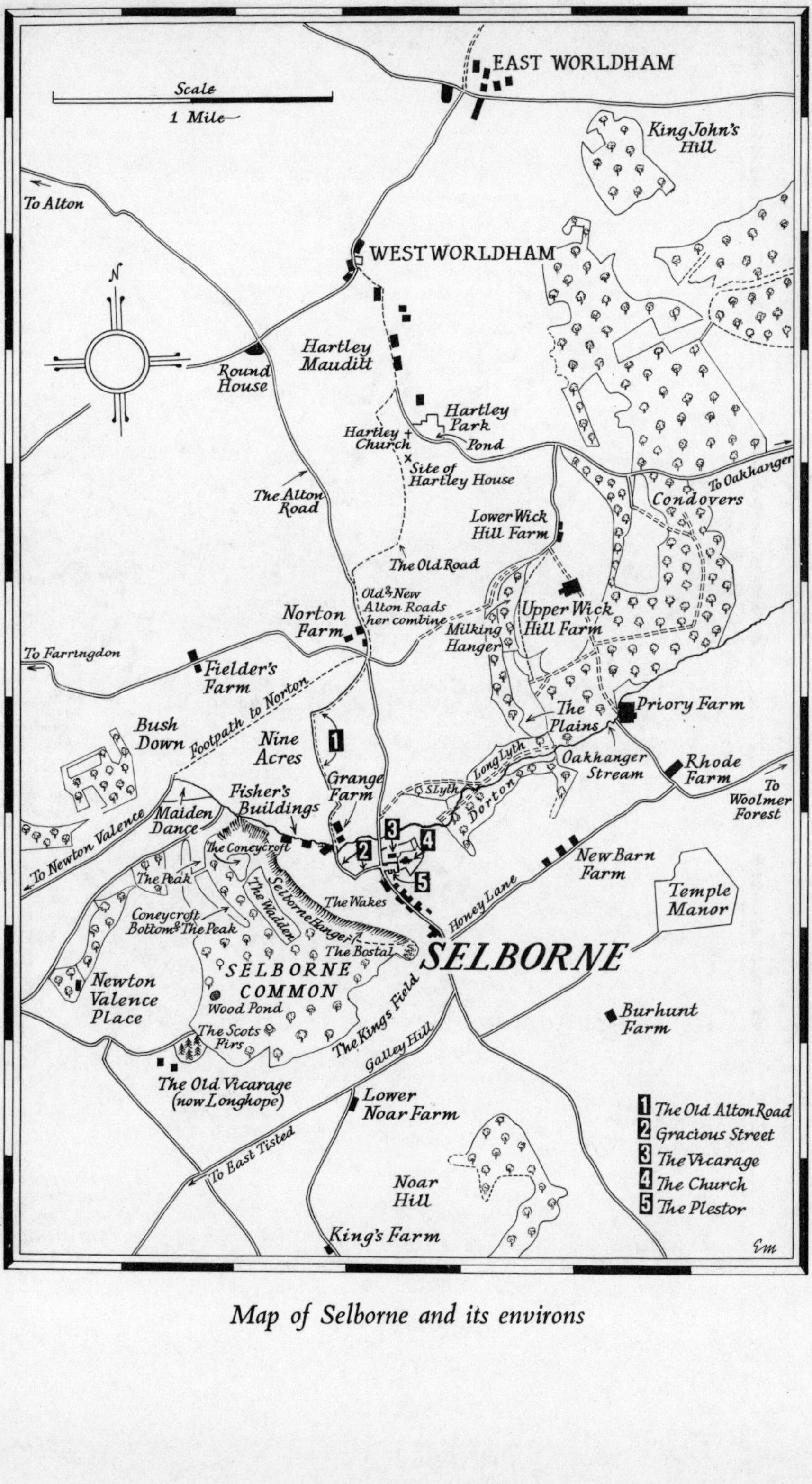

Map of Selborne and its environs

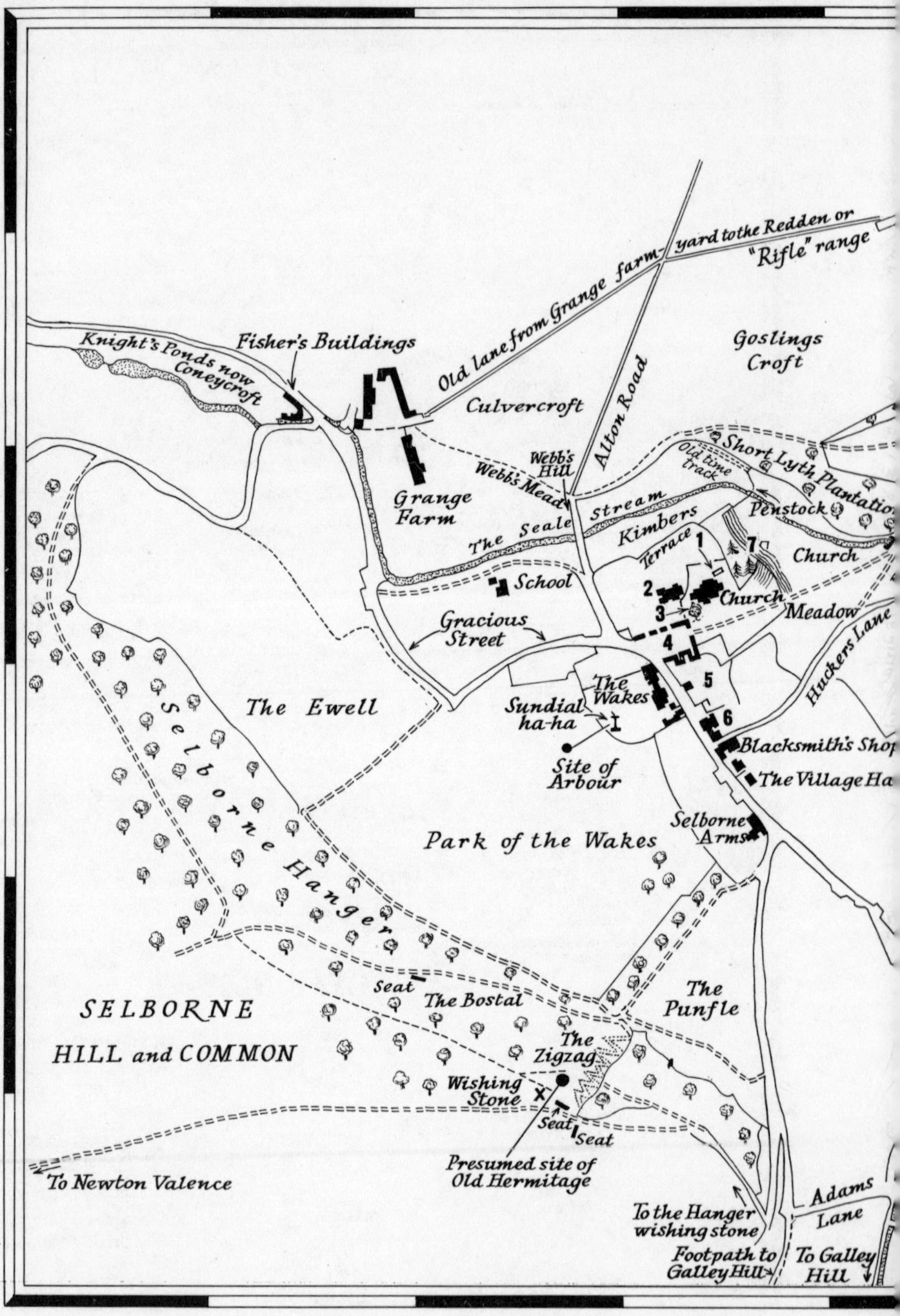
Knight's Ponds now Coneycroft
Fisher's Buildings
Old lane from Grange farm-yard to the Redden or "Rifle" range
Goslings Croft
Culvercroft
Alton Road
Webb's Hill
Webb's Mead
Grange Farm
Short Lyth Plantation
Old time track
Penstock
The Seale Stream
Kimbers
Terrace
Church
School
Church Meadow
Gracious Street
Huckers Lane
The Wakes
Sundial ha-ha
Site of Arbour
The Ewell
Blacksmith's Shop
The Village Ha
Selborne Hanger
Park of the Wakes
Selborne Arms
Seat
The Bostal
The Punfle
SELBORNE
HILL and COMMON
The Zigzag
Wishing Stone
Seat
Seat
Presumed site of Old Hermitage
To Newton Valence
To the Hanger wishing stone
Footpath to Galley Hill
Adams Lane
To Galley Hill

Map of S

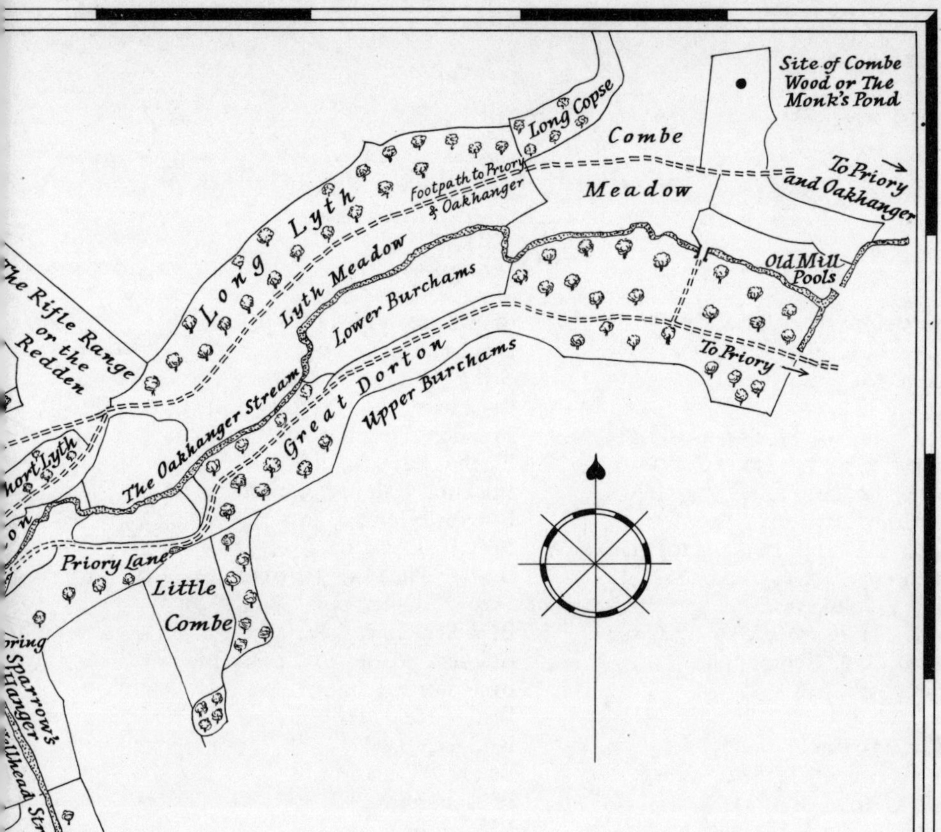
Site of Combe Wood or The Monk's Pond
Long Copse
Combe
Meadow
To Priory and Oakhanger
Footpath to Priory & Oakhanger
Long Lyth
Lyth Meadow
Lower Burchams
Old Mill Pools
The Rifle Range or the Redden
The Oakhanger Stream
Great Dorton
Upper Burchams
To Priory
Priory Lane
Little Combe
Sparrow's Hanger
Stream
Bridge Field
To Oakhanger & Borden
Honey Lane
1 Gilbert White's Grave
2 Vicarage
3 Yew Tree, Trumpeter's grave
4 The Plestor
5 Old Butcher's Shop
6 Queen's Hotel
7 The Castle Mound
0 500
Scale of Feet
Em

rne Village

Index